Funk & Wagnalls Guide to the

WORLD OF STAMP COLLECTING

Funk & Wagnalls Guide to the

WORLD OF STAMP COLLECTING

The Joys of Stamp Collecting for the Beginning and Advanced Philatelist

Viola Ilma

A Funk & Wagnalls Book
Published by Thomas Y. Crowell
New York

To Dick and Honor, with love

FUNK & WAGNALLS GUIDE TO THE WORLD OF STAMP COLLECTING. Copyright © 1978 by Viola Ilma. All rights reserved. Printed in the United States of America. No part of this book may be used or reproduced in any manner whatsoever without written permission except in the case of brief quotations embodied in critical articles and reviews. For information address Funk & Wagnalls, 521 Fifth Avenue, New York, N.Y. 10017. Published simultaneously in Canada by Fitzhenry & Whiteside Limited, Toronto.

Designed by Lydia Link

Library of Congress Cataloging in Publication Data

Ilma, Viola.
 Funk & Wagnalls guide to the world of stamp collecting.
 1. Postage-stamps—Collectors and collecting.
I. Title.
HE6213.I37   769'.56'075   77-22870
ISBN 0-308-10330-0

79 80 81 82 10 9 8 7 6 5 4 3 2

Contents

COLOR PLATES *(following page 148)*

Palais de Monaco

April 21, 1977

   On February 10, 1839, when Sir Rowland Hill
invented the first postage stamp, little did he
know of the exciting fame this small square piece
of paper would enjoy in the years to come!
   The postal stamps of the Principality of Monaco
depict, among many other subjects—the variety of
which have generated such great interest—the major
events of our history from its very origin in the
thirteenth century. Indeed, philatelists of the
United States, to whom I take pleasure in dedicating
these few lines, also study and appreciate the
history of their great nation through its stamps
and, therefore, acquire for themselves a thorough
knowledge of the progress achieved by man in all
fields, especially in the area of communications.
   As a few examples, insofar as the United States
is concerned, how could we forget the overland mail-
coach, linking for the first time, in 1858, the
civilized East to the Wild West? . . . What about
the Pony Express covering, in 1860, the "extraordinary" distance from St. Joseph, Missouri, to
Sacramento! . . . And then came the Empire State
express train and, as we leap over the years, our
amazing and incredible facility to converse from
one continent to the other through satellites,
simply by dialing a few numbers! And the United
States postal stamps also pay tribute to the

astonishing *Apollo XI,* enabling man to set foot on the moon—an accomplishment never to be forgotten!

   It should always be a rare privilege to leaf through a stamp album, not only for the pleasure of our very eyes, but also for the invaluable account shown of man's progress in our civilization. Stamps indeed enrich our knowledge and stimulate our interest in all the things that are peaceful, constructive and dignified for the betterment of mankind.

   I am sure philatelists of the United States fully share my opinion, for stamp collecting is not only a great hobby but a most enriching and peace-seeking occupation—a reminder of the past and an exciting exploration into the present!

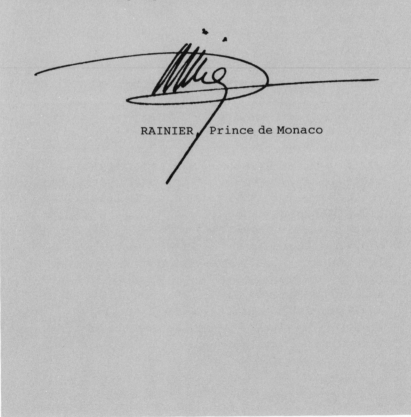

RAINIER, Prince de Monaco

His Serene Highness Prince Rainier III of Monaco.

Sardinian stamp, 20-cent blue, with pen cancellation applied
in MENTON, April 12, 1851.
(From the private collection of H.S.H. Prince Rainier III; by gracious
permission of H.S.H. Prince Rainier III)

Proof and block of twenty-five, "Series Charles III," first issue
of Monaco, 1885—unique.
(From the private collection of H.S.H. Prince Rainier III; by gracious
permission of H.S.H. Prince Rainier III)

The Fascination of Stamp Collecting

Rich man, poor man, beggar man, thief, doctor, lawyer, and two hundred million other people worldwide are participating in the biggest and grandest hobby in the world—stamp collecting. What is the lure that draws so many people to these tiny pieces of paper called postage stamps?

Stamp collecting acts as an enormous magnet. You don't recognize the pull at the start. It is like munching on potato chips—once you've taken one, you are helplessly compelled to try another and another. In the course of collecting, you may find yourself on a speaker's platform when you never thought you could face an audience; become a gold medal winner, something that never happened to you before; and probably meet people you never dreamed you'd ever know—far removed from your own specific circles. You will make interesting and often lasting friendships. Certainly you will get intricately involved in places you had never heard of, and may find yourself facing a millionaire or plumber who wants a stamp you possess. You may even lose your shirt by talking too much or being uninformed.

The Penny Red, used on a nineteenth-century valentine. (Courtesy of Harmers of New York)

Cupid plays his role, for the chase of valuable love letters in old attics has paid off handsomely. An elderly friend or grandparent may leave old letters, and you might be in for a pleasant surprise.

When you become a stamp collector you enter a sport *of* the people. You can get "ripped off" and "turned on." It's a ceaseless challenge that often becomes a lifelong love affair. You may drop it, you may pick it up, but you will never leave it.

A stamp is like a friend. The more you know about it, the better the relationship. The stamp has a birthday, it has anniversaries, it has a pedigree, and it has a destiny. It is useful to know about the first day a stamp is issued. In any case, all you have to do initially is to hold on to the free stamps you get on your mail or go into a post office and buy some stamps.

United States 24-cent Inverted Center, 1918, block of four, sold in 1976 by Harmers of New York, Inc., for $170,000.
(Courtesy of Harmers of New York)

Flying Upside Down

One of the most exciting moments in the history of United States stamp collecting is the story of Mr. W. T. Robey. He was an inexperienced and unknown stamp collector working as a stockbroker's clerk in Washington, D.C. At the time, early 1918, the first experimental airmail service between Washington, D.C., and New York—with an intermediate stop in Philadelphia—was planned. First flights were made in both directions on May 15, 1918. The United States Army furnished the planes and pilots. The Post Office issued a 24-cent airmail stamp, red and blue, with a picture of the early flying machine the *Jenny* for this event. On May 14, the Post Office distributed stamps to branch post offices in the three cities. Mr. Robey had friends in New York and Philadelphia who had asked him to put the new 24-cent airmail stamp on envelopes and mail them the day of this first flight.

Early on the morning of May 14, before going to his office, he went to the bank and took out $30 to buy the new stamps. He then went to the post office near his place of work. He walked up to a window and asked the clerk for the new stamps. The postal clerk told him that he had only a few stamps left. Robey looked at them, but they weren't well centered. The clerk mentioned that he would be receiving another batch at noontime. Eager Robey returned to the same post office promptly at noon, went to the same window, and got the same clerk. As promised he had a new batch. Robey handed him his three ten-dollar bills and got back $6, and was given a sheet of one hundred stamps. His heart stood still. When he looked at his sheet he noticed that all the airplanes were upside down. In his excitement he showed the postal clerk his find. Without comment the clerk closed his window and rushed to a telephone. Robey flew out of the post office with his upside-down airplane sheet safely tucked under his arm. He went to work to share his exuberance and excitement with his co-workers. He again left his office to try a few other post offices, but no inverted airplanes. By the time he got back to his office, two postal inspectors were there to greet him. They questioned Mr. Robey, but to no avail; he wouldn't even show his sheet, much less give it up. He just didn't budge. The inspectors left and Robey was the owner of the now famed 24-cent Inverted Airplane sheet.

Robey soon took his great find to a stamp dealer who offered him $500. He then went to another dealer who offered him $10,000. By the end of the week he sold his treasure for $15,000. He made a neat profit of $14,976 on his $24 investment. Today a single copy of the 24-cent Inverted Airplane stamp, properly centered, never hinged, sells for $70,000.

This find sheds a little light on the sheer excitement of stamp collecting. Actually Mr. Robey's original plan was to please his out-of-town friends. Once he'd gone to the post office and was told to come back, he did. Most important, he came precisely at noon; had he arrived at a later hour someone else might have become the proud owner. Had he not been observant, he might have just used the stamps for postage. He was not intimidated and refused to show his purchase to the inspectors. That he knew more than one stamp dealer also became a factor in his favor. He had enough sense not to accept the first offer, despite the fact that $500 is a lot more than $24.

Don't think for a moment, though, that the absorption of this fascinating hobby is just a world of once-in-a-lifetime rarities and dreams. The immediate potential always exists. It's a most pleasing thought that the average man can stumble onto what becomes a millionaire's passionate envy.

From Abyssinia to Zululand

A stamp is a practical item. You buy it, lick it, and bang it onto an envelope and mail it. The old image of a stamp collector is either a fat kid that no one on the block can stand or a dull recluse with thick glasses who sits at his desk hovering over a magnifying glass studying thousands of these little printed pieces of paper. This "weirdo" then, hour upon hour, year after year, puts each stamp one by one into a series of albums ranging alphabetically from A—Abyssinia (Ethiopia) —to Z—Zululand.

There are no rules on how or what to collect. Out of the twenty million collectors in the United States no two existing collections are exactly identical. You may accumulate stamps about fishes or Fiji, art or the Antarctic, mosquitoes or military history, dinosaurs or Denmark. You choose a subject or a country because it relates to some definition of your own personality, be it "way out," "methodical," or purely "classical"—you do your own thing all the way, and that's where the fun begins.

Curiosity may kill the cat, but it makes the stamp collector. No other hobby in the world catches in its breathtaking global arena the camaraderie that brings together kings, potentates, presidents, forgers, fakers, and you. Stamp collecting holds out an invitation to you to snoop around the globe and come out with an informal liberal arts education. It's a bridge to learning without boredom. Painlessly you learn about history. You're never alone, for your contacts emerge from your own investigative abilities. Inquisitiveness is rewarding. The developed qualities of keen observation, detection, and inquiry may make you a fine stamp collector. This book will show you how it can be accomplished.

Once hooked, it's like the common cold; you just have it. It doesn't do any harm; it's a seductive addiction that brings satisfaction and many good, hearty laughs. If you know what you're doing you may well, over a period of time, be making a sound investment.

Being at the right place at the opportune time can be most rewarding. When I was an enthusiastic novice, I realized that my hobby brought me to many places and allowed me to meet an assortment of people who weren't exactly the run-of-the-mill. I happened to be in Liberia the week that Monrovia, the capital, was preparing to celebrate Marshal Tito's arrival on March 18, 1961. Tito was traveling throughout Africa as an ambassador of goodwill. Much to my pleasure, President Tubman of Liberia sent me an invitation to attend the VIP banquet scheduled for that evening. While many wives of high officials and diplomats were at the hairdresser's that morning, I was visiting the postmaster, who had become a friend of mine. Sitting in front of his desk, I noticed that he had a pile of about two hundred envelopes which an official member of the Yugoslavian contingent had brought to him to be cancelled that day. The design on the envelope was printed in Yugoslavia to commemorate Tito's goodwill tour. The postmaster gave me two covers. I left his office delighted.

The pomp and ceremony was at its height at the banquet. The Yugoslavian naval officers looked handsome in their white uniforms. The guests at my own table seemed calm enough until I expressed my plan to have Marshal Tito and President Tubman autograph the two covers which had been cancelled earlier at the Monrovia post office. To guard the two heads of state, security was as tight as a drum. The friends at my table didn't want any fuss and preferred that I forget the whole thing.

Fortunately, in between dances, President Tubman had to leave the room and en route he crossed the ballroom floor alone. For me it was now or never. I dashed up to him with pen in hand and got his signature. Half of my plot had succeeded. Now my friends at the table were really uncomfortable. When the band struck up again, a tall, good-looking Yugoslavian naval officer came over and asked me for a dance. No sooner was I on the ballroom floor than I asked my partner to take my envelopes to Marshal Tito and have him sign them. He lost his cool and went straight to another officer who took the envelopes but forgot the pen. A few minutes later he was up at the dais. I could see Tubman leaning toward Tito pointing to his own signature. Tito smiled, the officer handed him a pen, and he signed. The officer stepped from the dais, walked over to me, bowed graciously, asked for a dance, and when he took me back to my seat, handed me my signed covers. All this for less than 25 cents, and no hairdo. With great relief, my friends at the table applauded. The next day I gave one of my two signed covers to the Liberian postmaster.

Cover signed by Marshal Tito and President Tubman.

SLEUTH CHECK

FIJI
Notice that on the top stamp the artist forgot to put a man in the canoe. The corrected stamp has a man in a canoe.

MONACO
Franklin Roosevelt has six fingers.

AUSTRIA
On the stamp on the left, the fellow's ears are upside down. On the stamp on the right, ears are right side up.

GUADELOUPE
The second camel has only three legs.

PAKISTAN
Stars and Crescent stamp to left, normal; stamp to right in reverse, an error.

(All of the above courtesy of Ira Zweifach)

Rose first-day cancel.
(Copyright British Post Office)

A Philatelic Rose Garden

Where does one begin? Why not choose a subject of beauty, love, and romance . . . the rose. Gather a philatelic rose garden of enchantment. Include the delicate Princess Grace rose from Monaco, the Algerian Rosa Odorata of North Africa, the pastel lemon Grandpa Dixon rose from Great Britain, and the gorgeous red, red Papa Meilland rose from Switzerland. Why not become a specialist, be a botanical philatelist, an expert and lover of flowers; even more specialized, a lover of the "Queen of Flowers," naming your collection "Roses on Stamps." No flower quite occupies the place in history equal to that of the rose. It is said that musk and damask roses flourished in the Hanging Gardens of Babylon. Roses were in abundance in the palace of King Solomon; they ornament the Taj Mahal. Cleopatra ordered garlands of Sweet Briars for her banquets and festivals. The Wars of the Roses were named after the White Rose of York and the Red Rose of Lancaster. Old Blush is the Last Rose of Summer celebrated by Sir

Thomas More which today is painfully chirped by some charity ball soprano. Perhaps the most famous rose garden ever assembled was at the château of Empress Josephine in Malmaison, France.

THE YEAR OF THE ROSE

Nineteen seventy-six was the year of the rose for England. Four stamps bearing roses were issued to honor the one hundredth anniversary of the Royal National Rose Society. The birthday of the Rose stamp was June 30, 1976, known as the first day of issue. What will be the destiny of this set of Rose stamps? What will be its philatelic career?

The 8½ pence value Elizabeth of Glamis, a salmon pink floribunda, bred from Spartan and Highlight, is named after Her Majesty Queen Elizabeth, the Queen Mother. The 10 pence stamp Grandpa Dickson is a pastel lemon yellow Hybrid Tea from a seedling Perfecta and Governador Braga da Cruz crossed with Piccadilly. The 11 pence stamp, which you are apt to receive on your mail from England, is the Rosa Mundi (Rosa Gallica Versicolo), a shrub rose with semidouble petals of twelve or twenty light crimson flowers, splashed with blush pink, white, and red, a sport from Rosa (Gallica Officinalis). The 13 pence, known in this set as the high value, is the Sweet Briar (Rosa Rubiginosa) or Eglantine.

The Royal National Rose Society has over sixty thousand members. The stamps issued coincided with the opening of the Royal National Summer Rose Show at Westminster. One hundred years ago the poet laureate of England, Dean Samuel Reynolds Hole, was lyrically called "the King of Roses." He was the Vicar of Caunton, who initiated the Grand National Rose Show, writing "a flood of roses at which the brotherhood might meet in love and unity to drink out of cups of silver, success to the Queen of Flowers."

The vicar did not receive a smashing response to his idea of an all-national rose show. Disappointed, he wrote, "I had thought better of mankind." How pleased he would have been one hundred years later to view the royal entrance of Her Majesty Queen Elizabeth, the Queen Mother, and Her Majesty Queen Ingrid of Denmark when they visited the centenary show of the Royal National Rose Society! His dream came true.

Stamp collecting relates enormously to observation. When you take a good look at the philatelic bouquet that can be put together from Great Britain, China, Algeria, Monaco, Switzerland, Luxembourg, Israel, and the United Nations, what is decidedly different about the British stamps?

The lone seventy-ninth stamp of Israel, known as the Desert Rose, is the oldest stamp in our Rose Garden, and it is from the youngest country. It was issued in the city of Jerusalem to honor the Desert Exhibition which was held from September 22 to 24, 1953. Israel then was only five years old. The theme "the desert shall rejoice and blossom like a rose" had become a reality. This stamp, like all of Israel's stamps, comes with and without tabs, which are marginal nonstamp pieces which explain something about the subject on the stamps.

The next set, consisting of two stamps, came from the Grand Duchy of Luxembourg. The Monaco diamond-shaped rose on a stamp was named after Princess Grace, and is the high value of a beautiful set of flowers on stamps issued May 16, 1959. The delicate pink Rosa Odorata stamp of Algiers was issued in 1969. Our yellow Royal Rose and Rose Hybrid were issued to publicize the handsome Flower Festival at Mondorf-les-Bains.

From the Republic of China (Taiwan) came the Charles Mallerin rose, known in China as the Black Rose; the Golden Sceptre, the yellow-edged-with-pink rose Peace, and the lush red Josephine Bruce rose.

The striking Iceberg rose from New Zealand was issued November 26, 1975.

The Turkish rose was issued June 4, 1960, honoring their spring flower festival.

PRO JUVENTUTE

For more than six decades, every December first the Swiss government has issued a set of stamps "Pro Juventute"—for the youth. What gives the stamps a special significance in addition to the postage value (face value) is a small surtax. The extra funds raised through the surtax are designated for youth projects. This income runs into the millions of dollars.

Like almost everything Swiss, their stamps are creations of pristine perfection. When the Pro Juventute stamps are issued, the schoolchildren sell them to their parents, friends, and relatives. Trained to use the profits constructively, the youth are introduced into the magic world of stampdom, and some become excellent collectors. It is delightful to imagine the snow falling gently at the foot of the Matterhorn or Jungfrau while boys and girls ski from village to village seeking orders for the Pro Juventute stamps. These sets, whether mint or used (used meaning that the stamp actually went through the mail) are worth owning.

On December 1, 1972, the Pro Juventute set was dedicated to "Famous Roses." This is certainly a grouping of roses to add to your garden. The lowest value is 10 centimes + 10 centimes. It is the breathtaking McGredy Sunset, a yellow, slightly tinted pink rose. Next comes the pink full-blossomed Miracle rose. The high value is a white, pink-lined rose called Madame Dimitrou and it is lovely. But the beauty of them all is the red, red rose we all dream of receiving . . . the renowned Papa Meilland.

THE STANLEY GIBBONS ROSE *(see Plate 1)*

Papa Meilland is one of the parent roses of the hybrid Stanley Gibbons Rose, bred by the famous rose growers Gregory's of Nottingham. Edward Stanley Gibbons was a pioneer in the fantastic world of stamp dealers. In 1856 at the age of sixteen, he launched his amazing career as a stamp dealer in a corner of his father's pharmacy in Plymouth, England. Eighteen years later he left the pharmacy business, already a well-known stamp dealer, and moved his stamp shop to London. Today, Stanley Gibbons, Ltd., is one of the largest stamp organizations in the world with a listing on the British stock exchange. It is practically impossible to be a stamp collector and not bring Stanley Gibbons into your life. How jolly a thought that a special rose is now the Stanley Gibbons rose and, believe it or not, you can order the rosebush from Stanley Gibbons Stamp Magazine, Ltd., at Drury House, Russell St., London, WC2B 5HD, England.

UNITED NATIONS

To complete our initial planting of a philatelic rose garden, there are four United Nations rose stamps—two from United Nations headquarters in New York and two from United Nations Geneva (Switzerland) headquarters—which were issued to honor the U.N. peace-keeping forces. No stamp collection of this rare beauty can afford to omit the Rosa Canina—wild rose breaking through barbed wire. This set is our spiritual conscience. Note the five languages in the frame of this U.N. stamp.

This, then, is an introduction to the elements that comprise a new stamp collection. We have chosen all the stamps in mint condition— that is, they have never gone through the mail. They should look as perfect as any stamp you might purchase in your post office today.

The goal we are aspiring to is perfection. The beauty of your stamps should be matched by the care with which you keep them. Their condition, if perfect, in the long run, will satisfy your aesthetic sense and quite possibly reap financial rewards.

An official Swiss
first-day cover.

PRO JUVENTUTE 1972

First-Day Covers

To blow the trumpet of the birthday of a stamp, some countries
throughout the world issue what is known as a first-day cover (or FDC).
The "cover" is an envelope. The design on the envelope is called a
"cachet." The postmark naturally includes the date of issue. The Swiss
FDC shown is an "official first day cover." From the cachet, note that
the design chosen was the Papa Meilland rose. The Swiss Post Office
also created a distinctive postmark in the form of a rose, in stamp
circles known as "a pictorial cancellation." This is a perfect example
of how you get involved. Naturally you will want to include this Swiss
festive beauty in your collection; it will look so superb in your album.

Just as your real flowers need a vase, your stamps need a house. To
cut those flowers you need gloves, but to handle your stamps you need
tongs. As we go along, we shall suggest how to "suit up" to become a
botanical philatelist.

Your First Album

If you receive a dozen roses today, will you take them to the kitchen
and stick them into an empty cardboard milk carton, or will you look
around the house for the most luxurious vase you possess, and lovingly
begin to arrange the roses for everyone's enjoyment?

The fresh roses you receive will fade only too soon, but the roses in
your stamp collection will bloom, and with time possibly flourish. Of
utmost importance is the selection of a stamp album to serve as a first
home for your treasures. Because of the rapid growth of the hobby,
many new types of albums are now available. They are planned so that

An album from the Royal Collection of Her Majesty
Queen Elizabeth II.
(By gracious permission of H.M. Queen Elizabeth II)

you can get the most enjoyment out of your collection. Designed to
insure satisfactory viewing, a good album can enhance your sense of
pride and attainment. A number of collections are housed in custom-
made albums, including the Royal Collection of Her Majesty Queen
Elizabeth II.

A stamp album is a miraculous brainrestorer. The pleasure lies in a certain
way of using one's mind. In collecting, every stamp is an event, a pleasure in
itself, and simultaneously, a step towards the growth of one's own collection.
Ayn Rand, stamp collector, author of The Fountainhead

Gone is the chaos of thousands of hinges. The chaotic throwing of
stamps into boxes and drawers is an antiquated, time-consuming technique. There are a number of fine houses that put out just the album
you need as a starter, an example of which is Lighthouse Publications,
Inc. They have a hingeless stamp album of sixteen pages, which are
snow white or jet black with transparent glassine pockets. The problem of hinges is nonexistent, because you do not need them. These
albums have double glassine interleaves which protect your stamps
from rubbing. You can open and shut your album hundreds of times
and leaf through your pages and find that they always look lovely. You
don't have to worry about filling empty spaces. You're not searching
for pictures to match your stamps. What you are doing is arranging
your special collection, as you wish. The hardcovers come in various
colors, which you choose to suit your own taste.

SHOP AROUND FOR AN ALBUM

There are many albums available. Visit a stamp dealer's store or go
to a stamp show. While you are looking around, you might notice some
albums that are well known before you decide on the one to buy.

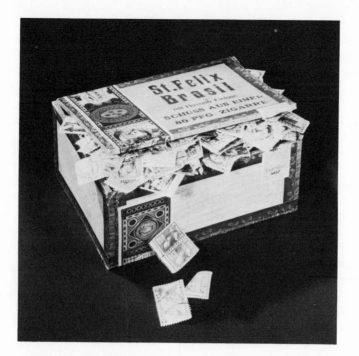

The old and new way of storing stamps.
(Courtesy of Lighthouse Publications, Inc.)

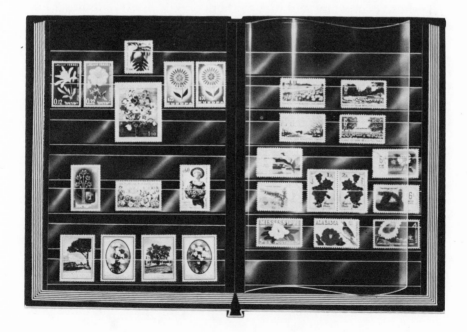

Collectors Institute, Ltd., 10102 F Street, Omaha, Nebraska 68125. Write for their attractive booklet, *Guidebook for Creative Collectors.* They emphasize that every collection should be a growing, improving, creative source to the hobbyist. Among many other items offered are stock card pages (8½" × 11") plus sheet protectors which are ideal as a starter. The way you control the look and placement of your stamps is paramount to your enjoyment. Good organization can help you to avoid the chaotic mass of directionless accumulations of stamps. Launch your stamp collecting career with discipline, beauty, and love.

H. E. Harris & Co. This is the world's largest stamp house. Their albums, accessories, catalogues, and stamps are renowned. They offer an all-purpose "Gem" album, ideal for developing special collections. They have a "New Collectors Club" that offers a "no-interest credit plan." Order your exact requirements, including stamps, but use moderation when you become faced with their plethora of engaging offers of all kinds of collections. Once you have made your decision concerning what to collect, stick to it. Your stamp dealer is certain to have all H. E. Harris products, and the company is represented at all major stamp shows throughout the country.

Scott Publishing Co. They, too, have stock pages to fit into a three-ring binder and a distinguished list of albums, as well as their famous catalogues, which you can order from your stamp dealer.

White Ace is a household name to many collectors. Their famous albums are available in all stamp stores and shows.

All these companies and many others offer "country albums." For instance, you can get an album that holds only United States stamps. Supplementary pages are offered to accommodate the stamps issued annually. Topical albums are also available, but you really don't have to go to the expense to buy one. All you need do is purchase a good weight paper, buy a three-ring punch machine, and a three-ring binder. The main purpose is to create a spotlessly clean and safe house to protect and display your own collection.

Now that you have your stamps and your album, you need tongs. These are like eyebrow tweezers, except that they are specifically made for stamp collectors. It is necessary to learn to pick up your stamps with tongs. They come in different shapes: spade tip, fine-pointed tip, spade tip bent, and pointed tip. Again, the decision depends upon personal preference, so try them all at your stamp dealer's. The tong you find most convenient to handle is the right one to choose.

Once you have your stamp album and your tongs, you are equipped for a fine beginning that should encourage your progress as a collector.

Let us assume you've attained these first three stages: You have your philatelic rose garden collection which, for the moment, consists of

Specialized United Nations album.
(Courtesy of United Nations Postal Administration)

A first-day cover album.
(Courtesy of Lighthouse Publications, Inc.)

How to mount a stamp.
(Courtesy of Lighthouse Publications, Inc.)

stamps from Great Britain, Israel, Luxembourg, China (Taiwan), Switzerland, Monaco, Algeria, and the U.N.; you have your album; you have your tongs.

You must remember always to store your album upright. This will allow the stamps to breathe more easily. They are much happier being looked at than being put into a silent steel vault.

Various size mounts.
(Courtesy of H. E. Harris & Co. Inc.)

HINGING

A number of companies manufacture hingeless albums. If you do not use a hingeless album, you must consider either mounts or hinges. Collectors Institute, Ltd., has Showguard mounts; Lighthouse offers Hawid mounts; and H. E. Harris has Crystal mounts. View them all before deciding. Don't be influenced by friends; be your own decision-maker.

Before clear mounts and hingeless albums came into existence, collectors attached what are known as hinges to their stamps in order to mount them in their albums. Some progress was made when peelable and prefolded hinges came into existence. To quote *Scott's Catalogue:* *"Condition is the all-important factor of price. Prices quoted are for stamps in fine condition."*

If you decide to use hinges, be sure to get the prefolded and peelable ones. In *Stamp Collectors Handbook* (Bonanza Books), Samuel Grossman states: "Stamps should *never be pasted down flat* in the album. Do not use paste, glue, or apply any adhesives for the purpose of attaching stamps. Nor should materials as mending tape, top of envelope, etc. be used for hinges. Good hinges are usually available from most stamp dealers. These should be thin and transparent and, of the utmost importance, they should be peelable enough that any can be removed with ease, and thereby avoid taking off part of the stamp or album page.

"When using a hinge, fold back the upper one-quarter and lightly moisten the gummed side. This part is then affixed to the top of the stamp, below the perforation. Then moisten the remaining ¾ of the hinge and attach it to the space in the album. Be sure not to apply too much moisture. Otherwise an overflow may cause the stamp itself to adhere to the album page. Never remove a wet hinge from your stamp or album. This is liable to make a tear or a thin spot. Wait a few hours until it is perfectly dry and then it will peel off easily." The reason for using a hingeless album or your own blank pages is that you can plan your collection so that it conforms to your specific needs.

You can start with a topical collection—stamps with roses or whatever your interest might be; or a country collection—all the stamps issued by your favorite country.

It's a strange phenomenon that each stamp you own begins to have a soul, a personality, a background of its own. Once people know you collect, they may give you stamps for your birthday, and perhaps for other occasions. Your collection begins to relate to old and new friends. You are now part of an enormous, generous, worldwide family, and your pages begin to tell the story of all sorts of experiences— all of this is ahead of you, as your collection grows under your skillful guidance.

SLEUTH CHECK

1. What country doesn't have its name on the stamp?
2. What three countries issued a set of four roses?
3. What organization (not country) issued a set of two stamps from New York headquarters and two more from Geneva headquarters?
4. What country has the name Helvetia in your Rose collection?
5. What country in this Rose collection issued stamps with and without tab?
6. How many stamps make a set of stamps?
7. What country in this Rose collection issued a set of semipostals to aid youth?

ANSWERS

1. Great Britain. Because Great Britain invented the postage stamp, only the monarch appears on the stamp. Therefore, you see the profile head of Her Majesty Queen Elizabeth II.
2. Great Britain, China, and Switzerland.
3. The United Nations is the only organization in the world permitted to issue stamps valid for postage. U.N. stamps are only valid for mailing from either the U.N. in New York or the U.N. in Geneva.
4. Switzerland.
5. Israel.
6. Two and upward to the number issued.
7. Switzerland.

Scott's Catalogue

On a sweltering August day in 1863, John Walter Scott, at the age of eighteen, arrived in New York City from London, England. All he had was a little trunk, but in that trunk was a meager possession of stamps that was to make him, along with young Stanley Gibbons, one of the great pioneers that laid the foundations of the great hobby of stamp collecting.

This was a unique era. Every place in the world was far away. Who could tell the difference between stamps from Brazil and India, or recognize a king on a stamp, much less figure out what country it came from?

Not only was a stamp hardly recognized as a world messenger but the business of writing a letter was a bit complicated. In those days the average American family had formulas for making ink: one part green vitriol, one part powdered dogwood, and three parts oak galls. They not only made their own ink but also their own pens, using feathers from around the farm. The elite ladies who wanted a fine point used quills of crow. Even today, fine-pointed pens are still called "crow-quills."

John Walter Scott became interested in stamps when he was fifteen years old. He was working for a mercantile house and became enamored of stamps on envelopes from foreign places. He was more than enamored; he latched onto as many as he could get. He no sooner arrived in New York City than he managed to meet the first United States stamp dealer in existence, with the unfanciful name of William P. Brown, who in 1860 had his sidewalk stamp business displayed in the open air at City Hall, New York City. This became typical in major centers throughout the world. (You will find the Paris open-air stamp bourse right near the Rond Point, as in 1878, halfway down the Champs Élysées. The bustling of stamp dealers trading and stamp lovers intermingled at this bourse is another reason you'll always love Paris.)

Young Scott sold his little grouping of stamps that were in his trunk to Mr. Brown for $10. Stories of old man Brown are legion, but one is of great importance: He gave Scott a hundred dollars' worth of stamps to sell. Within five years Scott established his own business at 34 Liberty Street, New York City. The following year he published his own catalogue, which was to become famous the world over—*Scott's Catalogue.* I suppose if one were to ask what made John Walter Scott and Stanley Gibbons stamp collecting pioneers one could say that to these two young men each and every stamp had a soul. They treated their stamps with love, respect, and appreciation. They were serious researchers. Their customers were important people, not only because they supported the embryo business but also because they were part of the vista that continues to bring endless pleasure to millions of people the world over.

Speaking of devotion, one legend has it that in 1883 Frédéric Bartholdi, sculptor of the Statue of Liberty, was a stamp collector, and the book the lady in the harbor embraces is a stamp album.

Most significant is that throughout all the years of the gargantuan growth of philately, the high standards of the top stamp dealers and auctioneers haven't changed, nor have their customers. None of them expects a Rolls-Royce for the price of a Ford.

Today, for the American collector and for many collectors worldwide, *Scott's Standard Postage Stamp Catalogue* is indispensable. It is necessary in every theater of the hobby. This includes you, the purchaser of stamps, dealers, and auctioneers.

The data included in this catalogue is the price exchange, a launch point, which is indicative of the value of each stamp. Just as stock market prices change, relating to supply and demand, so do prices of stamps. Primarily the catalogue is an indication of potential value. It is also an intimate armchair trip to every speck of land on this earth. It accounts for countries that have come and gone.

A Scott catalogue.
(Courtesy of Scott Publications, Inc.)

*From "Histoire de la Poste de Lettres,"
by Arthur de Rothschild*
THE CHILDREN'S STAMP EXCHANGE IN THE
CHAMPS ELYSÉES, PARIS, 1878

When astronaut Neil Armstrong first set foot on the moon, he became the first postmaster in space. He took engraved master dies of the United States' First Man on the Moon stamp with him. Subsequently, the First Man on the Moon stamp was issued September 9, 1969, printed from the plates made from that historic trip.

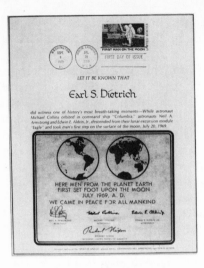

Special certificate with man on the moon stamp with first-day cancel.
(Courtesy of The Posthorn Inc., New York)

Ten Prized Dogs *(see Plate 2)*

The Ten Prized Dogs from the Republic of China are exquisite replicas of the original "Ten Hanging Silk Scrolls" painted by Lang-Shih-Ning now in the National Palace Museum, Taipei, Taiwan. Lang-Shih-Ning is one of the most prominent figures in the history of Chinese art. He was born Giuseppe Castiglione in Milan in 1668. At the age of nineteen he became a Jesuit. After eight years of training as a painter and architect, he was sent to China as a missionary. He was summoned to the palace in Peking, the capital of the Ching Dynasty, and over a period of fifty-one years served two emperors as court painter. He absorbed and made masterly use of an ancient Chinese art concept of great importance—"the order and harmony of nature." The ample space, the delicate feeling of movement, and the lines of trees and blossoms that Castiglione blended into his subject created a beautiful, spacious portrait.

The dogs pictured on each stamp were originally gifts to Emperor Chien Lung from dignitaries and high-ranking officials. Each dog was given a poetic name according to its form and color.

Issued November 16, 1971:

$1.00	Shuang Hua Yao	White Frost Hawk
$2.00	Shan Hsing Lang	Star Glancing Wolf
$2.50	Chin Ch'ih Hsien	Golden Winged Face
$5.00	Mo Yü Ch'ih	Black Young Dragon
$8.00	Ts'ang Shui Ch'iu	Grey Young Dragon

$1.00	Hsüeh Chao Lu	Black with Snow-White Claws
$2.00	Ju Huang Pao	Yellow Leopard
$2.50	Mo K'ung Ch'üeh	Flying Magpie
$5.00	Ts'ang Ni Ch'üan Jan	Heaven Lion
$8.00	Pan Chin Piao	Mottled Coat Tiger

The Chinese Postal Administration issued these ten stamps to "coordinate the Chinese Cultural Renaissance" in the Republic of China as well as to "arouse the public to awareness of the protection of animals."

The Chinese characters on the stamps read, "Postage stamps of the Republic of China" and the English wording "Republic of China" along with the value.

How to Read a Scott's Catalogue

This Puppy looks so sad because at first it's hard to find a stamp in *Scott's Catalogue—but you can.* The catalogue lists the stamps of nearly every country in the world and numbers them in the order in which they were issued in that particular country. To find a stamp you have to:

1. Know from what country it comes (most important).

2. Look through the pictures shown for that country and match them to your stamp. Our Puppy is second from the bottom in the second column.

3. Under or next to that picture you will find what the stamp design represents.

4. Under or next to that there is the letter "A," followed by a number —in this case "A255." This is the design number.

5. The next line tells you the process by which this stamp was printed: "lithographed and engraved."

6. On the left-hand side of the following line is the year, month, and day of issue: "1966, June 16." This is the date that would appear on a first-day cover.

7. The following line, from left to right, gives the *Scott's Catalogue* number: "763." Next comes the number "A255," which is the number

1965, Oct. 7 Photo. and Engraved
753   A245   1.50s gold, red & blk. 27   20
Issued to commemorate the 50th anniversary of the Union of Austrian Towns.

Lithographed and Engraved
1965, Oct. 25   Perf. 12   Unwmkd.
754   A246   3s blk., brt. bl. & red 45   35
Issued to commemorate the 10th anniversary of Austria's admission to the United Nations.

University of Technology, Vienna
A247

1965, Nov. 8 Engraved Perf. 13½x14
755   A247   1.50s violet   25   17
Issued to commemorate the 150th anniversary of the founding of the Vienna University of Technology.

Map of Austria with Postal Zone
Numbers—A248

1966, Jan. 14   Photo.   Perf. 12
756   A248   1.50s yel., red & blk. 25   7
Issued to publicize the introduction of postal zone numbers, Jan. 1, 1966.

PTT Building,
Emblem and
Churches of Sts.   Maria von Ebner
Maria Rotunda   Eschenbach
and Barbara
A249   A250

Lithographed and Engraved
1966, March 4   Perf. 14x13½
757   A249   1.50s dull yellow   23   14
Issued to commemorate the centenary of the headquarters of the Post and Telegraph Administration.

1966, March 11   Engraved
758   A250   3s plum   40   28
Issued to commemorate the 50th anniversary of the death of Maria von Ebner Eschenbach (1830–1916), novelist and poet.

1966, Apr. 19 Engr.   Perf. 14x13½
759   A251   1.50s slate green   25   16
Issued to commemorate the 200th anniversary of the opening of the Prater (park), Vienna, to the public by Emperor Joseph II.

Josef
Hoffmann
A252

Unwmkd.
1966, May 6   Engraved   Perf. 12
760   A252   3s dark brown   40   27
Issued to commemorate the tenth anniversary of the death of Josef Hoffmann (1870–1956), architect.

Arms of Wiener
Neustadt
A253

Photogravure and Engraved
1966, May 27   Perf. 14
761   A253   1.50s gray & multi. 25   17
Issued to publicize the Wiener Neustadt Art Exhibition, centered around the time and person of Emperor Frederick III (1440–1493).

Austrian
Eagle and
Emblem of
National
Bank
A254

1966, May 27   Perf. 14
762   A254   3s gray grn., dk. brn.
            & dk. green   40   32
Issued to commemorate the 150th anniversary of the Austrian National Bank.

Puppy
A255

Lithographed and Engraved
1966, June 16   Perf. 12
763   A255   1.80s yellow & black 27   22
Issued to commemorate the 120th anniversary of the Vienna Humane Society.

Lithographed
1966, Aug. 17 Perf. 13½ Unwr
Flowers in Natural Colors
764   A256   1.50s dark blue   22
765   "   1.80s   "   "   25
766   "   2.20s   "   "   45
767   "   3s   "   "   50
768   "   4s   "   "   70
769   "   5s   "   "   65
     Nos. 764–769 (6) 2.77

Fair
Building
A257

1966, Aug. 26 Engr. Perf. 13½
770   A257   3s violet blue   40
First International Fair at Wels.

Peter Anich, Map,   Sick Worker a
Globe and Books   Health Emble
A258   A259

1966, Sept. 1   Perf. 14x1
771   A258   1.80s black   27
Issued to commemorate the 200th anniversary of the death of Peter Anich (17—1766), Tirolean cartographer and far

1966, Sept. 19   Engr. and Li
772   A259   3s black & verm.   40
Issued to publicize the 15th Occupati Medicine Congress, Vienna, Sept. 19–2

Theater
Collectio
"Eunuch
by Tere
from a
1496
Edition
A260

Designs: 1.80s, Map Collection: T page of Geographia Blavania (Cronus, cules and celestial sphere). 2.20s, Pict Archive and Portrait Collection: View Old Vienna after a watercolor by An Stutzinger. 3s, Manuscript Collection: lustration from the 15th century "Livre Cuer d'Amours Esprls" of the Duke R d'Anjou.

Photogravure and Engraved
1966, Sept. 28   Perf. 13½x
773   A260   1.50s multicolored   22
774   "   1.80s   "   25
775   "   2.20s   "   32
776   "   3s   "   40
     Austrian National Library.

Scott's Catalogue, Vol. II, listing. (Courtesy of Scott Publications, Inc.)

given to the design, as explained above. Now you can see how the number of the design helps you find the catalogue number. Next comes the face value (in Austrian money): "1.80s." It means that an Austrian would have bought this stamp at the post office for one shilling and eighty groschen. Still on the same line is "yellow & black," which are the colors of the stamp. Following that is the number "27," which is the Scott catalogue value of 27 cents for *an unused* stamp. The last number "22" is the Scott catalogue value for a *used* stamp. The catalogue always follows that order. The prices given are only a guide to the market value of the stamp. It may be higher or lower, depending on supply and demand.

8. The last line gives you the reason for issuing the stamp.

For a collector it is most important to take note of all the information provided in the catalogue. You can soon recognize our Puppy as a commemorative stamp. He was issued to commemorate the one-hundred-twentieth anniversary of the Vienna Humane Society. When you get a catalogue, your eye naturally shoots to "How much is it worth?" Our little mutt is valued at 27 cents mint and 22 cents used. This only has meaning when you ask a stamp dealer "How much?" I called my favorite local stamp dealer. He sold me a single Puppy stamp for 25 cents mint and a used copy for 10 cents. Austrian stamps are recognized as sound; they hold their price and increase over a period of time in logical sequence. Austria does not create stamps to entice the ignorant collector. Their printings equal their postal demands. Thus, our little Puppy holds a dignified status. You won't find him in a packet offering, and he won't be involved in any rip-off stamp deals. Briefly, the darling has class.

First day of issue cover, Vienna, Austria. (Courtesy of Honor R. Holland)

Just a bit about my local stamp dealer. Alas, after many years in New York he recently moved to New Jersey. Did that lead me to another local dealer? Never. I learned long ago that your stamp dealer can become as important to you as a good lawyer. If you remain with him, he knows your ever-growing stamp interests and looks out for them. He can help you to build a first-class collection. Obviously the more you get to know about your stamps the more he can research along with you. There are many avenues that provide a marketplace to help you obtain the stamps you need. With my dealer there is little haggling, unlike the stamp dealer equivalent of the gillie-gillie type at Port Said. The longer you collect, the shorter the route of your search. This hobby is a broad, people-to-people affair, and your contacts unravel somewhat like the old Japanese dolls that fit into one another from very big to very little. But the pursuit can start with one responsible stamp dealer.

Our Puppy is the lead to putting together a topical collection on the subject of "Dogs on Stamps."

Rejected essay of "Babe."
(Courtesy of *Scott's Monthly Journal*)

"Babe"

What fabulous pedigreed dog would be chosen to be the model for a stamp to honor the one hundredth anniversary of the ASPCA? Would it be the Best-in-Show-pampered Pekingese? A stalwart, handsome German shepherd or a lovable pedigreed poodle? What dog in the United States could be the star of a luncheon at the Waldorf Astoria in New York City, with two thousand guests at $10 a plate to celebrate the first day of issue of a dog stamp?

The Society for the Prevention of Cruelty to Animals approached Norman Todhunter, one of the nation's top graphic artists. Naturally, it was the designer who chose the featured canine. Norman knew who his model would be. He wrote, "I have always felt that an artist should whenever possible select subjects for which he has the greatest empathy." And he had great empathy for his own dog, Babe. To make it perfectly clear, Norman Todhunter loved Babe. She was just a mongrel. Her mother was a Labrador retriever, but her father a heartless, unknown brute. Our model would represent the melting pot, a sort of mongrel strength, that was our country.

Babe was a hopeless model, according to Norman Todhunter. She hated flashbulbs. As soon as Norman began taking pictures of her, she proceeded to hide under the kitchen sink. Despite all her antics, three separate designs went to Washington, D.C. Todhunter's favorite sketch was rejected. These rejected designs are sought after by collectors, but almost impossible to come by. They are the very beginning of the process of producing a stamp. If you happen to meet an artist who is designing a stamp, start smiling at him, especially if he is not a stamp collector. Get the preliminary sketches he is apt to throw into the wastebasket. Be a step ahead of the archives.

The great day finally arrived. Babe, with a red, white, and blue ribbon was en route to the Waldorf Astoria to attend the first day of issue luncheon ceremony. How would she behave?

A temporary post office was set up in the Grand Ballroom. Eager collectors and noncollectors alike were getting FDC cancels, and some tried to get Norman Todhunter's autograph. In the midst of the hubbub, Ernest Kehr, author of *The Romance of Stamp Collecting* and

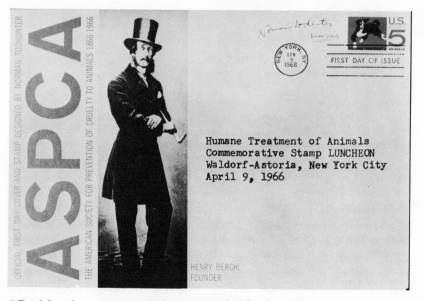

Official first-day program, ASPCA, autographed by the designer.
(Courtesy of The Posthorn, Inc., New York)

well-known philatelist, spotted Norman and Babe. He swiftly led them into a small anteroom where Ernie got Babe's paw prints for his special album, right next to Elsie, the Borden cow's hoof print. (Some of the other autographs in Ernie's album are Dwight D. Eisenhower, Queen Juliana of the Netherlands, Franklin D. Roosevelt, Francis Cardinal Spellman, and Neil Armstrong.)

Like the audience, Babe was bored by the speeches of the dignitaries and the presentation of albums that contained a United States sheet of fifty stamps bearing her portrait. Suddenly the lights dimmed. Two thousand people filled the Grand Ballroom, and the orchestra struck up the "Star-Spangled Banner." A lone spotlight welcomed the star of the show, Babe. Despite the fact that she didn't like men in uniform, she was flanked by her color guard, and together they marched to the center of the stage. Flash bulbs were popping everywhere. Babe didn't blink an eye. She knew this was her day, designated to remind the nation to be kind to all animals. One hundred fifteen million Babe stamps later, the designer reported that Babe was still deluged for paw prints.

Col. Henry W. Hartsfield, USAF, scheduled for the space shuttle *Enterprise*, 1980.
(Courtesy of National Aeronautics and Space Administration)

The World's First Space Traveler

Col. Henry W. Hartsfield of the United States Air Force (assigned to NASA as an astronaut scheduled to be on the space shuttle *Enterprise* in 1980) is attending stamp shows as guest of honor in NASA flying togs. The twentieth-century space age, with its sophisticated satellite communication, meteorology, and medicine, had its startling beginning when Laika, the world's first space traveler, orbited the earth in a Russian spacecraft called *Sputnik II*.

Following Laika came Belka and Strelka, and Chernushka and Zvezdochka who orbited in *Sputnik IV* and *V,* and helped to pave the scientific route to the heavens which put Yuri A. Gagarin of the Soviet Union into space and Neil Armstrong of the United States on the moon.

Mongolia, Ascension, Romania, and Bulgaria were a few of the countries that issued stamps to honor the dog pioneers of the space age. Reading *Scott's Catalogue* can give you a lot of information. For instance, the description of the two values of the 1957 Laika set from Romania reveals the difference between the two stamps. The designs are alike; the face value is the same. What then can you detect? The difference is the color.

To locate Laika in the set of five of 1963 from Romania is a bit tricky. You'll notice the lead picture shows a stamp of 20 bani value, and under it in small type "Centenary of 1958." Read on and you will see "Stamps on stamps 40b—Sputnik and Laika." That's your stamp. The catalogue number is C146.

All Scott numbers preceded by "C" are airmails. Can you locate the words *"Posta aeriana"* on the stamp?

This airmail set tells a few other facts. Our Laika is the lowest denomination in the set of five. The design incorporates a miniature reproduction of the 1957 Laika stamp. It is known as a stamp-on-a-stamp. This set embraces another topic relating to stamps that are issued to commemorate the Universal Postal Union.

The above three points suggest that you won't be the only person interested in that Laika stamp. You will have to decide if you want just one stamp—the Laika—or the entire set. Some dealers will sell only the entire set. Collectors have different points of view. Some swear that if the stamp is part of a larger set that costs more than $1 they won't buy it to obtain one stamp. The impatient collector will forfeit a few dollars. Melvin Garabrant, Vice-President of the American Topical Association, says, "If it's a good set I'll buy it." Why? "Because," he says, "the price value of the set increases every year. It advances the worth of an entire collection. If the time comes when you want to sell it, you'll get more for complete sets."

One's instinct is to save money and purchase the exact stamp one wants. In a way this stubborn attitude can be more rewarding. In its bimonthly journal, *Topical Time,* the ATA carries advertisements of dealers whose entire stock is categorized into topics. This is one way you can get that stamp by itself. The ATA also has a membership list whereby you can write to members who collect your topic. Here you can get into a swapping scene with your fellow "Dogs on Stamps" collectors.

188

Bobilna
Monument
A444

Black-winged
Stilt
A445

1957, Nov. 30

1192 A443 50b deep plum 20 5
1193 A444 55b slate blue 35 5

Issued to commemorate the 520th anniversary of
the insurrection of the peasants of Bobilna in 1437.

Perf. 13½x14, 14x13½

1957, Dec. 27 Photo. Wmk. 358

Animals: 10b, Great white egret. 20b,
White spoonbill. 50b, Sturgeon. 55b,
Ermine (horiz.). 1.30 l, White pelican
(horiz.).

1194 A445 5b red brn. & gray 5 5
1195 " 10b emerald & ochre 6 5
1196 " 20b bright red &
ochre 10 5
1197 " 50b blue green &
ochre 25 10
1198 " 55b deep claret
& gray 30 20
1199 " 1.30 l purple & orange 65 50
Nos. 1194-1199, C53-C54 (8) 5.91 1.65

Sputnik 2 and Laika

1957, Dec. 20 Perf. 14x13½

1200 A446 1.20 l blue &
dark brown 1.20 20
1201 " 1.20 l greenish blue
& chocolate 1.20 20

Dog Laika, "first space traveler."

Romanian Arms and Flags
A447

Designs: 55b, Arms, "Industry and Agriculture."
1.20 l, Arms, "Art, Science and Sport (soccer)."

222

No. C79 Surcharged and Overprinted:
"1913–1963 50 ani de la moarte"
Lithographed

1963, Sept. 15 Perf. 14 Unwmkd.

C145 AP31 1.75 l on 10b
yel. & brn. 75 18

Issued to commemorate the 50th anniversary of the death of Aurel Vlaicu, aviation pioneer.

Centenary Stamp of 1958
AP54

Stamps on Stamps: 40b, Sputnik 2 and
Laika, No. 1200. 55b, Yuri A. Gagarin,
No. C104a. 1.20 l, Nikolayev and Popo-
vich, Nos. C123 & C125. 1.55 l, Postal
Administration Bldg. and letter carrier, No.
965.

1963, Nov. 15 Photo. Perf. 14x13½

Size: 38x26mm.

C146 AP54 20b light blue
& dk. brn. 9 3
C147 " 40b brt. pink &
dark blue 21 3
C148 " 55b lt. ultra &
dk. carm.
rose 30 6
C149 " 1.20 l ocher & pur. 60 10
C150 " 1.55 l sal. pink &
olive gray 70 12
Nos. C146-C150, CB22 (6) 3.40 84

15th UPU Congress, Vienna.

Pavel R. Popovich
AP55

Astronauts and flag: 5b, Yuri A. Gagarin.
10b, Gherman S. Titov. 20b, John H
Glenn, Jr. 35b, M. Scott Carpenter. 40b,
Andrian G. Nikolayev. 60b, Walter M
Schirra. 75b, Gordon L. Cooper. 1 l.
Valeri Bykovski. 1.40 l, Valentina Teresh-
kova. (5b, 10b, 20b, 35b, 60b and 75b
are diamond shaped)

Laika stamp of 1957 (left) and 1963 (right) (Courtesy of Honor R. Holland)
and stamp listing from *Scott's Catalogue.* (Courtesy of Scott Publications)

The first-day cover from Bulgaria bears a stamp showing the dog pioneers of *Sputnik IV* and *V*. The stamp is tied to the envelope by a special commemorative cancellation. The outer circle spells their names, the three inner circles denote their orbits, and in the center is the world. To the left of this is a round cancel showing the date of issue and then the city, Sofia, in English and Bulgarian. The diamond-shaped cancellation is in four languages, "First Day." Can you figure them out? The cachet at the bottom of the envelope is the four little pioneers. This cover is known as a "handback" because it is unaddressed and has never gone through the mail.

Space dogs on first-day cover, Bulgaria.
(Courtesy of Honor R. Holland)

International Dogs on Stamps Show

CLASS I: SPORTING BREEDS

ENTRIES:

Pointer, San Marino.

Karelian Bear Dog, Finland.

Cocker Spaniel, Monaco.

Labrador Retriever, U.S.A.

(continued)

German Boar Hound, Dahomey.
(Courtesy of Honor R. Holland)

Arranging a topical collection is a lot of fun. I thought it would be amusing to classify our dogs along the lines of a real dog show. A love for dogs could lead you to track down the history of each breed, in order to put together a knowledgeable presentation of the topic and stamps at hand. The classifications are taken from the one-hundredth Westminster Kennel Club Dog Show.

Our alert Pointer is the low value in a good set from San Marino, situated on the top of Mount Titano, a country hardly bigger than a stamp. San Marino was the refuge of Garibaldi, the unifier of all Italy and the one responsible for the first democracy in Europe.

To see what is below the design on the stamp, you'll need a magnifying glass. At the left is I.P.S. OFF. CAR. Val. Roma, which is the name of the printer. To the right is the name of the designer, R. Franzoni. One-third of the stamp shows the coat of arms of San Marino, which you might wish to investigate further, if you are curious.

From the Principality of Monaco, where Princess Grace and her stamp-collecting husband Prince Rainier III reign, comes the prize-winning Cocker Spaniel, issued to commemorate the 1971 International Dog Show that was held in sparkling Monte Carlo.

The Karelian Bear Dog from Finland is the second value of three stamps—all dogs—issued to raise funds for their Anti-Tuberculosis Society campaign. The Labrador Retriever from the United States is a Hunting Permit stamp issued, naturally, to license hunters. On the back of the stamp there is a gray inscription that says, "It is unlawful to hunt waterfowl unless you sign your name in ink on the face of the stamp." The Hunting Permit stamps have been issued annually since

1934 and are better known as the "Duck stamps." To date, the Retriever is the only dog in this interesting special category. Where can you find it in *Scott's?* Quite naturally, under "U.S. Hunting Permits." The catalogue value is $30 mint and $1.75 used. Since every hunter has to sign his name on the front of the stamp, it is obvious that a perfect mint copy would be harder to obtain, because the purpose of getting the stamp is to obtain the necessary hunting permission. Certainly this Retriever carrying a mallard duck is expensive, but it is a smart and different addition to your collection. It's proof that you know your subject.

The German Boar Hound from the African Republic of Dahomey is depicted in a well-known painting of young Prince Balthazar by Velasquez. This stamp is cancelled "First Day of Issue" on what is known as a "Maximum Card." The cancellation, which is in French, commemorates the twenty-fifth anniversary of UNICEF, as does the stamp. You might wonder why a country in Africa sings praises to UNICEF. It is because UNICEF has aided underdeveloped countries by providing, food, medical supplies, and child care centers. A German Boar Hound would not likely appear in a dog show today, because he is a seventeenth-century dog. The Prince, however, has quite a twentieth-century haircut. You might notice that the stamp design matches the card. This is a nice item to own and gives variety to your collection. It's the kind of an item you can pick up at a stamp show.

"Perf," the philatelic poodle.
(Courtesy of *Minkus Stamp Journal*)

PERFS

Perf the Poodle didn't know that in the early history of stamps an Irishman, Henry Archer, bought a few sheets of stamps. He couldn't find scissors to separate them, so he proceeded to punch a row of holes along the margins of the stamps, making it easier to tear them apart. As a matter of fact, by experimenting with this action, he improved his system for perforating stamps, and in about the year 1847 he sold his brainstorm (now a model and patent of "A machine to pierce the sheet of stamps with holes so that each sheet could be torn apart") to the British Post Office for $100,000. The first perforated stamps appeared in England in 1854.

When Archer, the Irishman, put "teeth" on stamps, the vocabulary of his perforations became known in philatelic jargon as "perfs." As the intellectuals got into the act, they delved further into the fact that "perforate" comes from the Latin "per" which means "to," and "forace" means "bore," that is, to make a hole through anything by boring it or punching it.

In his superb book on stamp collecting, *Foundations of Philately,* Mr. William S. Boggs wrote, "Dr. LeGrand, a Frenchman, found that most stamps in his time were approximately two centimeters wide and therefore took two centimeters or 20 millimeters as the unit for gauging perforations." The gauge of the perforations is the number of holes in two centimeters, regardless of the size of the stamp.

Perforation gauge with stamp.

Our appealing dachshund from Luxembourg is perf 11½. Actually he should be facedown on the perf gauge, so that the design doesn't annoy your accurate measurement. The perforation gauge eliminates the need to count the holes to find the perf. By matching the holes or "teeth" of the stamp against the lines or dots on the gauge, you can quickly detect the perforation of a stamp. You can purchase a perforation gauge from most dealers and album manufacturers.

It makes sense to question why so much interest exists in the perf of a stamp. Perforation of a stamp is especially important if more than one perf has been used on the same stamp design issued. In *Scott's Catalogue,* for example, the Harding Memorial Issue of September 1, 1923, #610, is perf 11 and the catalogue shows it at 45 cents mint and 8 cents used. On September 12, 1923, #612, the same design, this time perf 10, is catalogued $9 mint and 75 cents used. The difference in value suggests it is indeed worth the bother to learn to read a perf gauge to measure the perfs in your stamps. To achieve the perfection, one strives for every existing variety. This begins to separate the accumulator from the collector. Extra knowledge can bring financial bonuses.

CLASS II: HOUND BREEDS

ENTRIES:

Newfoundland, St. Pierre and Miquelon.

Akito, Japan.

German Shepherd, Netherlands.

Newfoundland from Newfoundland.

Puli Sheep Dog, Hungary.

(Courtesy of Honor R. Holland)

DEFINITIVE—CLASS III

In our Class III entries, the little Akito from Japan is a definitive stamp. In *Scott's Catalogue* if the designated number of a stamp is a direct number, without a letter in front of it, you know that the stamp is either definitive or commemorative. If there is no listing as to what it commemorates, then it's a definitive stamp—that is, one that is easiest to purchase in the post office. It may be sold indefinitely, while a commemorative stamp has a limited time within which it is on sale. Also, often, if you don't ask specifically for a commemorative stamp, you may get the definitive that's on hand. Actually, from a philatelist's point of view, the study of a definitive stamp can be engrossing be-

CLASS III: WORKING BREEDS

ENTRIES:

Dachshund, Luxembourg.

Great Dane, Monaco.

Dachshund, Romania.

Borzoi, Russia.

St. Bernard, Albania.

(Courtesy of Honor R. Holland)

cause it's printed over and over again, creating shade varieties and other subtle differences that make for challenging detective work.

In my early days of collecting, I became interested in a definitive Spanish stamp depicting King Alphonso XIII as a baby. I had the chance to buy five pounds of used stamps of this definitive issue inexpensively. My Baby Alphonso stamps were soaking in the bathtub, in bowls, and even in the refrigerator and bureau drawers. I was looking for shade varieties and found many differences, since that particular stamp was available at the Spanish post office for a period of ten years.

Thus, if you really become involved, a study of the Akito could enhance your topical collection no end. Adding a few shade varieties to your collection puts you way ahead of anyone who doesn't take the time to do so.

The surtax of the seeing-eye German Shepherd was designated for social and cultural programs in the Netherlands.

One wonderful dog stamp comes from St. Pierre and Miquelon, two islands which belong to France and are located off the coast of Newfoundland covering an area of 93 square miles, with a population of 5,225, according to *Scott's Catalogue*. Their life-styles, told through their stamps, include fishermen, fishing, schooners, lighthouses, dog teams, rabbits, ice hockey, puffins, snow owls and, of course, the Newfoundland dog.

The "J" in front of the Scott number signifies that the Newfoundland dog from St. Pierre and Miquelon is a tax stamp with eleven different values. He's as expensive used as mint.

Vignette.

Proof of the frame.

Registered cover from St. Pierre and Miquelon to Wallaceburg, Ontario.

(Courtesy of Honor R. Holland)

It is quite delightful to stray from the beaten path to find unusual material that embellishes your collection. The design in the center of the stamp is known as the vignette. And doesn't our Newfoundland dog look smart and proud all by himself? The stamp beneath the vignette is the proof of the frame, and at this stage the finished product is ready to represent St. Pierre and Miquelon around the world.

The censored cover cancelled St. Pierre and Miquelon, dated 14–10–42, classifies this as a war cover of World War II. This cover has a curious postal history. To begin with, it's unusual for a tax stamp to be deemed acceptable for postage. This calls for further investigation. The 5-cent tax stamp is tied by a St. Pierre and Miquelon cancel dated 14–10, and underneath 42, which means it was marked October 14, 1942, to Wallaceburg, Ontario. Did you notice the censor tape marking with the number DB/106? On the back of the cover the tape reads "Examined by," making this a desirable World War II cover, for any value in this set "on cover" is worth having. The low value stamp was sufficient for the postal rate. Now you can understand why stamp fiends thoroughly examine boxes at stamp shows, hoping to find unexpected material. With only a population of 5,000, what amount of mail was sent using the high value stamps to Europe, Asia, or South America? If you keep your eyes open for unusual Newfoundland dog covers from St. Pierre and Miquelon, you may find one. If you do, grab it; it's a prize addition to your canine philatelic collection because in this case a used cover is more valuable than a first day of issue cover that never went through the mail. There are two more interesting definitives worthy of discussion, both from Newfoundland.

He's engraved, he's watermarked, and he's a lovable Newfoundland dog that appears on an interesting definitive set that was issued January 1, 1932, in Newfoundland. We have not yet discussed details of printing and printing methods but despite modern type printings, an engraved stamp has the appellation of "class."

You are familiar with watermarks if you've ever taken a good notepaper or letterhead and put it up against the light, for it's easy to see them. They existed long before the postage stamp. Basically they were applied to stamps to prevent forgery. Recognition of watermarks is very important because they help you classify your stamps. They come in all forms. On our Newfoundland dog the watermark is a coat of arms, but the most common watermarks are crowns, stars, letters, and designs. They can appear as single watermarks, one on every stamp to the sheet, or they can appear in multiples, repeats, and they emerge as normal, reversed, inverted, and in other forms. They can engage you in a jolly observation hunt.

Most of the time you can put your stamps up against the light and see watermarked paper; however, collectors use a watermark detector that resembles a black, shallow, glasslike tray. In it the stamp is placed facedown. You then put enough benzine or lighter fluid into the tray to cover the stamp. The watermark is seen immediately, there is no harm done to the gum or paper, and the stamp dries quickly. But don't smoke because you are handling inflammable fluid. Do not attempt to use this technique on stamps that are photogravure. As a matter of fact, always use the watermark tray with caution and care. Because some inks do not respond to the fluid, you should consult a fellow collector or catalogue before you undertake the procedure.

Recalled stamp of King Edward VIII.
(Courtesy of the Essay Proof Society of British North America)

King Edward VIII

The stamp of King Edward VIII was approved September 25, 1936. But with these words, "I have found it impossible to carry the heavy burden of responsibility and to discharge my duties as King, as I wish to do, without the help and support of the woman I love," King Edward VIII abdicated, making his the most poignant love story of the twentieth century, and voiding the stamp.

This approved but never issued stamp of Newfoundland created a swift change of a new definitive that would portray King George VI. What was done for a new definitive set? Our Newfoundland dog remained the 14-cent value but on the right-hand end the portrait of the king was added. Perforations of this stamp come in perfs of 14 and 13¼. Added to this, Holmes's handbook, a specialized Canadian catalogue on stamps of British North America, states, "Several re-entries, especially on the 14c value, exist." A reentry is a retouching of the die to improve the impression of the new stamp to be printed.

These extra bits of information aren't of much interest to the happy accumulator of stamps, but shifting into the rarefied position of a collector, your pursuit of knowledge of your stamp promotes you to the echelon where the "think kings" of stampdom reign. To tempt you to this consideration is totally irresistible.

A too-brief mention of specialized catalogues is necessary here and now. As with the Japanese wooden doll that has form after form as you unravel it, *Scott's Catalogue* yields general information at many levels.

Because I fell in love with this definitive Newfoundland dog, I got interested in a more detailed information catalogue of British North America, and for this specific area, I found Holmes's *Specialized Catalogue of Canada and British North America* and *The Essays and Proofs of British North America.* By the time you've read these books, you're well underway to knowing a great deal about our Newfoundland dog. If it weren't for the Duke of Windsor's love for Wally Simpson, his career as a stamp, where the portrait of King George VI replaced him, never would have come to pass.

WHAT IS A PROOF?

The first impression of a selected design showing the stamp as it will appear when issued. A proof may be in many colors and on different kinds of paper.

In *The Essays and Proofs of British North America,* you can read about all the proofs in existence. It is not all that impossible to own one. There is a society rather on the high-brow scale known as the Essay-Proof Society, and if you join, you will be in a position whereby you can begin the trek toward finding one proof. After this first victorious step, you'll be in line for more, and if you advance to this rarefied stage, you can first begin to call yourself a philatelist.

The master die of King George VI's head was added to the entire definitive set of 1932 which became the definitive set of 1936, and if you can add this to your topical collection then you are approaching the advanced stage of becoming an exhibitor. In any case, exposure to the Tiffany class is not a must, but why not look in the deluxe philatelic window?

The beginning die proof. Left: Dog motif extracted from the 14-cent value of 1932; right: King vignette from the special die made for this issue.
(Courtesy of Robert H. Pratt)

Composite die proof for the lettering used on the Newfoundland issues.
(Courtesy of Robert H. Pratt)

Finished die proof.
(Courtesy of Robert H. Pratt)

The stamp as issued.
(Courtesy of Robert H. Pratt)

CLASS IV: TERRIER BREEDS

ENTRIES:

Airedale, Poland.

Schnauzer, Monaco.

Fox Terrier, Poland.

(Courtesy of Honor R. Holland)

There is one stamp in this charming terrier group which you should query, having to do with the value of the stamp. If you have sharp eyes you will notice that it is the Schnauzer on the Monaco stamp where the value is written "o.00." The reason the value is shown this way is that the stamp is a specimen usually sent along with a press release to show the philatelic press what the stamp actually looks like. This specimen is a black-and-white glossy photograph suitable for reproduction in the press.

CLASS V: TOY GROUP

ENTRIES:

Pekingese, Republic of China.

Poodle, Hungary.

Pekingese, Republic of China.

Poodle, Czechoslovakia.

Poodle, Bhutan.   (Courtesy of Honor R. Holland)

In the Toy Group the only visible difference is on one of the two stamps from the Republic of China of the Pekingese dogs. Note that one stamp shows the 4.50 value normally while on the other two horizontal lines obliterate the value. The latter is a specimen. The airmail souvenir sheet of the poodle from Bhutan is in the "doghouse," philatelically speaking, because he comes from Bhutan, and he is sharing his doghouse with the Lhasa Apso in Class VI.

CLASS VI: NONSPORTING GROUP

ENTRIES:

Chow, Hong Kong.

Bulldog, Albania.

Lhasa Apso, Bhutan.   (Courtesy of Honor R. Holland)

The fetching bulldog comes from "SHQIPERIA"—doesn't look like Albania at all, does it? You can't get very involved in stamp collecting without researching the intrigue of language. "Shqiperia" is indeed the word "Albania."

His Majesty King Jigme Singye Wangchuck of Bhutan.
(Courtesy of the Bhutan Mission to the United Nations)

ABOUT BHUTAN

His Majesty King Jigme Singye Wangchuck rules over one million Bhutanese in a tiny kingdom smaller than Delaware situated in the Himalayas. The official religion is Tantric Buddhism introduced in the eighth century A.D. by Guru Rimpoche. Bhutan has three public schools, twelve junior high schools, seventy primary schools, and two technical schools. They have six general hospitals, twenty-five doctors, and fifty-one nurses for a total bed capacity of three hundred. For foreign guests there are three hotels and three guest houses.

FRIENDSHIP

How do our poodle souvenir sheet and our two irresistible apsos (well-known dogs from Tibet famed for fidelity to their masters) fall into the philatelic doghouse?

It all started when an American student at Oxford, Burt Kerr Todd, met a fellow student from Bhutan, a young lady from the royal family. She fascinated him with stories of social needs of her small country in the Himalayas. Upon graduation, Todd and two other student friends set out to visit the tiny state. When they finally got to the capital, Thimphu, they received a royal welcome. Todd fell in love with Bhutan. He was entranced with their ancient traditions, their gentle warmth and hospitality. Burt Todd, by the way, was a millionaire steel magnate. Because of his knowledge of United States industry, he was invited to become an honorary financial adviser to the Bhutan government. As important was his own desire to find a way to repay the endearing hospitality he received while in Bhutan. He wanted to help in the areas of health, social services, and transport.

This resulted in his approach to the World Bank for a loan. He was turned down. While in the elevator at the World Bank, he met a top United States official who had also attended the meeting. He told Todd not to be disappointed, that there were other ways. Did Todd ever consider the issuance of a postage stamp? Other countries balance their budgets this way, so why not Bhutan?

Todd presented this idea of revenue to the Bhutanese and he was asked to execute the program. He did, and in so doing, sent the philatelic world into a turmoil. Todd created a totally different concept of stamps—three-dimensional space stamps, steel industry stamps on steel foil, Buddhist Thanka paintings on silk, roses scented on stamps, and talking stamps on records that really play. The stamps were a huge success. Out of this revenue an airfield and a hospital were built, but also the stamps were "black-blotted," or considered phony.

Registered cover from Thimphu, Bhutan, to New York.

Today there is the Bhutan Philatelic Society, 1808 Mandeville Canyon Rd., Los Angeles, Calif. 90049, aiming to restore the postal reputation of Bhutanese stamps. From Bhutan, the manager of the Bank of Bhutan and a schoolteacher are members. In the United States, members come from Ketchikan, Alaska, to Louisville, Kentucky, from Jackson, Mississippi, to Salem, Oregon, from Puyallup, Washington, to New York City. These members are devoted to Bhutan.

The Steinway Collection

It takes a Frenchman to say unashamedly, "I am a lover." Monsieur George Herpin, back in 1864, was a lover of stamps. One evening, in search of a name for his newfound love affair, he consulted a Greek dictionary and found the words "philos," meaning love, and "atelos," meaning free from tax. He combined the two to make "philately." This rather awkward, pompous-sounding name stuck. Ever since stamp collecting was termed philately, people have confused it with philanthropy, Philadelphia, and psychosis. More importantly, millions of people like George Herpin have had an ongoing desire to become true philatelists.

One of the great lovers of stamps was Theodore E. Steinway, of the great firm of Steinway and Sons, makers of the "instrument of the immortals," the Steinway piano. He was the dean and one of the early pioneers of stamp collecting. Although he was one of the finest classical, learned, and active collectors in the United States, his true enjoyment was his "Music on Stamps," which became world famous.

Steinway created his own album pages to conform to his own way of arranging stamps, souvenir sheets, music cancellations, and postmarks. He classified his pages in groupings of composers, dances, marches, chants, pianists, operas, wind instruments, bells, drums, and primitive instruments.

On each page he drew two or three bars of music from what he considered to be the best works of the composer or artist. His stamps portrayed:

Bach	Handel	Pergolosi
Beethoven	Haydn	Schubert
Berlioz	Liszt	Smetana
Bruckner	Mozart	Spontini
Chopin	Paderewski	Johann Strauss
Dvořak		

Theodore E. Steinway with his stamps. (Courtesy of John H. Steinway)

From Steinway's album pages.
(Courtesy of John H. Steinway)

Theodore Steinway's two or three chosen bars of music, as headings for his album pages:

Bach: Passacaglia
Beethoven: *Moonlight* Sonata
Berlioz: *Damnation of Faust*
Bruckner: Third Symphony
Chopin: Polonaise
Dvořak: New World
  Symphony
Handel: "Largo"
Haydn: Sonata

Liszt: Sonata
Mozart: "Alla Turca"
Paderewski: Minuet
Pergolosi: *La Serva Padrona*
Schubert: *Unfinished* Symphony
Smetana: *The Bartered Bride*
Johann Strauss: The Beautiful
  Blue Danube

Steinway Village cancel.
(Courtesy of John H. Steinway)

In 1871, Steinway and Sons purchased a 400-acre tract of farmland which was later to become the northern end of Long Island City. They built a model village for their employees, known as Steinway Village, which had its own post office and thus the Steinway cancellation.

Steinway and Sons sponsored concert artists such as Anton Rubenstein and his pupil Josef Hoffman, who played the Steinway piano at Steinway Hall, which was superseded by Carnegie Hall. It was at Carnegie Hall that the Steinways presented a young pianist they discovered in London who was a thunderous success in the United States. He was Ignace Jan Paderewski, who later became premier of Poland.

In 1919 Poland issued a stamp of Paderewski as premier to commemorate the First National Assembly. When the great artist was in the United States for a concert, Theodore Steinway had that Polish stamp ready for Paderewski to autograph. Said he, "Do me a real favor." To which the great pianist replied, "Of course. What is it?" "Autograph this stamp, don't autograph any other."* Steinway, a true lover of stamps, successfully obtained the only one of its kind. This autographed stamp remained one of Steinway's favorite jewels in his musical stamp collection. Catalogue value today is 8 cents.

Like many ardent stamp collectors, Steinway often gave philatelic gifts to his fellow stamp aficionados in the world of music. Singers such as Lily Pons, Lauritz Melchior, and Enrico Caruso were beneficiaries. Caruso was an accumulator who picked up stamps in cities and countries where he sang, including Naples, Milan, Moscow, St. Petersburg, Buenos Aires, Mexico City, London, and New York.

In 1933 Germany issued a significant set of nine stamps honoring

---

*When this collection was sold, the new owner found that he had two autographed pieces from Paderewski. Rather than destroying one, he gave it to the High School of Music and Art, New York City.

Paderewski autograph on Paderewski stamp.
(Courtesy of John H. Steinway)

the fiftieth anniversary of Richard Wagner's death. They portrayed scenes from nine of Wagner's music dramas. Steinway put together a souvenir card. He purchased five hundred Wagner sets at a dollar a set as soon as they were issued. He then went to the Steinway archives and chose a painting of Richard Wagner at the Steinway Grand Piano, which the company gave him on the occasion of his first Bayreuth Concert in 1876. After having this painting reproduced for his souvenir card, Steinway then mounted the Wagner set onto the card. His opera friends weren't the only lucky recipients of the VIP souvenir card. He sent one to his good friend and avid stamp collector President Franklin D. Roosevelt. He didn't forget his other stamp-collecting friends including Jascha Heifetz, the violinist, Piatigorsky, the cellist, and the late Cardinal Spellman. (Cardinal Spellman's stamp collection became the basis of the Cardinal Spellman museum in New Weston, Massachusetts.) A number of stamp dealers were on his list as well as top stamp auctioneers and friends from leading philatelic societies. Collectors and noncollectors from all walks of life sent Theodore Steinway gifts to add to his musical collection. (Once you let your friends know about your collecting interests, you'll be amazed at what may be given to you.) Today the $1 Wagner set is listed in *Scott's Catalogue* for $188.95 mint and $195.75 used.

Steinway was a leader in encouraging and supporting stamp exhibitions. This letter from Harold Ickes, Secretary of the Interior under FDR, to Theodore Steinway, on the occasion of the Third International Philatelic Exhibition held in New York City, of which Steinway was chairman, is a delightful reflection that flows from one collector to another:

As I grow older, I find myself more and more deeply interested in four things.

They are, in brief summary:

Progress—the steady and consistent advancement of humanity onward and upward toward a civilization freer, happier, and more notably humane;

Education—the improvement of our democracy in terms of a culture that is based upon philosophy, art and science, through both individual and co-operative effort;

Conservation—the preservation of the precious material and spiritual resources of our country and our people;

Peace—the development of a practical good-neighborliness in the world.

All of these great aims, I believe, may be promoted by and through philately. They have been and will be stimulated by the universal system of postal communication which now correlates the most distant communities of the earth. The little scraps of colored paper that we call stamps have been and will continue to be the instruments of that network—important, interesting and valuable in themselves; symbols of an age which is destined to prosper, not to perish.

To fellow philatelists, assembled in New York for the Third International Philatelic Exhibition, I send greetings and best wishes.

> Harold Ickes
> Secretary of the Interior (APS 9529)

Theodore Steinway is now one of the immortals of stampdom. He was the president of the Collectors Club of New York, America's most prestigious stamp club; purchased the basis of the Collectors Club Library, which today is the most important philatelic library in the country; was one of the founders of the Philatelic Foundation, whose major activities consist of expertizing stamps; and was a member of the American Topical Association, his membership card was #2000.

On September 8, 1972, Liechtenstein issued a set of three stamps, "Pioneers of Philately," of which the highest value portrays Theodore E. Steinway.

Today John Steinway, executive of Steinway and Sons, like his father, is a collector. Specializing mainly in Egyptian stamps, he is a trustee of The Philatelic Foundation. He relates with great zest stories of his father's antics and pleasures in collecting. One anecdote concerns the time Theodore Steinway had a duplicate of a much-sought-after, expensive, and elusive United States Trans-Mississippi high value stamp. He gave the duplicate to Jascha Heifetz, who upon re-

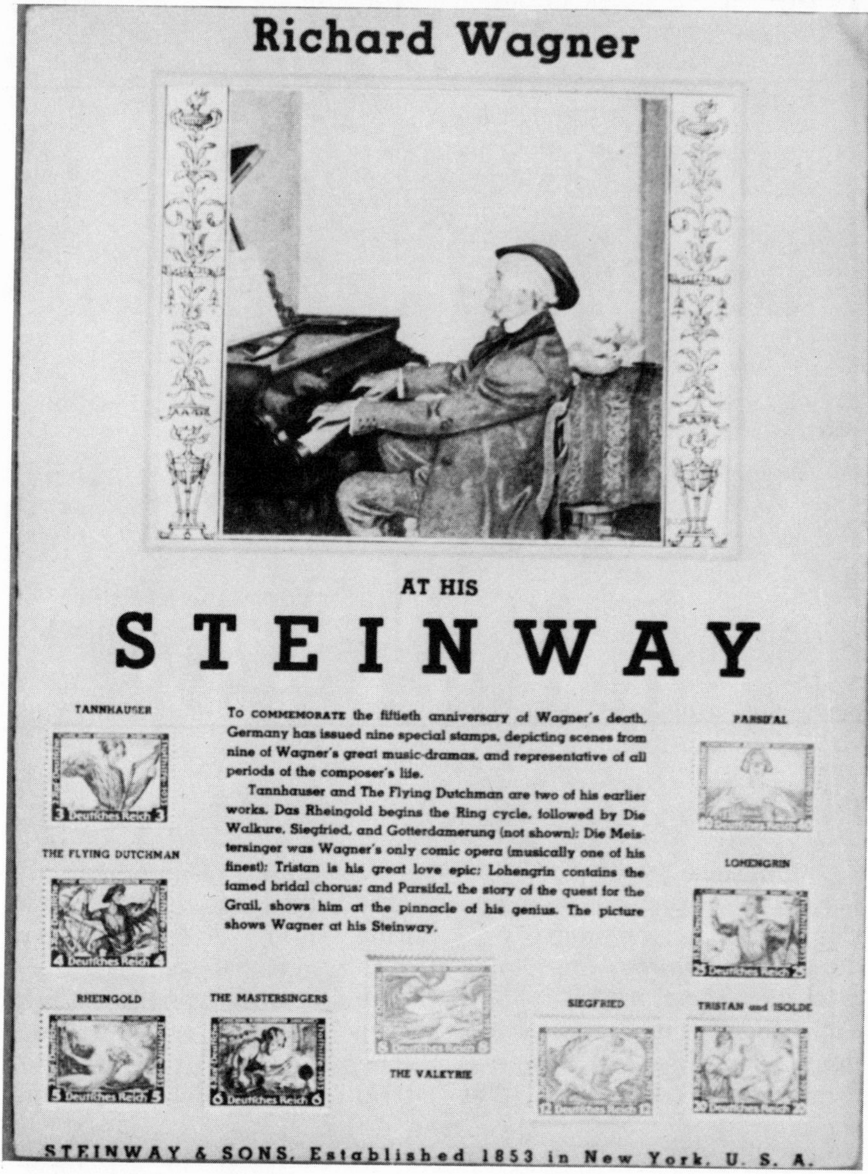

Steinway's gift.
(Courtesy of John H. Steinway)

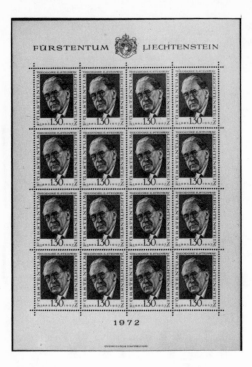

Stamp honoring Pioneers of
Philately, 1972.
(Courtesy of John H. Steinway)

ceiving it, exclaimed to Steinway: "Please, please don't tell Piatigorsky!"

Some Steinway Immortals

Dame Nellie Melba (1861–1931), first famed Australian opera star,
sang with Enrico Caruso. She received the D.B.E. (Dame of the British
Empire) for her charitable work during World War I. The caloric
dessert Peach Melba was named after this great star.

George Enescu (1881–1955), studied music with gypsies as a boy.
Violinist and composer, he is most known for his fiery gypsy "Second
Roumanian Rhapsody." He was a teacher of Yehudi Menuhin.

Ignace Jan Paderewski (1860–1941), premier of Poland, pianist,
composer.

Richard Wagner (1813–1883), great composer of operas: "Tannhäuser," "The Flying Dutchman," and the Ring Trilogy.

Gustav Mahler (1860–1911), Austrian conductor and composer. Director, Vienna State Opera; conductor, New York Philharmonic Orchestra. He wrote nine symphonies and was the last of the romantic
school of Vienna.

George Gershwin (1898–1937), famed American composer of
"Porgy and Bess," "Rhapsody in Blue," "An American in Paris."

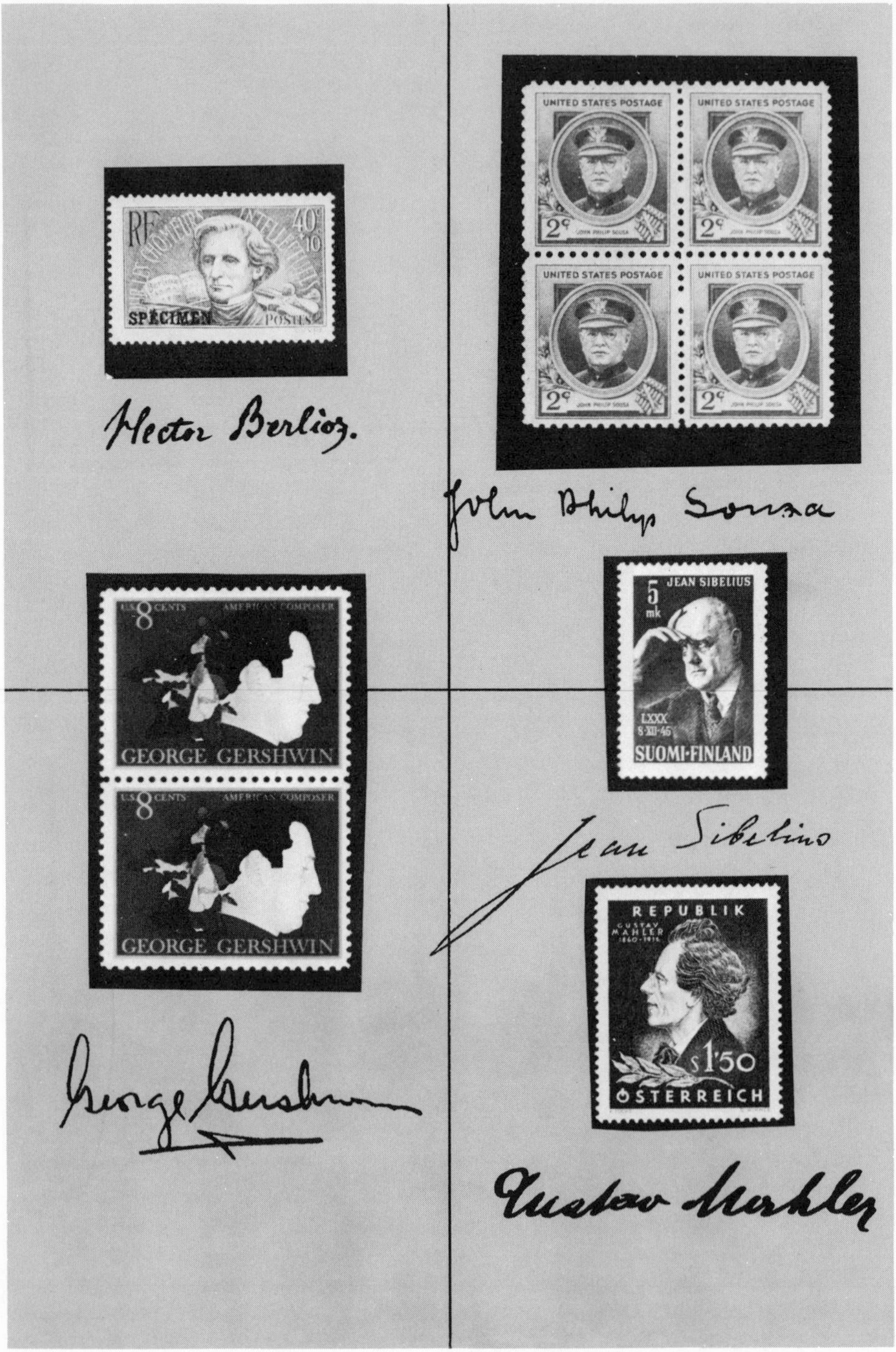

Hector Berlioz.

John Philip Sousa

George Gershwin

Jean Sibelius

Gustav Mahler

John Philip Sousa (1854–1932), composer of America's great march music. He received the Medal of Honor from Congress for "Stars and Stripes Forever." Bandmaster of the United States Marine Corps.

Victor Herbert (1859–1924), American composer of light operettas. Best known are "Babes in Toyland" and "Naughty Marietta."

Hector Berlioz (1803–1869), famous French composer best known for his "Symphony Fantastique" and "Romeo and Juliet."

Jean Sibelius (1865–1957), Finnish composer best known for his "Finlandia."

Enrico Caruso (1873–1921), Italian tenor, the greatest tenor, it is said, of all times, first sang "La Bohème" at the La Scala Opera House, Milan, 1902. *Tosca* and *Pagliacci* were his stupendous operas. To equal Caruso is every tenor's dream.

Joining a Local Stamp Club

One day in New York City, I found a stamp dealer near my home, although at that point I didn't even know a *Scott's Catalogue* existed. The very first stamp dealer I encountered was Bruno. His office, on Lexington Avenue, has the flavor of an old W. C. Fields movie. It is a one flight walkup, whereupon you enter a room consisting of tables and chairs, with ashtrays that are cleaned annually.

Bruno is an old-fashioned stamp dealer, content to make a reasonable profit and please his customers. It was at Bruno's that I became part of a network that is almost impossible to describe. Once, a man there told me he was president of an African stamp society, and that led to a meeting at my home. It was there that I met a member of the ATOZ Stamp Club. Finally I was introduced to the founder, Melvin Garabrant.

ATOZ members collect everything from A to Z, thus the name. The club is a "tiny jewel" with no more than two dozen members. It's a philatelic leadership and watchdog group especially concerned with exhibition judges and juniors.

A stamp club, especially on a local basis, is one vital source that teaches you the ins and outs of what to look for in advancing your collection, and where to buy and why. Occasionally within a local club you meet quasi-stamp dealers who earn a bit of money on the side and find welcomed material for you when they learn what your interests are.

An extra offshoot of a stamp club is its ever-increasing social aspect. Friends bring their friends and their friends, too. A banker, a plumber, a watchmaker may comprise the diverse membership.

Above all else, a local stamp club or a specialized club can be a source of marvelous friendships. I developed an admiration for one lover of "Music on Stamps," George Guzzio. He is the director of the ATA Judges Accreditation. Like Theodore Steinway, he collects classical stamps, but for sheer joy, his romance of a lifetime is in his "Music on Stamps." His Mozart collection alone is a many-time gold medal winner, both national and international.

George Guzzio himself is baroque in life-style, liking all that is artistic and elegant. There is hardly a phase of philately, classical or topical, with which he isn't familiar. He is the par excellence agent for the elusive collector who prefers to be "unknown." Our sample of Guzzio's collection is limited by space, but the flair of the material gives you a light introduction that may take you from the ordinary to the informed.

Left, the wrong notes; right, corrected notes. (Courtesy of George T. Guzzio)

The Wrong Notes

Can you imagine waltzing into a post office to purchase a block of four stamps only to return to notice the musical notes on those stamps were incorrect? You had read in the press that this stamp was honoring Robert Schumann, and for the fun of it you played the musical notes from the stamp on your piano. However, instead of hearing Schumann's "Mondnacht" (moonlight), you heard and recognized Schubert's "Nachtlied" (nightsong). The stamp had the face of the right composer, but the notes of another. This actually happened to one unsuspecting collector. Like Paul Revere, he alerted the entire musical world, philatelic and otherwise. How delightful to think the stamp designer, the printers, the proofreaders, and the high government officials all missed this musical mixup! The stamp was withdrawn in two days and finally all was resolved; the correct notes appeared on a new stamp forty-two days later and as a result the "normal" stamp and the "error" live happily ever after in many albums. Democratic Germany could get a good night's sleep, for nightsong and moonlight and Schumann and Schubert were unraveled at last.

Hungarian souvenir sheet, Franz Liszt, issued May 6, 1934.
(Courtesy of George T. Guzzio)

Stamp Shows: Souvenir Sheets

From time to time, a country will issue what is called a souvenir sheet. In 1934 the Hungarian Philatelic Society had its fiftieth anniversary, as well as a stamp show, to celebrate the event. The government issued a special souvenir sheet using the stamp of Franz Liszt that came from a definitive set, now reprinted into a souvenir sheet.

From the outset this sheet was special. The entrance fee to the stamp show was 70 filler. Thus, with every ticket purchased, plus 20 filler, you could obtain the souvenir sheet (about 50 cents). Only 50,-000 were printed. Today this is a scarce item that *Scott's Catalogue* lists at $40 mint and $35 used, if not more. Because at the actual show many were purchased for the subject matter, and because the souvenir sheet was especially created for that particular stamp exhibition. Over the years the popularity of music on stamps heightened the scarcity. By being at the right place at the right moment you can find an item which, over a period of time, steadily increases in value.

It isn't a bad idea to buy a special souvenir sheet if you happen to be at a stamp show, for like a promising plant, it may grow in value.

Becoming a Specialist

Once you begin to accumulate both mint and used stamps you start to look for ways to take advantage of all that happens in the diversified world of the mails, such as finding postmarks, cancellations, postal stationery, first-day covers, commercial covers, meters, and air letter sheets. This brings added excitement to your stamp-collecting enjoyment. The range of postal discovery is mind-boggling. There is a stamp society that fits the description "different strokes for different folks" in every conceivable area of philately. Each society is a gold mine of information and membership and for the most part costs a nominal fee of from $3 to $5 annually.

Our "Music on Stamps" parade of corner cards, postal stationery, cancellations, FDCs, meters, and precancels will give you an idea of the varied choice in store for you. The 25-cent purchase might be the find of your lifetime.

Corner Cards

In the good old days stamps weren't multicolored; topics of every subject known to man were not on stamps to lure the recipient to take notice. The repeated rendition of a George Washington definitive or Ben Franklin was all too commonplace.

Businessmen, when grandpa or great-grandpa was a lad, used the left-hand corner of an envelope to expose their products for direct-mail campaigns. These envelopes were known as corner cards. Theodore Steinway had the largest collection of corner cards related to music ever assembled. W. W. Johnson & Co. were out to sell violin players their steel violin strings. Without the marketing apparatus that exists today and without lists this outfit probably wrote to every music center in the country, addressed, "To Any Violin Player." The postal advertising rate at that time (circa 1873) was 1 cent. The stamp is

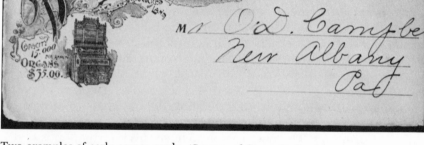

Two examples of early corner cards. (Courtesy of George T. Guzzio)

Benjamin Franklin (Scott 144a) with a cancellation known as a "killer" applied to prevent the reuse of the stamp. With the charm of this pitch, let's hope they reached a fiddler's heart and his pocketbook.

The corner card from Washington, New Jersey, was the headquarters for the Beethoven Organ Co. Note the reasonable prices: pianos, $175; organs, $35. This was postmarked Washington, New Jersey, January 4, 12:30 P.M., 1899. The stamp is tied to the cover by a Washington, New Jersey, cancel and an "eye" cancel with number 1 in the center, known as a "killer" cancel.

Box Creepers

At any number of stamp shows, big and small, local and national, you are bound to find a stamp dealer with boxes and boxes of envelopes and postal cards. This is the happy hunting ground of the "box creepers" who have the true philatelic instinct. Contentedly, they're searching for corner cards, cancellations, slogans, letter sheets, etc. They are the heartbeat of the hobby, always learning, and surprise! Once in a while they make real discoveries, some even profitable.

Postal Stationery

If you are collecting "Music on Stamps," and you find a mint postal card imprinted with the stamp design of your tête-bêche mint copy of Johann Sebastian Bach, you have found a worthwhile addition to your collection, worth about 50 cents. By becoming a box creeper you have located a mint copy attached with a reply card. Now you can start looking for the reply card actually sent through the mail. With persistence, you'll find one.

The first postal card was issued in Austria in 1869. It was the idea of Dr. Emmanuel Hermann, a professor of political economy at the Vienna Neustaat Military Academy. Printed on it were the words, "The postal authorities do not assume any responsibility for the contents of the written communication." The following year the British issued a postal card. Socially it was considered unworthy of response. Regardless, the postal card became an instant success.

There is a remarkable and informative postal stationery catalogue called *Higgins and Gage*. It describes each and every piece of postal stationery worldwide in minute detail. It defines changes of color in paper, errors in type, and offers a variety of type changes due to different printings. The only reason to have this information is that if you want to poke around and know all you possibly can find out, it's all there. It's an eye-opener to help you develop what is my crazy specialty: a "want list." Latching onto this rarefied sphere that only specialists encounter, you get positive direction as to what exists, thanks to distinguished research done by many knowledgeable collectors before you ever gave stamps a thought. It's like chasing down a family tree: the more you know about what actually exists, the easier it is as a box creeper to know what you are looking at and looking for. Then, too, you may do some original investigation that makes you rather special.

A want list can become a useful chart or list that disciplines both your budget and your route to realizing the objectives you set out to attain. If you've found a suitable stamp dealer, let him know your want list so he can help you as you move along.

A Bach postcard and a Berlin postcard with special fiftieth anniversary of the Richard Wagner Music Festival, Bayreuth. (Courtesy of George T. Guzzio)

Cancellations

Collecting cancellations and postmarks is a hobby within the hobby of stamp collecting. On the whole, it is inexpensive and downright attractive. Topical collecting is an excellent introduction to this special kind of observation. Cancellations and postmarks come in every form imaginable: square, circular, rectangular, oval, octagonal. They give added emphasis to a date of significance, an event, or accent the special importance of a particular stamp or set of stamps.

The oldest-known music cancellation from Vienna, Austria, June 6, 1892, and a special cancellation honoring the American singer Marian Anderson's visit to Haiti, 29 April 1950.
(Courtesy of George T. Guzzio)

First-Day Covers

The first day of issue of a stamp has become as lively an event as would be the celebration of your birthday. To beautify as well as to give official sanction to the birthdate of the issuance of a stamp governments issue what is known as an official first-day cover. Occasionally, the cancellations tied to a stamp are as exquisitely executed as the stamp. In 1975 Sweden put out a 7 Krona stamp honoring ballet depicting Romeo and Juliet. This stamp was selected as the most beautiful stamp of Sweden for that year in a contest held by the Swedish postal authorities. The dancers on the stamp are Annali Alhanko and Per Arthur Segerstrom of the Swedish ballet. The cancellation of a ballet slipper made this first-day cover irresistible.

You might have noticed that the beautiful ballet first-day cover of Romeo and Juliet and the special cover of the Austrian ballet stamp with the special Salzburg cancellation were unaddressed. For the past ten years, first-day cover lovers have coveted unaddressed covers simply because they look beautiful. These are known as "handbacks," because they are taken to a post office and cancelled, and then handed back to the owner; they never go through the mail. Serious collectors snub these covers, and yet they are growing in popularity. Personally, I would prefer to have these same items, but sent through the mail.

As we move into the collecting of classical stamps, we enter into the spectacular area of forged cancellations, which are mainly on scarce stamps, where the cancel is on a used stamp. The thievery comes later —and there's lots of it. Even dodging fakes, forgers, and rip-off artists has its peculiar intrigue. It's like a horse race—you simply set out to beat the system.

For the box creeper, meter and slogan cancellation chasing is fun. It's relatively inexpensive, especially when the meter or slogan cancel comes to your door. Open up your mail with loving care, as someone may want your meter mail. Furthermore, you may want to swap for a beautiful cancellation that you'd never seen before that would be perfect for your collection—no, not money—a swap.

Whenever I have the opportunity to go to a stamp show, especially in and around New York, I usually can be found among the box creepers at one of the popular booths, like Moe Luff's. He is a buyer and seller of slogan cancels and the author of a most useful catalogue, which resulted from the increasing interest in them. He has compiled and priced 6,550 different United States slogans, and listed them alphabetically and topically with the current market price. In black, heavy type he writes, "What makes value? Rarity—Demand—Condition." At any stamp show or stamp dealer's store, large or small, look at the boxes of covers that some dealers have at their tables. Often the material you find is worth the entire visit to the stamp show.

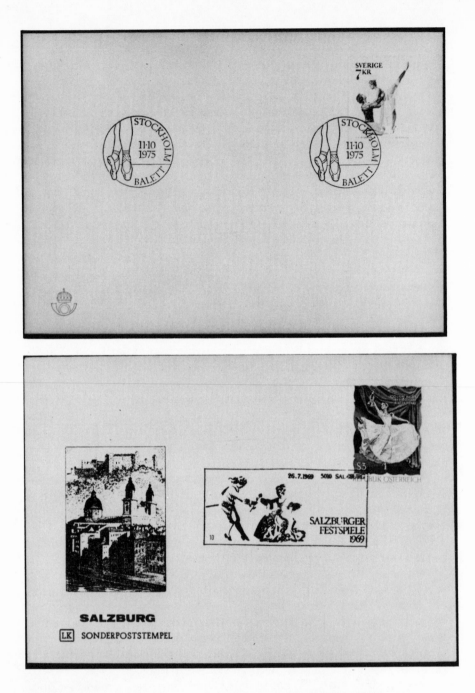

"Romeo and Juliet," voted the most beautiful stamp of Sweden in 1975 (Courtesy of Carey Leigh Brown), and special Salzburg Festival cancel on the "Blue Danube" stamp of Austria. (Courtesy of George T. Guzzio)

Precancels

Did you ever notice that stamps you buy on envelopes have the name of a city and state between two lines overprinted on the stamp? It's third-class mail and usually an advertising or promotion pitch from a large corporation. This type of stamp is known as a precancel.

Precancels came into being in 1890 when the U.S. Post Office approved them to expedite the handling of mass bulk mailing needs of seed companies, patent medicine makers, and mail-order houses. Precancel passionates say if you want a barrel of fun with a minimum of expense and a maximum of pleasure, collect precancels.

There are two types of precancels: those made locally are called "city types" and those that are overprinted by the Bureau of Engraving and Printing are known as "Bureau types."

One of the most knowledgeable precancel stamp dealers is Mr. W. Scott Partridge of North Carolina, a specialized precancel dealer. He sends out a "Dear Collector" letter that is a seductive invitation to the precancel maze. For $1 he can send you the *ABC's of Precancel Collecting*, and is willing to sponsor you into the Precancel Stamp Society, publishers of the pamphlet. You couldn't possibly imagine all that there is to collect in this sphere, with only two lines and the name of the city and state overprinted on a stamp. For instance, on Bureau prints alone there are eleven styles to track down.

Some people collect all precancels; others just Bureau prints. Slimming down, there are precancels with cancellations from one state; still others collect towns and types. (The *ABC's* pamphlet says that a

Top, line pair tagged; gap pair, precancelled. (Courtesy of R. E. Beresford)

Right, imperforate line pair, precancelled. (Courtesy of Jacques C. Schiff, Jr.)

First-day cover autographed by Dick Cavett.
(Courtesy of Albert Lolio)

complete town collection would contain 20,000 precancels!) Even more particular is a collection of precancels on ghost towns. On and on it goes . . .

If you want to get onto this tack, write to Mr. W. Scott Partridge, P.O. Box 5447, High Park, North Carolina 27269.

Liberty Bell Booklet Panes

Booklet panes are familiar to those of you who go to the post office to purchase them because they are convenient to store in a wallet or purse. Some people must notice, even if on a subliminal level, that sometimes there are five stamps in two panes with the sixth spot housing a stamp bearing a label such as "Have Fun with Stamp Collecting" or a switch—the booklet pane of the same stamp has seven stamps with a label like "Paying bills? Use postal money orders." Another booklet pane of the Liberty Bell stamps actually has eight thirteen-cent stamps. That's only the beginning of differences that suggest booklet panes or "bookletry" may be indeed a specialized field of collecting. Because it does not have a vast following, it might well be the extra collecting beat to pursue.

The Liberty Bell Booklet Detecting Exercise

To the everyday stamp buyer, a booklet is a convenient object to put in your wallet. A collector has another kind of eye. John Caffrey, an expert in this specialized area, in an informative article, "Bookletry: A Taxonomical Introduction," states: "It is much more complex and challenging than may be apparent at first glance. I do not pretend to exhaust the subject, only the reader."

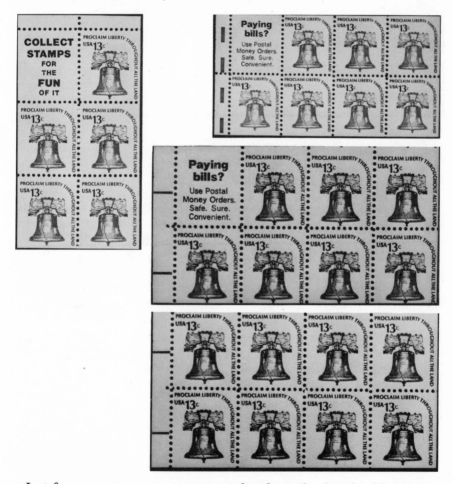

Just for your amusement, can you decide in the four booklet panes shown here:

1. Which booklet pane consists of five stamps and a label (an advertisement)?
2. Which booklet pane has vertical bars in the margin or selvage of the pane?
3. Which booklet pane of seven stamps has horizontal bars and a label?
4. Which booklet pane has eight stamps with horizontal bars?

By checking off what you view, you learn what you are missing. As long as they are sold at the post office you have the chance of picking up what you are missing, but not the five-stamp with label, because this is only available from vending machines.

The misperfs from the booklet panes in strips and pairs from the Liberty Bell issue we call "freaks and varieties." This is one of the ways you get involved with an inexpensive stamp that at first seems ordinary.

Misperforation.
(Courtesy of Jacques C. Schiff, Jr.)

BELLS IN YOUR MUSIC COLLECTION

The continuing saga of the 13-cent Liberty Bell presents an interesting choice to you the collector. You could either include it in a music collection for the fun of it or you can also start to look at the booklet panes you buy in your post office and see what you come up with. By starting a small list of what you find, you can keep your eyes open for the missing ones in newspaper ads and shows. You can watch your mail for examples of used copies or you can try to find copies with the label used on a cover and eventually you will have a small and interesting collection. Remember, the everyday stamp—the definitive—is the one almost everyone takes for granted until it has gone off sale and has been replaced by either a new postage rate or new design. The challenge and fun begin in trying to collect something that was once right in your post office.

Coils

In the United States not only are the stamps of booklet panes sometimes issued as coil stamps but the post office also issues a special series known as "bulk rate" stamps. These stamps are issued only in coil form. Coil stamps were created for use by big mailing houses. They come in rolls of five hundred to many thousands which are placed in machines that affix the stamps automatically. They are somewhat elu-

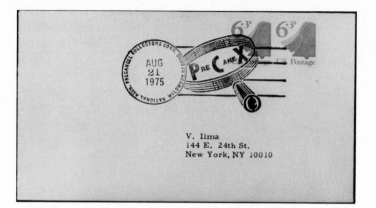

Bulk rate coil stamps on a cover with Precancel Collectors
Convention hand cancel.

sive because many people throw away the envelopes from these advertising mailings. It is because of this that another ATOZ member,
Dick Beresford, has found a lot of fun in collecting them. He tries to
find them on envelopes and to gather as many of the precancelled
town names as he can. He picks up pairs, line pairs, and almost anything he can find. The first of the new "bulk rate" stamps was a
6.3-cent stamp showing bells. He has all of these and since he found
that he could buy these unprecancelled through the philatelic windows at larger post offices, he has used them on covers to get fancy
cancellations from shows and special events. Just about every day he
receives many responses to his inquiries for covers and town precancels. He has found a few dealers who specialize in this area that is not
expensive but a lively pursuit.

A Mind
for the Sound
of Music

If you have a romantic heart it isn't difficult to become emotionally attached to the life and music of Wolfgang Amadeus Mozart. He was born in Salzburg in 1756. At the age of six he was performing at the Schoenbrunn Palace in Vienna for Empress Maria Theresa, her consort husband, Emperor Francis I, and the archduchess, Marie Antoinette. One of the composer's favorite presents from the empress was a small and exquisite pocket writing case in silver, with silver pens —an encouraging gift of rare beauty for the musical prodigy. The world would come to know the royal suit (made of lilac velvet with a matching waistcoat embroidered with leaves and flowers) given to him by the empress. The coat and waistcoat were edged with bands of gold embroidery. Because the suit was modeled for a royal prince, it had a little sword, according to Goethe, who at the age of fourteen, attended one of Mozart's concerts. He was impressed with the "little sword and wig."

The seven-year-old Mozart played on Christmas Eve at Versailles for Louis XV. As the king's guest for two weeks at the palace, he adored the fairyland magnificence of the Gardens of Versailles and the splendor of the fountains. He performed not only for Louis XV but also for the queen, the dauphin, and Madame Pompadour. In between concerts, he romped through the grandeur of the mirrored halls, spellbound by the sparkling chandeliers. The Paris music critic of the *Correspondence Literature* wrote that Mozart was "unbelievable."

At the age of eight Mozart played for King George III and Queen Charlotte at St. James's Palace in London. It was in London that he first heard the Italian operas which so impressed him. He accompanied the queen as she sang. It was in 1765, at the age of nine, that Mozart gave his first concert consisting of music he had composed, including six sonatas for violin and piano published in Paris. At fourteen he composed operas and gave concerts throughout Italy.

Wolfgang Amadeus Mozart

The greatness of Mozart was attested to by another master of music, Franz Josef Haydn, who in speaking to Mozart's father Leopold, said to him, "I tell you, calling God as my witness and speaking as a man, that your son is the greatest composer I know either personally or by repute. He has taste, and in addition, the most complete understanding of composition."
Letters of Mozart translated by Bozman

In the short life span of thirty five years, Mozart composed six hundred musical works covering all the major categories. Among his works are some twenty two operas, fifty two symphonies, sixty religious pieces and numerous sonatas, concertos and other compositions of rare quality.

The following pages depict the basic stamps issued for Mozart, supplemented by examples of postal history, usage, stamp production phases & other various elements.

The Man & his Works

Introductory page of Mozart exhibit from the collection of George T. Guzzio.

Mozart, age seven.
(Courtesy of George T. Guzzio)

Mozart, throughout his travels, was in love with stagecoaches. "The rumble of the coach wheels, the rhythm of the horses' hooves, the crack of the coachman's whip" put snatches of melodies into his mind: Handel, Bach, Italian operas, and his own music. In one of his earliest remaining letters he wrote: "My heart is quite enchanted because I find this journey so cheerful. Our coachman is a fine fellow, whenever the road allows him the smallest opportunity he drives fast."

The stagecoach in the mid-eighteenth century was a most important development in the growth of the posts. It provided the first dependable means of transport, not only for royal personages but also for the

French mail coach, 1840.(Courtesy of the Swiss PTT Museum, Bern)

public. Until then letters were delivered by royal messengers. Because of expense, kings decided to allow passengers to ride on stagecoaches along with mail carriers. Mail coaches replaced horse and foot messengers in England, introducing speed into communications. Postal networks throughout Europe were delivering mail from town to town and from one country to another, but mail service within a city itself was needed. On April 1, 1772, Josef Hardy set up a postman's service that spread over a three-mile radius of Vienna. This became known as the "Clapper Service" because when the postman was approaching a street he used a clapper to alert the people to his arrival. He picked up the mail six times a day, hand-stamped each letter showing the date and hour, and took it to the nearest branch post office for its further destiny. These early hand stamps of the "Clapper Post" are much sought after. In the collectors' jargon, they are "nice pieces of the early postal history of Austria."

Mozart's stagecoach journeys activated his musical curiosity. He became fascinated with the skill of a certain coachman's use of the "posthorn." The coachman, also known as the postilion, blew his posthorn to announce his arrival as he passed through the villages. Mozart wanted to experiment with the posthorn instrument, an unusual idea to introduce into an orchestra.

On August 3, 1779, Mozart performed his Posthorn Serenade #9, D Major, K320, in Salzburg. Five years later he wrote his great C Major Mass, of which Robert Schumann wrote, "There are things in this world about which nothing can be said such as Mozart's C Major Symphony, much of Shakespeare and pages of Beethoven."

While Mozart was in Vienna writing his opera *Don Giovanni* in 1787, a rough, thickset young teen-ager with a pockmarked face managed to meet him. He actually wanted to take a few piano lessons from Mozart. Mozart's inner reaction was "another meaningless piano

Austrian posthorn, stamp day issue, 1976.
(Courtesy of the Austrian PTT)

Hanover block of four tête-
bêche, 1860 issue reprint.
(Courtesy of R. E. Beresford)

player." There were other people present in the room when the
young man sat down and struck one chord. Mozart was immediately
surprised, and upon hearing the young pianist play, Mozart said to his
friends, "He should be watched. He will soon make noise in the world
of music." Before the young teen-ager left, Mozart said, "Please, may
I have your name once again?" "Yes," the student replied, "Ludwig
van Beethovan."

The difference in the Beethoven single stamp (Fig. 1) and the identical stamp in pairs is that the pair is imperforate (Fig. 2). The normal
stamp is part of a large definitive set, but the imperforate stamp was
never issued. *Scott's Catalogue* says that it exists; and so it does. The
"imperf" pair obviously means the stamp has no perforations. This
pair comes from the only known sheet of one hundred stamps. Sometimes imperforate sheets of a stamp are run off the press by a government mainly for dignitaries or government officials. These, over a
period of time, get into the hands of a few collectors, and, needless to
say, a very pleasing item to find.

Fig. 1, normal stamp.

Fig. 2, imperforate pair.

The block of four of Handel (Fig. 3) with marginal inscription is a test of your ability to observe. There is an error that appears on every sheet. Can you find it? (Clue: the engraver's error appears in the upper right stamp of the block.) (Wrong date, 1585 instead of 1685.)

The Handel stamp became a perfin. Note the P.O.L. perforated initials (Fig. 4) which stand for police. This perfin was made for the official use of the German police department, and it came in three different size initials, labeled Type A, Type B, and Type C. The perfin enthusiast chases after all three.

You could easily mistake a perfin for a damaged stamp; it is not. Actually, punching holes into a stamp was the brainstorm of an Englishman, Joseph Sloper. In 1868 he patented a machine for perforating railroad tickets that led him to the stamp-perforating business. In a hassle with the British Post Office authorities, Sloper presented a case history of a man who had stolen eight thousand postage stamps from a large firm. His selling point of perforating initials into postage stamps for security reasons was accepted. Since he had the patent of his machine to perforate initials into stamps, either he himself could do the job for corporations or sell them his machine whereby they could perforate their own initials on their own stamps. Either way, he had it made. Handel wrote the *Messiah* in twenty-four days. It took Sloper two years to work out his deal with the British Post Office.

There is a club that exists for perfin passionates known as the Perfin Stamp Society. This is only one of the many side alleys of collecting that's neither too expensive nor oversubscribed. Those knee-deep in it are highly entertained. Furthermore, it's wide open and has great possibilities for original research.

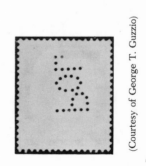

Fig. 3, block of four of Handel with error.   Fig. 4, one of the perfin types.

The stamp of Joseph Joachim (1831–1907), violinist, conductor, and composer, was issued to commemorate the centenary of the Berlin Music School. The visible overprint (Fig. 5) "muster" means specimen. Postal officials of many countries distribute sample sets of their stamps to the Universal Postal Union for distribution to member countries. The overprint "specimen" or in German "muster" invalidates the stamp for postal use.

I learned such a specimen existed after five years when I found it in the marvelous Holmes's *Specialized Catalogue on British North America. Scott's Catalogue,* of course, is the bread of your philatelic table, but a specialized catalogue on any country is the caviar, as it provides the extra touch of unique information gathered by the profound students of philately.

The German catalogue known as *Michel* is worldwide. This specialized catalogue is printed in Germany. *Michel* gives a good deal more data on each stamp than *Scott's,* including the name of the designer, engraver, numbers printed, and further descriptions of the background of the designer of each stamp, plus a picture of each stamp. The catalogue describes booklets and provides other information.

It's amazing how after a period of time you can begin to read German, French, Spanish, and other languages to find secrets hidden in foreign catalogues. It was in *Michel*'s specialized catalogue that I found the information on the perfins of our Handel stamps. It is not necessary to learn such minute details, but it's one further step toward the making of a true collector.

A set of four imperforate stamps (Fig. 6) was issued to commemorate the one-hundredth anniversary of the birth of the Russian composer Rimsky-Korsakov. Imperforate stamps collected in pairs present a positive proof of nonperforation. Note the wide margins between the stamps, canceling any doubt that the stamps may have been perforated. These Soviet imperf stamps were valid for postage. The same set was also issued perforate.

Fig. 5, a specimen overprint.

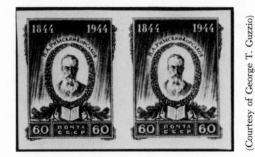

Fig. 6, imperforate pair.

(Courtesy of George T. Guzzio)

Face to Face

In the imperforate pair of stamps from Hungary (Magyar) you can see what is known as a se-tenant imperforate pair (Fig. 7), meaning that the stamps are joined together but differ in design. Franz Liszt faces right, Frederic Chopin faces left. *Scott's* lists Franz Liszt as #1168 and Chopin as #1169, and states "#1168 and #1169 alternate in the sheet, forming horizontal se-tenant pairs."

Franz Liszt (1811–1886), Hungarian pianist and composer, was a child prodigy educated in Vienna by the sponsorship of several Hungarian aristocrats. Liszt was considered to be the greatest piano virtuoso of the century, and his *Liebestraum* and Hungarian rhapsodies are his best-known works.

Frédéric Chopin (1810–1849) was the incomparable Polish composer. Chopin's scherzos, ballads, preludes, and nocturnes have never been surpassed.

Here is a definitive stamp of Ludwig van Beethoven in a gutter pair (Fig. 9) from the country of the Saar, which no longer exists. A gutter occurs when sheets of stamps are divided into panes. They are most desirable to acquire and will add another dimension to your collection.

One of this pair of German stamps of Johann Sebastian Bach (1685–1750) is upside down, known as tête-bêche (Fig. 10). This variety is usually found in booklet panes. The tête-bêche pair is two unseparated stamps, one of which is upside down next to another in normal position. Naturally, if you tore them apart you wouldn't know the difference.

Here is Bach in a tête-bêche gutter pair (Fig. 11). The only way to get this is from an unsevered sheet before it is manufactured into a booklet. To do so one should contact a stamp dealer who specializes in Germany.

Fig. 7, imperforate se-tenant pair. (Courtesy of George T. Guzzio)

Fig. 8, Frédéric Chopin.

Fig. 9, Beethoven
gutter pair.

Fig. 10, Bach tête-bêche pair.

Fig. 11, Bach tête-bêche gutter pair.

Fig. 12, Beethoven
Altona local.

(Courtesy of George T. Guzzio)

Altona Locals

Locals are private stamps usually operative within a certain town, city, or district. The most famous American locals are the stamps of Wells Fargo—the company that ran the dashing, dynamic Pony Express. This local of Beethoven (Fig. 12) is from Altona, a suburb of Hamburg, and was issued in 1889.

National clubs which specialize in areas mentioned in this section are:

American Postmark Society
Box 193
Port Huron, Mich. 48060

Booklet Pane Collectors Club
10500 Rockville Pike
Rockville, Md. 20852

Fourth Class Cancellation Club
Crete, Nebraska

Meter Stamp Society
34 Laurelton Ave.
Jackson, N.J. 08527

National Association of Precancel
   Collectors
Box 121
Wildwood, N.J. 08260

The Perfins Club
10550 Western Ave. SP94
Stanton, Calif. 90680

Postmark Collectors Club
3487 Firstenberger Road
Marion, Ohio 43302

Precancel Stamp Society, Inc.
12045 Hickory Hills Court
Oakton, Va. 22124

United Postal Stationery Society
Box 1407
Bloomington, Ill. 61701

U.S. Cancellation Club
855 Cove Way
Denver, Colo. 80209

The American Topical Association

The American Topical Association is the best source of information, fellowship, and inspiration if you want to begin with a topical collection. For an $11 annual subscription they will supply a membership directory that lists all 12,000 members in over ninety countries with addresses and collecting interests.

If, for instance, you cannot read Urdu, Portuguese, Slovene, Swedish, and a host of other languages, simply contact their translation service. ATA has a "think tank" of translators covering the globe.

For your membership you also get the *Topical Time*, a newsy and useful bimonthly journal. It includes new issues worldwide and checklists of an infinite variety that can save you time and money. It reviews all major new philatelic publications geared to topicals and includes interesting articles by collectors who specialize in their own fields. In addition, *Topical Time* has a list of handbooks written by specific ATA study units.

It is inexpensive to join an ATA study unit. When you become a member of a unit, you may have limited knowledge, but you will soon find out that they need your participation in many different areas. There is an ample need for writing, if you have this ability, and it's quite thrilling to see tales of your collecting interest in print. You might volunteer your services in the varied responsibilities of stampdom, such as carting exhibition frames to a stamp show in your station wagon. You really can get involved. This adds to the pleasure, the sharing, the growth, the tears, and the successes of all the activity that goes on within an ATA study unit. By joining one, you're not just a computer number—the stamp club becomes yours; you are welcomed and needed.

One of the added features of *Topical Time* is the advertisers who cater to topical collectors. These ads bring you much-needed contacts that enable you to purchase material of interest on a topical basis. I noticed the following on an ad headlined "Approvals for a Specialist":

Americana	Medicine
Antarctica	Min. Sheets
Biology	Music
Boy Scouts	Olympic
Centenary	Osaka
Chess	Railroads
Churchill	Red Cross
Eisenhower	Religion
Europa	Rotary
Exhibition	Dr. Schweitzer
FDR	Ships
Inv. Center	Space
J. Kennedy	Sports
Lincoln	U.N. (Worldwide)
Lions	UPU
Maps	Football
Airmails	Insects
Arphila	Painting
Bicentennial	World's Fairs
Concorde	
Copernicus	

The founder of ATA, Jerry Husak, recognized the new trend of topical collecting before it had achieved any status at all. Today it is zooming in popularity and has added a dimension of great importance to the collector, who in turn has enormous influence on the increase of interest in stamp collecting.

For information about the American Topical Association, write to: American Topical Association, 3306 N. 50th St., Milwaukee, Wisconsin 53216.

Art in Miniature

(See Plates 3, 4, and 5)

The Lascaux Cave Paintings

In 1940, not far from Bordeaux, France, four young boys were exploring caves. While clearing away branches to get into the entrance of Devil's Hole, which was blocked because of a thunderstorm, the oldest of them, who was seventeen, slid down a shaft and landed in the underground. Joined by his friends, he got a lamp, and while walking through the grotto, one of them happened to notice animal drawings on the wall. These were the famous Lascaux Cave paintings (Fig. 1), (Paleolithic art, 20,000–15,000 B.C.), the oldest form of pictorial communication known to man.

The Artist and the Postage Stamp

Indeed, the postage stamp has become the global envoy of the history of art by using works from all artistic disciplines. Exact miniatures of the great masterpiece paintings that are on exhibit in the Louvre in Paris, the Prado in Spain, the National Museum in London, the National Gallery of Art in Washington, D.C., and many others, are reproduced on stamps. You can be an armchair connoisseur and join the many collectors whose passion and love for art is building a miniature art collection.

An Artistic Philatelist

Irwin Rosen is the president of the New York chapter of the Fine Arts Philatelists, a stamp club solely devoted to the fine arts on stamps. His career as an import manager of the fine arts department of a distinguished import-export house is such that one can't tell which love affair came first: the job or the hobby. He and I struggled to make a selection from his vast and glamorous "Art on Stamps," a beautiful collection including singles, multiples, first-day covers and proofs in all their stages, especially the stunning art stamps of France.

In 1974 he set up the Impressionist Exhibit that came from the Louvre to the Metropolitan Museum of Art. (The Met is one of his firm's clients.) One can imagine Irwin matching his stamps, proofs, and first-day covers to the paintings he handled, which included works by Mary Cassatt, Monet, Degas, Matisse, and the "father of modern art," Cézanne. Can you locate them in our miniature art collection?

The Masterpieces in Miniature: Pre-Fifteenth Century

The Lascaux painting is followed by an Athenian vessel (Fig. 2) painted by Euphronius (510–500 B.C.) and an Etruscan painting, *The Musicians* (about 480 B.C.) (Fig. 3), both fine examples of early Roman and Greek art. The delicate stamp from Ireland comes from the Miniature Book of Kells, ninth century (Fig. 4), and a miniature of *Monks in Abbey Workshop* (circa 1040) (Fig. 15) was issued by Luxembourg. The *Pietà*, detail of the *Entombment*, fresco, 1264, was issued by Yugoslavia (Fig. 5).

Moving into the Gothic style, from Belgium comes the *Portrait of Lady Talbot*, by Petrus Christus, 1415 (Fig. 6), and the painting *Madonna and Child* by Roger van Der Weyden (Fig. 19). From France comes the beautiful art stamp, *The Departure for the Hunt* (Fig. 7). This miniature decorates the page of the calendar devoted to the month of August in the manuscript painted for the Duke of Berry's "The Very Rich Book of Hours." The Duke of Berry (1340–1416) was an avid collector of objects of art and all things elegant. He sent his private messengers from France to England to purchase greyhounds of the finest breed. "The Book of Hours" was the work of Paul of Limbourg and his two brothers. This is considered to be the finest early French book in existence, and it is now in the Condé Museum in Chantilly, France.

If It's Art on Stamps . . .

If you would like to begin to collect art on stamps and want to concentrate on a country dedicated to art, you can start with a beautiful album, "Art in France." In 1961, France began to issue jumbo-sized stamps of the great works of art of France. These include "The Furrier," stained-glass window from Chartres Cathedral; "The Triumph of the Virgin," stained-glass window from Notre Dame Cathedral, Paris; "The Lady and the Unicorn," fifteenth-century tapestry; and the paintings of Paul Cézanne, Georges Braque, Georges de la Tour,

Honoré Daumier, Jean Dominique Ingres, Pierre Auguste Renoir, and too many more to mention.

The editor of "Art in France," Pierre DeBrimont, writes in the preface of this album, "As philatelists completed their album of art reproductions, these connoisseurs gradually became aware that they were building a collection not only of striking and colorful postage stamps, but a museum gallery of authentic miniature engravings, the official reproductions of some of the greatest art treasures in the world." This art on stamps album not only has a place for each large stamp but also an excellent background of the history of the painting, as well as specifically related philatelic information. For instance, the album mentions that in the "Miniature from the Manuscript of 'The Very Rich Book of Hours' of the Duke of Berry," a variety known as the "white sky" exists. It occurred during the printing of sheets numbered 52123 and 52124, where the yellow tint is missing on every one of the twenty-five stamps that make up the sheets. The album has a place for the variety. If you have a penchant for French ⸱⸱⸱ ⸱⸱ you may write for details to: P. Ruinart, Imaginary Museum of Art on Stamps, Rue des Terreaux 2, Lausanne 1003, Switzerland. For some guidance you may want to find out about the Fine Arts Philatelists: Box 1606, Midland, Michigan 48680, Att: Jewel Sonderegger.

Do you recognize our Early Renaissance choices? One is the *Battle of San Romano* by Paolo Uccello (Fig. 9), from San Marino, another is the *Adoration of the Child* by Fra Filippo Lippi (Fig. 8), from the Central African Republic, and lastly, *Grandfather and Grandson* by Domenico Ghirlandaio (Fig. 11), from the Republic of the Congo. It was with Ghirlandaio, then the most famous master in Florence, that Michelangelo spent his apprenticeship.

India issued a set of four stamps portraying Michelangelo's *Creation* (Fig. 12), which is in the Sistine Chapel, St. Peter's, Rome.

THE BIRD WATCHER—SIXTEENTH CENTURY

Thomas Craven writes, "Leonardo da Vinci is perhaps the most resplendent figure in the history of the human race." The stamp chosen for your enjoyment of Leonardo da Vinci was issued by Argentina. The original painting hangs in the Louvre museum. It is a detail from the *Virgin of the Rocks* (Fig. 13), which was painted between 1478 and 1483, during da Vinci's first years as an independent artist. The great painter of the High Renaissance was a constant visitor to the bird shops. He bought birds, took them out of their cages and observed their flight. They were the models for sketches of his ideas about the possibility of a flying machine, the earliest forerunner of an airplane known.

St. Paul by El Greco (Fig. 14), was painted by the sixteenth-century artist who lived and painted in Spain and was rediscovered by the modernists.

A HUMAN ONLOOKER—SIXTEENTH CENTURY

Popular in the sixteenth century was Peter Brueghel, the Elder, of whom Aldous Huxley wrote, "Other artists pretended to be angels, painting the scene with a knowledge of its significance. But Brueghel resolutely remains a human onlooker."

BAROQUE—SEVENTEENTH CENTURY

The Baroque era of great painters when people were painted more realistically, included some artists in our miniature art collection. Can you recognize the paintings of Peter Paul Rubens, Frans Hals (Fig. 17), Murillo (Fig. 16), and Velásquez (Fig. 18)? Rembrandt was the last of the spiritual painters; from Togo, we found the stamp of his famous *The Anatomy Lesson* (Fig. 10).

NEOCLASSICISM—NINETEENTH CENTURY

The period of neoclassicism brought artists influenced by revolt and revolution. Napoleon gave Jacques Louis David the title of "Premier Peintre de l'Empereur." In 1792 he was elected to the National Assembly through the influence of Marat, Danton, and Robespierre. Sarah Newmeyer in her book *Enjoying Modern Art* wrote, "David became not only the official painter of the revolution, but virtual art dictator of France." From Grenada, we added John Louis David's *Crossing the Alps* (Fig. 20).

From England comes *The Hay Wain* (Fig. 25), landscape by John Constable.

IMPRESSIONISM—NINETEENTH CENTURY

We are all a bit more familiar with the *La Bohème* era of the fabulous impressionists. The United States issued a stamp honoring the impressionist painter Mary Cassatt (Fig. 21), who lived in Paris, was a pupil of Degas (Fig. 24), and a friend of Paul Gauguin (Fig. 23), Cézanne, Manet (Fig. 22), and Renoir. She not only held her high place among her peers, but also was a loyal friend to them. She was a prim young lady from a socialite family in Pittsburgh. With her life established as a painter in Paris, she appealed to her many wealthy friends in the United States to buy the paintings of her fellow artists Degas,

Gauguin, Renoir, and Manet. Because of her endless insistence to convince them to buy more than one painting, they began to respond, "Enough is enough!" Today a single Gauguin may sell for $3 million.

It is rather amazing to think that Gauguin, who was called "the civilized savage," started out as a successful Parisian stockbroker before becoming an artist. With his talent and love for painting, he finally went broke, retreated from civilization, and went to Tahiti. His exotic paintings in vivid colors brought the beauty of Tahiti to the world. His influence on modern art for the next generation was profound, but Gauguin died of loneliness, despair, and poverty.

POST-IMPRESSIONISM—TWENTIETH CENTURY

Leading the young French painters of the twentieth century was Henri Matisse. He was the most prominent figure of the art movement called the Fauves. In 1905 Matisse and a number of young painters were given a special room in the Grand Palais de Champs Élysées— and this was considered extraordinary. Some art critic labeled this grouping "the cage of the wild beasts" (Fauves), and the name stuck.

As a young man, Matisse was studying in Paris to become a lawyer. At the age of twenty-two he happened to get appendicitis. His mother, to ease the boredom of his recuperation, bought him a box of paints, and the moment he began to paint he was "transported to paradise." Matisse's career as a lawyer ended before it began. *The Blue Nudes* by Henri Matisse (Fig. 26) is one of the handsomest of the smashing series of French art stamps which fit in the beautiful album "Art on Stamps."

CUBISM AND EXPRESSIONISM—TWENTIETH CENTURY

It must have been a remarkable time in Montmartre, where Picasso (Fig. 27), Braque, and other unknown young painters filled the back room of a tiny restaurant with tobacco smoke and the electricity of their minds. The departure from old art concepts to cubism, which experimented in structure, challenged the onlooker to participate in reaction concept. This was a startling departure that radically changed the concept of art appreciation.

Leader of the expressionists in our miniature collection is *The Honeymooners of the Eiffel Tower* (Fig. 28) by Marc Chagall. He, with his airy, lovelike tenderness and use of bright romantic colors, deviated from the cubist technique.

Our miniature art collection of stamps from the Stone Age to Picasso presents the beginning as well as the end of the cycle of art. The caveman paintings are man's first message before the written word existed. Primarily it was primitive art that inspired Picasso and many of the modernists like Robert Delaunay—*Joy of Life* (Fig. 29)—that followed him, creating a pictorial sense of the future.

Mrs. John Douglas by Thomas Gainsborough; *Don Antonio Moreiga* by Francisco de Goya; *Old Time Letter Rack by Peto and Mlle. La Vergne* by Jean Liotard, issued by the United States, 1974.
(Courtesy of U.S. Postal Service)

Letters Mingle Souls

The importance of a letter or a message has never changed. Today when we seal an envelope, we overlook the amazing service it performs: it keeps a message private. This is a privilege for which our forefathers and theirs before them struggled for over a thousand years.

The letter at your doorstep today may bring you news of a fantastic event in your life, but it also should be recognized as part of a record of the history of communications. The first abstractionists were the scribes from Babylon and Egypt who in 5000 B.C. chiseled their messages on tablets that over the centuries evolved into letters as we know them today.

Countdown to
a Stamp

There is an appointed time for everything . . .
A time to be born, and a time to die;
A time to plant, and a time to uproot the plant . . .
A time to weep, and a time to laugh;
A time to mourn, and a time to dance . . .
A time to love, and a time to hate;
A time for war, and a time for peace.
                                    Ecclesiastes 3:1–8

KNOTTY SCRIBES

Before Columbus discovered America, in the Inca Empire's capital at Cuzco, Peru, there were official scribes whose specialty was the tying and deciphering of the *quipu*, or knot letter. The *quipu* consisted of knots prearranged on strands of ropes which only the sender and the receiver could comprehend. The *quipu* recorded heads of cattle and sheep; one knot equaled ten, a double knot one hundred, and a triple one thousand. The cord, or main strap, was made up of dangling threads in a variety of colors, from which hung a second strap in other colors. All colors represented a code signifying ideas and objects: white for peace, red for war, and yellow for gold.

THE CHASQUI WORE WHITE FEATHERS

The Inca messengers famed for their incredible speed were known as Chasqui. They wore caps of pure white feathers. They not only carried a *quipu* which they delivered on foot (no horses existed until the Spanish conquistadores brought them) but they also memorized an added message to go along with the *quipu*. The Chasqui would then pass the *quipu* and the memorized message on to the Chasqui at the next post house, and so on went the relay. Upon arrival in any

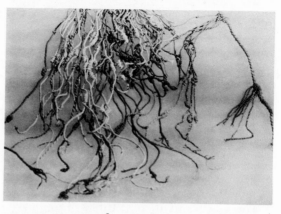

Eight-hundred-year-old
quipu knot record of the old
Incas.
(Courtesy of Herbert Rosen)

village, these mercurial messengers caused great excitement, interest, and anxiety because they were the conveyors of news, good or bad. They used the 2,500 miles of roads to carry word of distant uprisings, which could be quickly suppressed by dispatching large armies back along the roads. The Incas and the Aztecs provided the first posts available to the public.

BEAN LETTERS DELIVERED BY FLEET RUNNERS

The Chimu tribes of northeast Peru had a system of writing codes on lima beans. Bean letters were delivered by fleet runners in the same way the postman delivers a letter to you.

SPEECH CURLS

One of the earliest records of writing from ancient Mexico is on a mural depicting "The Rain Gods' Heaven," from a palace painting, *The Paradise of Tlaloc.* It pictures a string of speech curls rolling out of mouths of little men. This is now known as a form of glyph writing.

Speech curls or glyph writing.
(Courtesy of the Peabody Museum of Archaeology and Ethnology)

The World's First Parcel Post—A Fishy Story

It seems that the Aztecs' fondness for fish led to the development of fleet runners who were employed solely to distribute fish to the villages. It is said that the emperor's fish, brought from the seacoast to Tenochtitlán (now Mexico City), arrived 24 hours after it was caught —scoring time: a mile every six and a half minutes. This could very well be called the world's first parcel post.

Skull Messages

The Greeks in ancient times chose a slave, shaved his head, wrote a message on his skull, and fed him well while his hair grew thicker and longer, covering the message. When he reached the point of his assigned destination, his head was shaven and the message read. One thing was certain: he couldn't read the missive on his own head. Security programming was underway.

The World's First Written Message

> He who would excel in the school of the scribe must rise at dawn.
>
> Sumerian proverb

Man has lived on the earth over two million years, yet it was only five thousand years ago in Mesopotamia (now Iraq), between the Tigris and Euphrates rivers, the cradle of civilization, that writing was born. It was ruled by Sumerians who invented the first system of writing known to man: cuneiform script.

Writing Bricks

A wedge-shaped reed was used to impress messages on clay tablets or "writing bricks." The tablet was then baked in the hot sun. After the message was thoroughly baked in the hot sun, it was carried in the palm of a Babylonian runner to the addressee. The tablet shown here, baked in 2300 B.C., is one of the world's first written messages—no, not a love letter, but a message about brewing beer. One ancient Babylonian proverb (circa 2300 B.C.) suggests time hasn't changed the quality of man's inhumanity to man: "You can have a lord; you can have a king; but the man to fear is the tax collector."

A cuneiform tablet (c. 2300 B.C.) from Babylonia.
(From the collection of the late Edith Faulstich, courtesy of Fred Faulstich)

Hammurabi, ruler of the Babylonian kingdom, with cuneiform writing, circa 1800 B.C.
(By permission of the British Museum)

The Ishtar Gate, German Democratic Republic.

Reconstruction of the Ishtar Gate in the State Museum of Berlin.
(By permission of the State Museum of Berlin, German Democratic Republic)

Countdown to a Stamp 89

MOONSTRUCK: 2000 B.C.–A.D. 2000

Recently, one of IBM's most brilliant mathematicians, Bryant Tuckerman, spent forty hours on one of the corporation's most complex computing machines calculating the motions of the sun, moon, and planets for six hundred years as they moved over ancient Babylon. Scholars at IBM who can read cuneiform script are hard at work tracing the astronomical motions of Babylon two thousand years ago.

It was the Babylonians who wrote the signs of the Zodiac. The ancient stargazers used them to foretell the future. *Time* magazine reported in "History by Computer" that "The Babylonians believed that the motions of heavenly bodies had an intimate influence on human affairs. . . . As the Babylonians recorded events, they were likely to include the positions of the moon on that day, or the location of some of the planets."

THE FIRST MAILS

Although it is impossible to ascertain the exact date the first mails were carried, we do know that it was several centuries before the birth of Christ, as is shown by the following passage from the Bible: "So the posts went with letters from the King and his princes throughout all Israel and Judah and . . . passed from city to city throughout the country of Ephraim and Manasseh, even unto Zebulun."

The king under whom all this took place was Hezekiah, who ruled Judah from 726 to 715 B.C. Although this post was only an occasional affair, it paved the way for the Persian postal system.

The Flood.

WE HAVE FOUND THE FLOOD

If you travel to Baghdad, the railroad will stop at Ur, the great capital of ancient Mesopotamia, where the talented and creative Sumerians lived. It was also the city of Abraham. The Babylonian version of the story of the Flood, written on cuneiform tablets in 1700

B.C., was discovered by Sir Henry Chesewicke Rawlinson, and it took thirty years to decipher. It revealed that the authors were Sumerians, living in Ur. G. S. Wegener writes in his *6000 Years of the Bible,* "And it was from Ur in Mesopotamia that Sir Leonard Woolley, the British archeologist, in the summer of 1929, electrified the world with the message: 'We have found the flood!' . . . Woolley had excavated a group of mounds on 'high hills' surrounding the staged tower known as Tell Muqayyer, near the Persian Gulf. Woolley had found the city and in six years of painstaking labor had laid it bare in all its splendor. The land where 'all mankind had turned to clay' had been found. The flood of the Bible was no longer a legend." In the tomb chamber dating back to 2500 B.C., Sir Leonard unearthed seventy-four skeletons, golden cups, tableware, musical instruments, and thousands of clay tablets.

THE FIRST POSTMASTERS—THE SCRIBES

At about the same time the Sumerians introduced clay tablets, the ancient Egyptian scribes devised hieroglyphics—writing chiseled into stones, and often painted in colors of great beauty. Scribes were professional men we can honor by calling them the first postmasters of the world. If the kings and generals couldn't read or write, the scribes could, and therefore they held the intellectual and political plums to success. Scribes, too, were collectors. They were collectors of what they had learned. The scribes as postmasters handled all aspects of written communication. They supervised the making of clay tablets, organizing and writing of royal chronicles, writing of personal royal letters, and writing of business letters. They dispatched messengers and they were superior scholars studying diligently and recording for history what IBM is trying to fathom through its intricate computers today.

BREAKTHROUGH ON THE NILE

Important to the evolution of a letter was the Egyptians' use of the papyrus plant that grew on the banks of the Nile. They made papyrus on which they were able to write from the tall water reed. Strips unwrapped from the inner stalk were moistened and pressed to form scrolls about 30 feet long. Actually, letter-sized sheets were either glued or sewn together and rolled up. The scribes whittled a reed into the shape of a little brush.

An Egyptian messenger.

Letter written on papyrus-leaf.

THE DISCOVERY OF PARCHMENT

Pergamon, an ancient Greek town in Asia Minor (now Bergama in western Turkey), had enormous pride in its great library. The famous library in Alexandria, Egypt, was in feverish competition with the Pergamon library. By holding back delivery of papyrus, the Alexandrians put themselves in an advantageous position. But the Pergamons invented parchment. They took animal hides, soaked them, scraped off all the meat and hair, stretched the skins, and dried them in the sun. Parchment, which is more durable than papyrus, was an important step toward the envelope we so easily take for granted.

For centuries the Middle East used parchment scrolls that fit into gold and silver protective containers, which could be worn by messengers crossing rivers. Parchment scrolls took on a look of great importance then and still manifest it today in the form of diplomas and documents of distinction.

THE PERSIAN POSTAL SYSTEM

King Cyrus the Great, builder of the Persian Empire, is considered to be the founder of the postal relay system which employed messengers on horseback by day and night. The king's stables were set up at intervals equal to the distance a horse could travel in a day without becoming exhausted. Each stable had grooms to look after its horses. An intelligent man was appointed to each station who would deliver to one courier the letters brought by another. This was called "postriding." Xenophon wrote of the mighty ruler's mail service, "A letter travelled faster than a crane could fly."

If you have visited the General Post Office on Thirty-third Street in New York City, you may have noticed the immortal words of the Greek historian Herodotus praising the Persian postal system: "Neither snow, nor rain, nor heat, nor gloom of night stays these couriers from the swift completion of their appointed rounds."

The clay cylinder discovered in Babylon in the fifth century records the victory of King Cyrus over Babylon in 539 B.C. It is a declaration concerning the human rights in occupied cities. (In 1971 Iran presented a copy to the United Nations and Ethiopia issued three stamps in 1972 which were replicas of this historical document to honor the two-thousand-five-hundredth anniversary of the birth of the great Persian Empire.) In G. S. Wegener's book *6000 Years of the Bible,* he describes the victory of King Cyrus, "The Persian king Cyrus defeated the Babylonians and in so doing put an end both to the rule of Babylon and the captivity of the Jews. Their years of longing for homes and for the holy city of Jerusalem, their weeping 'by the waters of Babylon,'

The Edict of Cyrus the Great at the United Nations.
(Courtesy of the United Nations/T. Chen)

Ethiopian stamp commemorating the two-thousand-five-hundredth anniversary of the founding of the Persian Empire by Cyrus the Great.

were over. Two years later they returned to their own country. . . . The Persians are perhaps the only example in history of a people who called themselves 'liberators' really being liberators and not oppressors."

THE ROMAN WAY

Centuries later, Julius Caesar adopted the Persian courier system of using mounted messengers, later developed by Emperor Augustus. In Otto Hornung's colorful *Encyclopedia for Stamp Collecting*, he writes, "Courier routes were established along the Roman roads, which were already in excellent condition. In addition to messengers on foot and on horseback (tabellarii), carriages were introduced into the service. All along military roads stations were built manned by permanent garrisons of messengers, horsemen and carriage drivers. In addition, there were spare horses, and supplies of fodder and food. The whole establishment was called *cursus publicus* and the individual stations *mansio* or *statio*. The word 'posts' came from the Roman *posita statio* from which we derive both post office and postage stamp."

The Chinese Caesar, Shih Huang-ti, builder of the Great Wall of China (246–210 B.C.), set up the first courier system along the imperial roads of China. Prince Shotoku during the Nara period (A.D. 710–784) introduced the relay system and stations to Japan.

FIRST USE OF PAPER

In A.D. 105 Tsai Lun, during the Han Dynasty, fashioned paper out of old bark, jute, old rags, and fishing nets. Long before western Asia, India, and Europe learned about paper, the Chinese were perfecting its use.

The Great Wall of China.

Tsai Lun, inventor of paper, Han Dynasty, A.D. 105.
(Courtesy of the Directorate General of Posts, Republic of China)

First Appearance of the Word "Posts"

The first appearance of the word "posts" occurs in the accounts of Marco Polo's travels in the year 1298 in China. Glowingly, he describes the fabulous postal system set up by the great Mongolian leader Kublai Khan, who improved the postal system that his grandfather, Genghis Khan, developed. Ernest A. Kehr, in his book *The Romance of Stamp Collecting*, writes, "In China the Kublai Khan set up a system that was unmatched for nearly six centuries. An idea of the vastness may be imagined when one realizes that about 10,000 postal stations were dotted throughout his empire and were webbed together by maintained roads. Kublai Khan's system used boats for crossing rivers, camels and carriages for transporting passengers and second class mail." Each station had from fifty to as many as four hundred sturdy and swift Mongolian horses, usually furnished by the nearest town or village. The riders, who often had to travel more than two hundred miles a day, were well trained, and nothing but the most exacting service was tolerated. Marco Polo reported that in cases of emergency, they rode at night and if there was no moon a man ran before the horse with a torch, which slowed the pace considerably. In addition to the horsemen, there were foot messengers, who by running in three-mile relays could cover more than a hundred miles a day. These men wore a girdle of bells to give notice of their approach to a station, so that another runner might be ready, and a clerk carefully recorded the time of arrival and departure of each messenger.

Résumé of the organization of the postal stations of Kublai Khan.
(Courtesy of the Directorate General of Posts, Republic of China)

Charlemagne—Postal Planner

During the early part of the ninth century, Charlemagne conquered all of Europe, except England, Scandinavia, southern Italy, and Moslem Spain. He was the first to create the shape of Europe. Using the

Charlemagne attending school.

best features of the postal relay system of Cyrus the Great, he set up his own postal organization, which became the groundwork for the postal system of the Holy Roman Empire.

"Although Charlemagne could read but couldn't write, which was not unusual in the ninth century, he slept with a tablet under his pillow, so he could practice the alphabet." He sponsored programs to encourage literacy, granted scholarships, and promoted the value of education—all of which led to the establishment of universities. On Christmas Day, A.D. 800, Charlemagne's triumph was consecrated in St. Peter's in Rome and he became the new head of the Roman Empire of the West. The stamp issued by France in 1966 pictures Charlemagne attending school with a page holding a book for him.

> The letter is a voiceless messenger and the messenger is a living letter.
>
> Epictetus, A.D. 80

THE MEDIEVAL MESSENGER, A STUDY ON DEFINITIVES*

The medieval foot messenger carried his letters in his hand along with a spear. This protected him from the wolves, dogs, and men he might encounter while trekking through the forest. He could brush away the fallen branches or logs and if necessary he could vault over streams. The professional city messenger appeared in the early part of the thirteenth century. More elegant, he wore a uniform, carried a lance, and sometimes a leather bag.

*For a study on our medieval messengers, Swiss definitives, we are indebted to Lauretta Garabrant, a member of clubs such as the Helvetia Society, the Eire Philatelic Society, and ATOZ representative to the Federation of New Jersey Stamp Clubs.

In 1960 two medieval messengers appeared in a Swiss definitive set. The 10-centime value also has a tiny dog. Can you spot him? A definitive has many varieties, and because of many printings over a period of time, it has a long and often complex life.

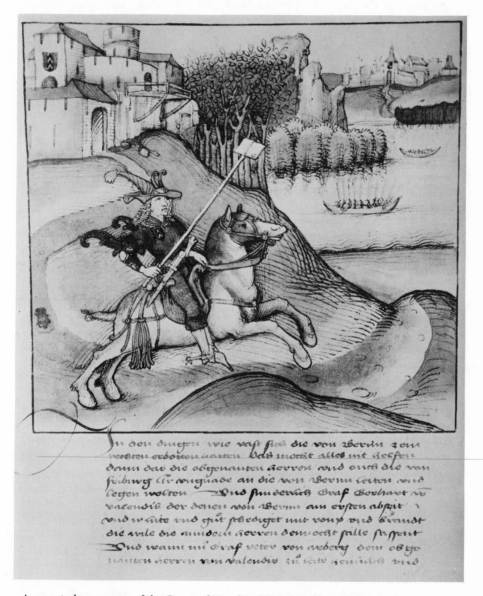

A mounted messenger of the Count of Neuchatel-Valangin bringing the declaration of war to the city of Bern, from a design of 1500.
(Courtesy of the Swiss PTT Museum, Bern)

THE SWISS DEFINITIVES, 1960–1961

(See illustrations on pages 99, 100, 101, and 102).

First Lauretta shows tête-bêche pairs that were taken from sheets printed for the manufacture of booklets. The sheet contains ninety stamps. Then come pairs with inter-space. Can you see the difference? These are "gutter pairs."

HORIZONTAL COILS

In the second exhibit page, she displays the same medieval messengers. This time they are "horizontal coils" with control numbers. On the 5-centime value is a medieval messenger. He has four strokes on his lance which *Scott's* lists as Type I. The same stamp exists with three strokes on the lance and is known as Type II. A study such as this is sometimes referred to as "nit-picking" or even "fly-specking"—that is, to study and find constant varieties in an issue of stamps. Sometimes this is accidental.

MORE "NIT-PICKING"

On the third page we have more "nit-picking." We view the same "horizontal coils" but without control numbers. Can you locate two horizontal lines above the arch of the gate of the Cathedral of Lucerne? In *Scott's* this is listed as Type II. On Type I there are three shading lines above the gate. Now you can understand the accusation made about these alert nit-pickers. The truth is you can get slightly jealous when they observe so much. Observation, you can realize, has a lot to do with the start of a real collection and a real collector.

FIND THE NAIL

Can you find the nail on the top of the lance on the fourth page? On "vertical coils," control numbers appear only on every five stamps. If you live in Switzerland, there is an easy solution, for these coils are in vending machines. The regular stamps have a nail on the lance. The coil stamps do not.

It is worth noticing the way Lauretta has placed her material and the uncomplicated way she has written up her pages.

WHERE TO FIND MATERIAL

In order to find material like that which appears in this collection, you can write: The Swiss PTT, 3000 Bern 33, Switzerland. The Swiss are very good in helping the collector get up-to-date material.

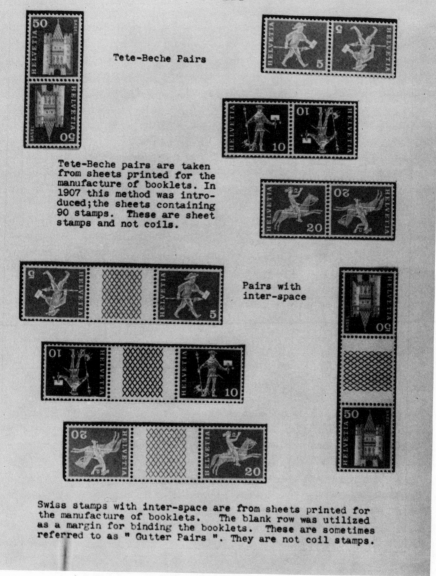

Tete-Beche Pairs

Tete-Beche pairs are taken
from sheets printed for the
manufacture of booklets. In
1907 this method was introduced; the sheets containing
90 stamps. These are sheet
stamps and not coils.

Pairs with
inter-space

Swiss stamps with inter-space are from sheets printed for
the manufacture of booklets. The blank row was utilized
as a margin for binding the booklets. These are sometimes
referred to as " Gutter Pairs ". They are not coil stamps.

Tête-bêche pairs.
(From the collection of Lauretta Garabrant)

1960-1961
Horizontal Coils
with control numbers

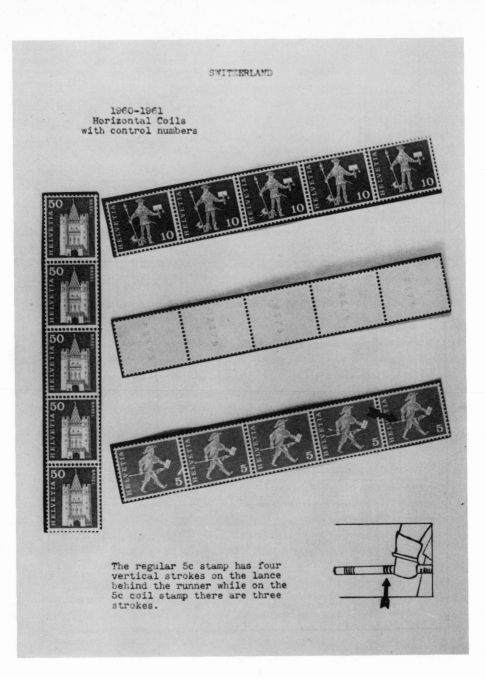

The regular 5c stamp has four
vertical strokes on the lance
behind the runner while on the
5c coil stamp there are three
strokes.

Horizontal coils with control numbers.
(From the collection of Lauretta Garabrant)

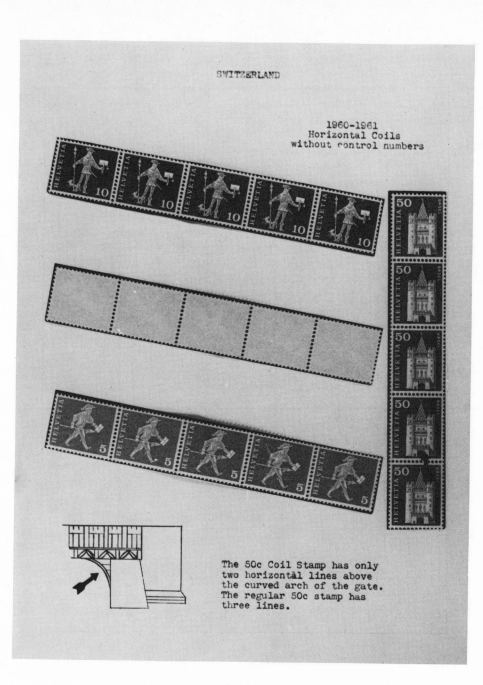

The 50c Coil Stamp has only two horizontal lines above the curved arch of the gate. The regular 50c stamp has three lines.

Horizontal coils without control numbers.
(From the collection of Lauretta Garabrant)

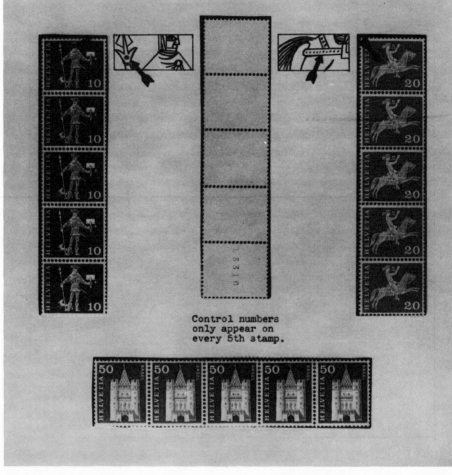

SWITZERLAND

1960-1961
Vertical Coils

The illustration of the 10c value of the regular sheet stamp shows the top of the lance fixed by a nail. The coil stamps are missing the nail.

The illustration of the 20c value of the regular sheet stamp shows 10 points on the mules harness below the tail. The coil stamps show only 9 points on the harness.

Control numbers
only appear on
every 5th stamp.

Vertical coils.
(From the collection of Lauretta Garabrant)

Saint Benedict, patron saint
of Europe, founder of the
Benedictine monastery of
Monte Cassino.
(Courtesy of Melvin Garabrant)

THE DALE CARNEGIE OF THE ELEVENTH CENTURY

From the Benedictine monastery of Monte Cassino near Naples,
Deacon Alberich, in the eleventh century, wrote a thesis on "How to
Write a Letter." Sounding like an instructor at Dale Carnegie's today,
he outlined in five parts the ingredients necessary:

Part I: The Salutado—introduction or greeting
Part II: The Capitatio—make an attempt to please the receiver to favor
the writer
Part III: The Narratio—state the purpose of the letter
Part IV: The Petitio—make the request in mind
Part V: The Conclusio—conclusion best suited to the tone of the letter.

This was written in Latin nine hundred years ago. "The Benedic-
tines had 3,600 establishments alone. Their monks travelled from one
monastery to the other maintaining communications that often covered great distances by month-long journeys."

MEDIEVAL LETTER WRITERS

Medieval direct-mail entrepreneurs were getting into action. One
merchant's letters that have survived are those of Francesco di Marco
Datini of Prato, a town near Florence. He amassed more than 150,000
letters of business contacts from Italy, France, Portugal, Flanders,
England, North Africa, and the Levant. Two friends, and two of the
most prolific writers of the twelfth century, were Thomas à Becket,
Archbishop of Canterbury, and John of Salisbury, noted British ec-
clesiastic, who became Bishop of Chartres. In 1176 John of Salisbury
wrote Thomas à Becket, "I made a detour through Paris. When I saw
the wealth of goods, the cheerfulness of its population, the regard the
clerks enjoy, the majesty and glory of the Church, the various occupa-
tions of its philosophers, full of admiration, I thought I saw angels and
descending Jacob's ladder which was touching the sky. Enraptured by

this pilgrimage, I had to confess, 'the Lord is in this place, and I knew it not.' " And this phrase of a poet comes to mind: "Happy exile it is, for the one who has this city for an abode."

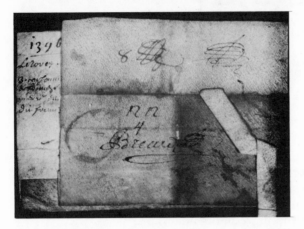

Letter on parchment from a monastery, 1396.
(From the collection of the late Edith Faulstich, courtesy of Fred Faulstich)

THE UNIVERSITY POSTS

The medieval world of the twelfth and thirteenth centuries was anything but the dark ages. It was an era of tremendous scholarship. In 1224 at the University of Naples "flying messengers" or *Nunci Volante* didn't actually fly. They sometimes took from two to three weeks to deliver a letter. Parents have always welcomed news from their children at school, and most of the students' correspondence consisted of the familiar jargon contained in a letter to home. One such letter records the following message, "I am studying with the greatest of diligence, but the matter of money stands greatly in my way." Emperor Frederick II of the Holy Roman Empire often called on wealthy and distinguished citizens to loan money to such students.

THE UNIVERSITY OF PARIS

The University of Paris, founded in 1250, held its first classes at Notre Dame Cathedral. By 1296 the University had its own messenger service. Messengers carried letters for students and for private individuals and they traveled to the farthest reaches of Europe. Eventually their services became available to the general public and until the late seventeenth century they constituted the most significant postal system in France. "These messengers had many privileges. For one thing, they were exempt from military service and most important had the support and protection of the king." The profit from the messengers made it possible for the university to pay the professors.

Madonna and Child from a window in the
Cathedral of Notre-Dame de Paris.
(Courtesy of Irwin Rosen)

St. Thomas Aquinas.

MEDIEVAL SCHOLARSHIP

The philosopher Abelard, better known for his love of Héloise, while
at the University of Paris, was considered to be the first European
intellectual. An outstanding number of great scholars, scribes, and
monks were translating books from the Greek and Arabic into Latin,
including the writings of Pliny, Plato, Euclid, and Ptolemy. These
scholarly attainments were responsible for the advance both of science and technology, especially in the fields of astronomy, medicine,
algebra, and trigonometry. Aristotle presented the newly founded
University of Paris with a more or less complete system of scientific
thought. It was at the same university that St. Thomas Aquinas, known
as the "Dumb Ox" because of his slow deliberation of speech, wrote
Summa Theologica, which was to become the foundation of official
Roman Catholic philosophy.

MOMENTS OF TRIUMPH ON THE POSTAGE STAMP

One reason that the postage stamps of the world are so fascinating
is that they embrace in pictures moments of great triumph and pride
throughout the history of man. They reflect the continuity of progress,
and the story behind each stamp, by each country's own choice, tells
exactly what they treasure most. France, during the twelfth and thirteenth centuries, built more than one thousand cathedrals and
through its postage stamps has created miniature masterpieces of its
magnificent stained-glass windows which to this day remain unmatched.

Detail from a stained-glass
window from the Cathedral
of Chartres ("The Furrier").
(Courtesy of Irwin Rosen)

THE STAINED-GLASS WINDOW FROM CHARTRES CATHEDRAL

One of the most beautiful stained-glass windows to appear on stamps is that of Chartres. Only 54 miles outside of Paris, the windows survived the ravages of war. To understand the gargantuan task accomplished in the making of the Chartres stained-glass windows, one must note that from 1210 to 1240, one hundred seventy-three panes of stained glass totaling 21,000 square feet were completed for the sanctuary.

The kings of France and their devout nobles were major donors to the edifice. There were forty-two corporations at the time, resembling our present-day TV sponsors, that were large donors as well. Each company's contribution was unique, as its pane of stained glass depicted a scene representing its particular trade. The French stamp "The Furrier" was a miniature engraving of a Chartres stained-glass window. You can see the furrier doing what he does best: selling.

ST. FRANCIS OF ASSISI

The stupendous cathedrals of the Middle Ages were monuments of faith and technological achievement. The business of living was found in order and freedom. The spiritual leader was St. Francis of Assisi, who sacrificed his wealth to work for the poor. His interest was neither theology nor palace power, but concern for the world of man. His influence became a tower of inspiration and strength in the oncoming High Renaissance, especially to the mighty Leonardo and Michelangelo.

MEDIEVAL PROSPERITY

Throughout Europe trade fairs became popular. Weavers, die makers, butchers, and goldsmiths were forming guilds. Iron for armored suits was displayed for knightly purchase power. Horseshoes were being mass-produced. The Forest of Dean in England executed an order for five thousand pairs for Richard the Lion-Hearted in the Third Crusade. In 1966 Great Britain issued a set of eight stamps commemorating the nine-hundredth anniversary of the Battle of Hastings from the Bayeux tapestries. The earliest representation of horses working in the fields appears in the border of the famed tapestry. During the Middle Ages farmers found a way to increase horse-power by hitching horses one behind the other to distribute weight. All over Europe the austere Cistercian monasteries were tending vineyards while their fellow lay brothers in England were rearing sheep to keep up with the ever-growing demand for both wool and parchment. The most romantic of nobles and knights were troubadours.

Medieval messengers
from an old drawing.

"The Bayeux Tapestry" depicting the battle of Hastings.
(From the collection of Honor R. Holland)

TROUBADOURS AND MINNESINGERS

The troubadours at first traveled in the south of France. They made slang popular and dumped the pompous Latin of the Church. Their poetry, lyrics, and songs, often bawdy, helped make the everyday language full of hearty laughs and enjoyment. The courtly knights were gallant, generous, and madly successful in their rounds of romance and lovemaking. German minnesingers, like the French troubadours and the Italian *trovatori*, had much interest in romance and love. One persistent knight, so the story goes, was Knight Ulrich of Liechtenstein. He kept singing his verses of love to his lady fair for ten years and finally was granted an interview, but he did not receive yes for an answer.

Souvenir sheet from Liechtenstein.
(Courtesy of John H. Steinway)

MILADY, IT'S COLD OUTSIDE

As the knights and nobles traveled around from castle to castle, they unfolded tapestries of knighthood and romance. These were usually carried on muleback, trailing behind their prominent masters. After reaching a castle the knights entered and proceeded to hang up the tapestries, which were used primarily to decorate the dreary walls of the castle and to keep out the cold and drafts. This set the stage for a festive air and sumptuous festivities.

In 1970 Liechtenstein issued a work of art in the form of a souvenir sheet commemorating the eight-hundredth anniversary of the birth of Wolfram von Eschenbach, famous minnesinger of love songs. He was the medieval hero of lyrics and poetry. The border of this postal jewel is printed in gold. On the top of the souvenir sheet of four stamps is our hero's name and on the right-hand border the word "maze" is written in gold, symbolizing the knighthood qualifications of "character, moderation, restraint, and decorous modesty." The word "Zuht," meaning "breeding, virtue, gallantry, propriety, and kindness" appears, as does "Triuwe"—the importance of sincerity, steadfastness, and constancy when one's word is given. The lowest value portrays the famous minnesinger honored. The 50-rappen value is the Austrian minnesinger, knightly poet Reinmar der Fiedler, famous for his minstrel songs. Knight Hartman von Starkenburg, 80-rappen value, is overhauling his weapons. The high value, 120 rappen, is the painting of Friedrich von Hauser, a minnesinger from a powerful baronial family, best known for his amorous poetry. His portrait on the stamp in the souvenir sheet is as the writer of love poetry aboard a ship departing for the Crusades to the Holy Land. In its totality this exquisite souvenir sheet portrays knightly, chivalrous ideals of the Middle Ages: moderation, discipline, and faith.

> Every man has in him the tastes and instincts of a cultural historian.
>
> Jacques Barzun

Tannhäuser "max-card," which enlarges on a postcard the design of a stamp. Wagner used the story of Tannhäuser for his famous opera. Design from a fourteenth-century Manesee manuscript.
(Courtesy of George T. Guzzio)

This stampless cover bears two red wax seals affixing a red silk thread, an example of a method used by the aristocracy to demand attention and privacy. This small letter, sent by a nobleman to his sister, asked for money to buy a new horse to gain prestige in his regiment. It was delivered to "Aix" (Aachen), February 12, 1641, addressed to "Madame de la Rogue, *ma soeur* [my sister]." This cover dates from the Thirty Years War. (From the collection of E. Herbert Mayer)

STAMPLESS COVERS, OR PREADHESIVE SNOOPERS

Philatelically, the Middle Ages launched us into a most intriguing phase of the hobby. One may find old envelopes and letters folded like envelopes, despite the fact that at the time stamps were nonexistent. These covers or folded letters on parchment, calfhide, and sometimes paper are known as preadhesives. They were either delivered by a messenger or, in later years, by mail.

Collectors enamored of this specialized phase of philately are usually history buffs—specifically military history. I met one such person, Herbert Mayer, at a stamp auction. He had his eye and his heart set on a seventeenth-century silk thread cover, and eventually acquired it. While talking to him, I sensed his tremendous enthusiasm. His conversation went something like this: "Yesterday I took the day off from business and set out to get a military stampless cover in auction. I was willing to spend up to $300, but guess what . . . I got it for only $30. You must mention in your book that this type of collecting is not always expensive."

I should imagine that this is a field for newcomers who have a flair for history and genealogy. The difference between collecting stampless covers and a first-day cover of roses is like weighing the difference between a mink coat and a pair of blue jeans. Of course, you can have both.

THE POSTS

The posts during the early fourteenth century became as necessary to a man of power and leadership as feet to a runner. The posts conquered distance, and therefore made the posts masters of com-

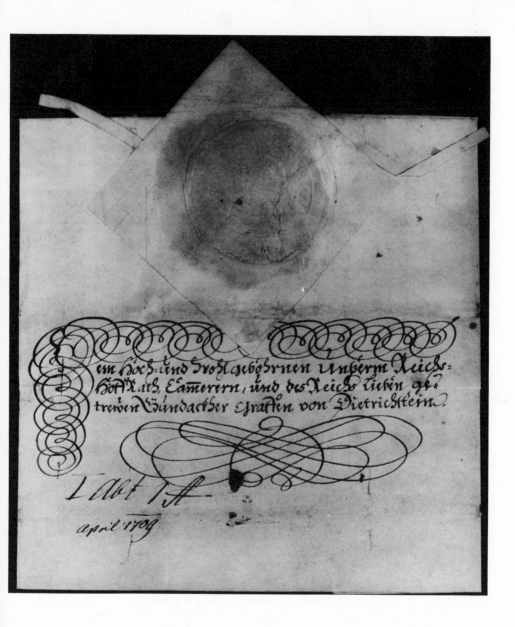

Another example of a handsome stampless letter is this letter from the emperor
Josef I (1678–1711), instructing his chamberlain to accompany the king of Den-
mark on his trip from Bassano, Italy, to Innsbruck, Austria, and to entertain him.
The emperor was at war with France over the Spanish Succession (1701–1714)
and the king of Denmark was on the side of the Empire.
(From the collection of E. Herbert Mayer)

munications. Capitalism was on the march, and anyone designated to become master of society turned his attention to the art of communication.

Italian bankers and merchants from Milan, Florence, and Venice began to put modern techniques of business to work. Letters of payment, which could be cashed in other countries, were inaugurated. Business began to function from the commanding horizon of a desk. Venice controlled the shipping business of all Europe, including the tourism of pilgrims to the Holy Land. The Venetian Republic owned a fleet of ships that made scheduled voyages between Venice and the Black Sea, Syria, Egypt, Flanders, and England.

Signboard of the Thurn and Taxis Imperial Post in Germany.
(Courtesy of the Swiss PTT Museum, Bern)

"We Invented the Mails"—Thurn and Taxis

Prince Johannes von Thurn and Taxis, a fifty-year-old bachelor, is one of the biggest landowners in the world today, and one of the ten wealthiest men in West Germany. He lives in the feudal castle in Regensburg, Bavaria, which his family has occupied since 1790. To get to the castle, which is larger than Buckingham Palace, you have to go through twelve courtyards where you might be greeted by Napoleon, his little brown dachshund. The billionaire prince, recently interviewed in *The New York Times,* said, "I don't collect art. I surround myself with ancestry." He continued, "We, meaning the family, invented the mails and got the monopoly on the mail service for the Holy Roman Empire in the Fifteenth Century. Before that, we were robber barons, really pirates, of Northern Italy."

The first modern postal enterprise was founded by the couriers of Bergamo. Prominent in this enterprise was the family of Tasso, later to become the princely house of Thurn and Taxis. In the year 1200 they established a postal service with the central seat in Venice and opened offices in Venice and Rome. They organized mounted posts and relays throughout the Papal States, and introduced in 1500 a regular postal course from Venice to Rome and back. This was just the beginning of the epic extravaganza of the remarkable aristocratic Thurn and Taxis family, who for generation after generation, over a period of six hundred years, did exactly what the twentieth-century Prince von Thurn and Taxis said, "[They] invented the mails." Like the Rothschild banking family, the Thurn and Taxis royal family stuck together, and so did their fortunes.

EARLY RENAISSANCE PRINCE INNOVATES THREAT LETTERS

One reckless, ruthless, and successful ruler during the early Renaissance who launched a courier service from 1387 to 1402 was Duke Gian Galeazzo Visconti of Milan. As conqueror of northern and central Italy, he recognized the meaning of speed. Rare and interesting folded letters have been found in the Visconti's archives that introduced the sign of the gallows to urge messengers to speed up delivery. Added was a sign of stirrups, which meant the letter was to be delivered on horseback, and for emphasis the word *cito* (haste) was applied—forerunner of the special delivery letter. With the gallows and all the other markings, the Visconti's threatening message was clear: "This letter is to go by horseback, day and night, by postal rider, not just rapidly but with the speed of lightning under the penalty of the gallows." Like all such admonitions, this official threat had about the same effect as the modern warnings on packets of cigarettes. This form of request for special delivery was continued up to the seventeenth century.

Letter from Verona to Venice dated November 17, 1524, with gallows marking indicating special haste and stirrups indicating change of horses and five *cito* marks, to emphasize haste.
(From the collection of the late Edith Faulstich, courtesy of Fred Faulstich)

A Duke of Sforza cover dated 1458 with the world's first postmark.
(From the collection of the late Edith Faulstich, courtesy of Fred Faulstich)

The world's first postmark in detail.
(Courtesy of the Society of Philatelic Americans)

THE WORLD'S FIRST POSTMARK

Succeeding the Visconti was the wealthy and powerful Duke Sforza of Milan who created the world's first postmark. The cover reproduced here, dated 1458, shows the postmark "Mediolanum Cursores" (Milan Couriers). In the center of the postmark is the coat of arms of the Duke. These rare postmarks were dry impressions, for stamp ink was not in use at that time. The vertical strike is a merchants' shipping mark which was used for identification up to the beginning of the nineteenth century. What makes this cover most interesting is that the letter was not sent from one government official to another. Rather it is correspondence from one private individual to another. This is considered proof that the princely postmarks were used for general postal services in the time of the early Renaissance.

The Mediolanum Cursores with the arms of Sforza and initials F. S., perhaps for ordinary mail.
(Courtesy of the Society of Philatelic Americans)

The Mediolanum Cursores with the arms of Sforza and initials S. S. for mounted courier.
(Courtesy of the Society of Philatelic Americans)

THE THURN AND TAXIS MONOPOLY CONTINUES

> The Posts . . . it was one of those wells into which all things flow.
>
> Count Leonard von Taxis

The billions of letters that go through the mail every day throughout every corner of the entire world can hardly be taken for granted. The mails are the personal arteries from the heart of every society.

The first of the Thurn and Taxis family to become wealthy was Francis I, who created the first international postal system for Emperor Maximilian I. A decree accepted November 15, 1516, by the emperor, which Francis probably wrote, states, "The King will procure and deliver to the postmasters licenses from the Holy Father, the Pope, from the King of France and, as it is necessary, from other princes and rulers through whose countries these posts will run so that closed cities, ferries, bridges and other places will be opened to the posts." Francis managed to include the following statement in the decree and contract: "Nobody should be Postmaster and Minister of Couriers other than a Von Taxis." Following Francis came his brother, Count Leonard, who was appointed Grand Postmaster of the Holy Roman Empire.

Each generation of Von Taxis sons, brothers, cousins, and nephews in one way or another extended the facilities of the post. When the Royal House could no longer pay the Von Taxis for their know-how, they resolved the problem with a suggestion made by Francis. To assure a profit, they secured permission to transport paying passengers

Francois I of Thurn and
Taxis.
(Courtesy of Doris Tusty)

Alexandrine de Rye,
Countess of Taxis.
(Courtesy of Doris Tusty)

as well as deliver mail to private people. By the seventeenth century
Prince Leonard II was hereditary postmaster of the realm. His
mother, Alexandrine de Rye, Countess of Taxis, had been the first
postmistress of the Netherlands post.

Prince Eugene Alexander was made hereditary prince of the German Empire by Leopold II. Knighted as well, he established the
princely house of Thurn and Taxis.

As a result of the War of the Spanish Succession, the family lost
control of the Netherlands posts. This forced the next Taxis, Anselme
Francis, to make his headquarters in Germany. It took twelve years
for the building of his palace to be completed. Alexandre Ferdinand,
who succeeded his father, contributed huge sums of money toward
the castle's expense, and in turn he was appointed the principal deputy of the empire. He received the credentials of ambassadors and
entertained the leaders of Europe lavishly. In 1748 he moved to Regensburg Castle where Prince Johannes von Thurn and Taxis "sur-
rounds himself with ancestry."

By the beginning of the nineteenth century, Prince Charles had an
annual net income of millions of dollars. Thurn and Taxis had a staff
of twenty thousand people, and possessed tens of thousands of horses,
and many castles and estates. Their postilions were instantly recognized all over Europe by the yellow trumpet embroidered on the front
and back of their tunics. They sounded the posthorn and carried a
special passport.

Prince Charles was to be the last in the affairs of the post from the
princely house of Thurn and Taxis. Prussia, in 1867, bought the Thurn
and Taxis posts for three million thalers in cash. It was Dr. Heinrich
von Stephan, postmaster of the North German Confederation in 1874,

Alexandre Ferdinand
of Thurn and Taxis.
(Courtesy of Doris Tusty)

Prince Charles of Thurn
and Taxis.
(Courtesy of Doris Tusty)

François Rabelais.

King Louis XI of France.

Erasmus of
Rotterdam.

Box used by state messengers
of Bern, Switzerland, for carrying parchment letters in
the sixteenth century.
(Courtesy of the Swiss PTT Museum, Bern)

A Turkish imperial messenger of 1572.
(Courtesy of the Swiss PTT Museum, Bern)

who invented the postcard and organized the Universal Postal Union (to which almost every nation belongs). He headed the transfer of the Thurn and Taxis post, ending the glamorous, aristocratic story of "the Princes of the Posts."

THE FIRST ROYAL POSTAL SERVICE OF THE MIDDLE AGES

In 1464 King Louis XI of France organized the first regular messenger service with definite routes and relay stations throughout France. He did not allow the postmaster "in pain of death" to make post horses available to anyone, regardless of rank, without his personal order. He did, however, make the post available to private people. The trouble was that the rates were so high that the ordinary person could not take advantage of the royal offer. Louis XI laid the basic foundation for the French postal system that exists in France to this very day.

A QUIET REVOLUTION

Rabelais, author of *Gargantua,* apropos of a small pamphlet he had written, was to say, "More copies of this would be sold in two months than people would buy the Bible in two years." He was referring to the invention of a printing press with movable type with which its inventor, Johann Gutenberg from Mainz, Germany, printed his first book, the Holy Bible, in 1456.

Erasmus, the famous fifteenth-century scholar from Rotterdam, was to set a record by writing more letters than any other person in the world. He had a staff of young men he called "formuli" that he sent around the globe. Some of his messengers were gone for as long as two years with their bags of letters to the north, south, east, and west. Erasmus had brilliant correspondences with popes, cardinals, kings, princes, nobles, and men of letters and scholarship worldwide. When his "formuli" messengers returned, they would bring bags full of mail as well as manuscripts, books, and gifts from his distinguished correspondents.

By 1500, there were printing presses in 183 towns throughout Europe. Printing made new ideas in politics and religion available to thousands of thinking men all over Europe. The Bible was no longer the monopoly of the Church, universities, and abbeys. Through the use of the printed word, thinkers like Erasmus could reach a far wider audience. His *In Praise of Folly* was one of the first books to influence all of Europe.

Sir Brian Tuke, first British postmaster, painted by Hans Holbein, the Younger, 1516. (Courtesy of the National Gallery of Art, Washington, D.C.)

The First British Postmaster

It was Erasmus who gave Hans Holbein the Younger letters to his friends in England, one of whom was Thomas More. Hans Holbein the Younger settled permanently in England, and became court painter to King Henry VIII. His major task was painting portraits of the royal household. The handsome painting of Sir Brian Tuke, the first British postmaster, signifies the importance of the man and the posts. The British postal system began as a royal courier service.

History has shown us that as a country's economic picture improves, parallel to it, usually, is the introduction of a postal organization. In 1516 King Henry VIII set up a permanent postal establishment and appointed Sir Brian Tuke the "Master of the King's Post." Sir Brian Tuke established regular schedules for the post instead of running them only when required, as had been the practice before.

At the time Sir Brian Tuke was postmaster, Henry VIII, a good Roman Catholic, went to the pope to annul his first marriage to Catherine of Aragon because she could not give him an heir. The pope refused him. King Henry broke with the Church, married Ann Boleyn, and fathered Elizabeth I. He established the Church of England and declared himself as its head.

"Hast for Lyfe for Life Hast"
—Elizabethan Special Delivery Letter

By the time of Elizabeth I, a few letters other than government correspondence were being carried by the post.

This Elizabethan letter with "Haste post Haste-etc." marked with

Elizabethan letter with endorsement "Hast for Lyfe for Life Hast," and marked with a gallows sign. (Courtesy of the British Post Office)

the gallows sign indicates that it was to be treated as a special delivery letter. The matter concerned either an execution or a reprieve for a condemned prisoner.

During the reign of Charles I, the Master of the King's Post was Thomas Witherings. To determine postal rates, he considered not only the destination of a letter but also its weight and size.

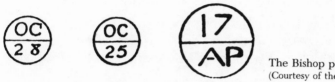

The Bishop postmarks.
(Courtesy of the British Post Office)

THE BISHOP MARK

In 1660 Colonel Henry Bishop became postmaster general of Great Britain and Ireland. When asked about delays in the post, he replied, "A stamp is invented that is put on a letter showing the day of the month that every letter comes to the office so that no letter carrier may care detayne a letter from post to post, which before was usual."

THE PENNY POST

In 1680 when William Dockwra introduced the penny post in London, he was providing a needed public service. Interestingly enough, at that time no official in any country comprehended the need in larger cities for better communications within their own boundaries. No public service existed for sending a letter. Usually one sent a servant, and if one did not have a servant, one hired a paid messenger. That is where Dockwra stepped in.

First he organized a house-to-house delivery service. Second, he charged a flat fee of one penny. And lastly, he introduced a mark to indicate that the postal fee had been paid. His service was so successful that the penny post not only benefited London but also the Crown Post as well, for now every man had a post office just around the corner, and more letters were written than ever before. Dockwra's operation became so successful that when the Duke of York became King James II in 1685, he took away the penny post from Dockwra and incorporated it into the postal system.

(1)

The Practical Method

OF THE

PENNY-POST:

Being a Sheet very neceſſary for all Perſons to have by them,

For their Information in the Regular Uſe of a De-
ſign ſo well Approved of, for quickening Corre-
ſpondence, Promoting Trade and Publick Good.

*With an Explaination of the following Stamps, for the
Marking of all Letters.*

Hereas *William Dockwra* of *London* Merchant, and the reſt of the
Undertakers, (who are all Natives and free Citizens of *London*)
out of a ſence of the great benefit which would accrew to the numerous Inhabitants of this Great City, and adjacent parts, (with
hopes of ſome Reaſonable Encouragement hereafter to Them-
ſelves) have lately ſet up a *New Invention* to convey Letters and
Parcels, not exceeding One Pound Weight, and Ten Pounds in
Value, to and from all Parts within the Contiguous Buildings of
the Weekly Bills Mortality for a Penny a Letter or Parcel, whereby Correſpondency, the Life of Trade and Buſineſs, is and will
be much facilitated ; and having for above a year paſt, with great
pains, and at ſome Thouſands of Pounds Charge, reduced the
ſame into Practice, which does manifeſtly appear to be for the Publick Good ; yet as all new
Deſigns at firſt uſually meet with Oppoſition and great Diſcouragements, rarely (if at all) pro-
ving beneficial to the Firſt Adventurers, ſo hath this alſo incurr'd the ſame Fate hitherto, eſpe-
cially from the Ignorant and Envious ; but the Undertakers do hope that all People will be
Convinced, by time and experience, which removes Prejudice and Errors, and renders all New
Undertakings Compleat ; for the Attainment of which good Ends, they have with great In-
duſtry, much expence of time, and at a Chargeable Rate, made ſuch Alterations in their
former Methods, as (they hope) will now give Univerſal ſatisfaction. And whereas there
has been much Noiſe about the pretended Delays and Miſcarriage of Letters going by the
Penny-Poſt, which has riſen through the great Miſtake and Neglect of other People, as
the Undertakers can ſufficiently Evidence, by many Authentick Certificats which they have
ready to produce, for the Juſtification of their due Performance in General, yet has there
been ſo many Cauſeleſs and Unjuſt Reflections caſt on ſo Uſeful an Undertaking, that they
hold it highly Neceſſary to undeceive the World, by ſhewing ſome of the grounds from whence
they ſpring, *viz.* Some Men ſuppoſe, and confidently Alledge their Letters are Miſcarried,
(or at leaſt Delayed,) becauſe they have not always an immediate Anſwer, when perhaps

A   the

Announcement of the penny post.   (Courtesy of Harmers International)

First-day cover commemorating the coronation of Napoleon.
(Courtesy of The Posthorn, Inc., New York)

The Rosetta stone.
(Courtesy of the Oriental Institute, University of Chicago)

Egyptian stamp honoring
Jean François Champollion.

Europa— From Charlemagne to Winston Churchill

When Charlemagne was crowned ruler of the Holy Roman Empire by the pope in A.D. 800, he had united most of Western Europe under his rule.

Napoleon, who introduced the metric system, a civil code, and a world court, had his dreams of a United Europe. He said, "I wanted to find a European system, a European code of laws, a European Court of Appeals . . . throughout all of Europe." Actually, he consolidated practically all of Europe from Scandinavia and southern Italy to Spain and Portugal. By 1807 he was emperor of France and king of Italy. His brother Joseph was king of Naples, and his brother Jerome, king of Westphalia. Prussia, Austria, Switzerland, and Belgium were parts of Napoleon's domain. One of his marshals, Bernadotte, was king of Sweden. When he invaded Spain and Portugal, he made his brother king of Spain. He bestowed the title of king of Rome on his son by Marie Louise.

The Rosetta Stone

In 1799 Napoleon returned to Egypt and defeated a Turkish army which had landed at Aboukir. Wanting to consolidate his power in France, he left his Egyptian forces under the command of General Kléber.

While some of Napoleon's engineers were digging near the Rosetta branch of the Nile (1799), a worker's shovel struck a huge slab of stone. The face of the slab was covered with writing in three different languages: hieroglyphics, demotic (hieroglyphic script), and Greek. A schoolboy in France named Jean François Champollion was intrigued by this amazing discovery and resolved to solve the mystery of hieroglyphics. After twenty-two years of studying Greek, Hebrew, Coptic,

Syriac, and Arabic, he finally broke the code. The Rosetta stone turned out to be a priestly decree honoring Ptolemy V (196 B.C.). Libraries of Egyptian writing came alive and the discovery also shed new light on biblical stories.

Letter addressed to General Kléber during Napoleon's Egyptian campaign with Rosette handstamp.
(From the collection of the late Edith Faulstich, courtesy of Fred Faulstich)

Arc de Triomphe max card.
(Courtesy of R. E. Beresford)

The Arc de Triomphe

The Arc de Triomphe, which has been on many stamps of the world, was built at the wish of Napoleon. It was his desire to have all the battles he won forever inscribed. To date, 386 names of great generals who participated in wars of the First Republic and the Empire are inscribed in it. On December 15, 1840, his funeral cortege passed through the Arc de Triomphe to his final resting place, Les Invalides in Paris. This honor has never been given to any other French hero. The arch is the largest of its kind in the world.

Folded letter to Sir Nathan Rothschild, April 20, 1814.
(Courtesy of E. Herbert Mayer)

Sir Nathan Rothschild

Military stampless covers during the fascinating Napoleonic era are of great interest to the collectors of military mail. This folded cover addressed to Sir Nathan Rothschild in London from Lamonier, April 20, 1814, was mailed the day Napoleon took leave of his troops at Fontainebleau and departed for Elba. The letter was sent via an English prisoner-of-war transport. The front of the cover shows a black strike, "Transport Officer, Prisoner of War, G.R." and a crown, also blue "Two py pence, Unpaid, Bge St. Welter" and manuscript "2" and backstamp with arrival markings. Sir Nathan was known for his elaborate news-gathering service on the continent.

Sir Winston Churchill

Sir Winston Churchill was the first great leader who envisioned a United States of Europe. In a speech he made in Zurich, Switzerland, in 1946, he said, "We must re-create the European family in a regional structure called, it may be, the United States of Europe, and the first step will be to form a Council of Europe. If at first all the states of Europe are not willing or able to join a union, we must nevertheless proceed to assemble and combine those who will and can."

The Council of Europe

Two years after Winston Churchill spoke, Belgium, France, Luxembourg, the Netherlands, and the United Kingdom met. A Council of Europe was formed "to bring together the closest economic, social and cultural co-operation to safeguard their common heritage."

By 1955 the distinguished French premier Robert Schuman proposed a "European Economic Community," which was the birth of the "Common Market." Out of an interest in the history and purpose of uniting Europe came the ardent army of philatelists who collect "EUROPA."

Since 1956 most member countries have issued commemorative stamps using a common design. The first of the common design Europa stamps is shown here on what is called a "multiple die proof." The stamps are in similar colors from both France and Luxembourg.

The collective die proof depicting a cog wheel and a sheaf of wheat symbolizing the Europa concept of free economy and mutual prosperity was issued by France in 1957. The important difference is the two values on the same proof. This is a fine example of the term "collective die proof."

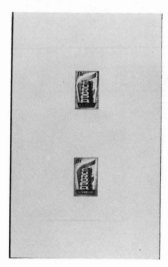

Multiple die proof.
(Courtesy of Melvin Garabrant)

Collective die proof.
(Courtesy of Melvin Garabrant)

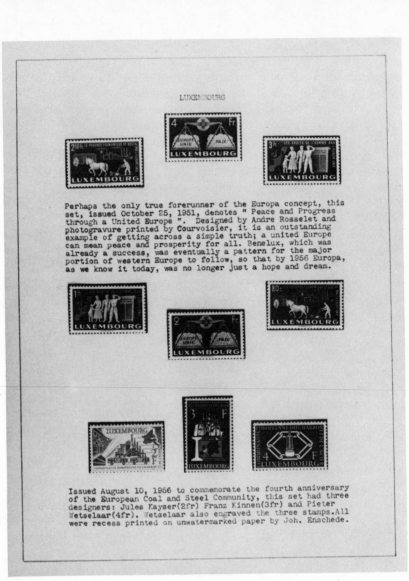

LUXEMBOURG

Perhaps the only true forerunner of the Europa concept, this set, issued October 25, 1951, denotes " Peace and Progress through a United Europe ". Designed by Andre Rosselet and photogravure printed by Courvoisier, it is an outstanding example of getting across a simple truth; a united Europe can mean peace and prosperity for all. Benelux, which was already a success, was eventually a pattern for the major portion of western Europe to follow, so that by 1956 Europa, as we know it today, was no longer just a hope and dream.

Issued August 10, 1956 to commemorate the fourth anniversary of the European Coal and Steel Community, this set had three designers: Jules Kayser(2fr) Franz Kinnen(3fr) and Pieter Wetselaar(4fr). Wetselaar also engraved the three stamps.All were recess printed on unwatermarked paper by Joh. Enschede.

A page from a Europa collection.
(Collection of Melvin Garabrant)

Europa stamp "CEPT" of Monaco.

Europa Alphabet

When you collect Europa, you get involved with endless initials of the alphabet. Each set of initials can be a collector's specialty. For instance, the initials CEPT represent the Conference of European Postal and Telecommunications administrations. A big specialized catalog called *Europa* is an eyeful on the interesting and varied concepts of Europa. To list just a few:

> CEA: European Confederation of Agriculture
> CEEA: European Community for Atomic Energy
> CECA: European Coal and Steel Community
> CEH: European Time Table Conference
> CERN: European Center for Nuclear Research
> EBC: European Brewing Convention
> NATO: North Atlantic Treaty Organization

NATO is a reminder of a fine Europa collector I once met who, as a result of chasing down information on NATO, came up with more knowledge of the organization than some of its top officers.

The Europa Study Unit *(See Plate 6)*

Tied in with this enthusiastic Europa collecting is the Europa Study Unit, a stamp club full of talent and vitality. Membership in this club is $1 annually. Most of the members send in checks voluntarily because the Study Unit offers so much research and current news not really available elsewhere.

This ever-growing club issues a formidable handbook, containing more than 1,800 entries plus information on dates of issue, designs, numbers issued, varieties, and more. The handbook is mimeographed and can be happily housed in a three-ring notebook. This type of handbook makes sense because it increases in size constantly; supplementary pages are sent throughout the year to Europa members. Added to this they have periodic auctions which are most useful to club members who wish both to buy and sell Europa material.

"One of the great challenges of Europa collecting is that the topic is an interesting exercise for the imagination. Some only collect the yearly Europa issues. Others, taking a liberal view, collect anything and everything that can be conceivably connected with the unity of Europe. Most collectors fall in between."

For any type of designer—be it of fabrics, dishes, ideas, directions or outstanding antiques—the 1976 Europa issues from all the member countries are not only a treat to the eye but also an education in "arts and crafts" that is unique. In the late eighteenth century, Sweden presented an ornamental tile stove made in the Marieberg China Factory (Fig. 1). In the same set issued is a stamp depicting a nineteenth-century Lapp spoon of elk horn, now in the Nordic Museum in Stockholm (Fig. 3). A stunning Byzantine goblet was the design chosen by Cyprus (Fig. 2), from France came a 1787 porcelain plate from Sèvres (Fig. 4), and from Iceland a wooden bowl (Fig. 5).

Turkey offered a decorated pitcher (Fig. 6) and a ceramic plate (Fig. 13) made by the Sumerbank Yildez Porcelain Industry Enterprises in Istanbul. Ireland chose to portray a striking Delftware bowl with interlaced sides, popular in that country during the second half of the eighteenth century. It was produced in Dublin at the factory of Henry Delamain (Fig. 7).

Switzerland issued a stamp depicting a richly decorated eighteenth-century pocket watch from the La Loche Horological Museum (Fig. 8).

Greece, as could be expected, issued examples of ceramics, and one of these stamps is a Florentine jug of Western Macedonia (Fig. 9).

The eighth-century Tassilo cup from the Benedictine Abbey of Krimsmunster is Austria's striking stamp. This cup dates back almost a thousand years or so and is named for Duke Tassilo II, first cousin of Emperor Charlemagne (Fig. 10).

Luxembourg's design depicted a red terra cotta soup tureen (Fig. 11). Norway issued a bishop's bowl in the shape of a miter made of faience that was created by the Herrebo Potteries near Halden dating from the late 1760s. This is now in the Oslo Museum of Applied Arts (Fig. 12); Finland presented a stamp with a knife from Bogri with a golden sheath and belt (Fig. 14). Lastly, San Marino offered a stamp, silver in color, of a chiseled silver plate by Agostino Ruscelli of the Giuseppe Arzilli goldsmith shop (Fig. 15).

These sets alone could influence you to become a Europa collector. If you would like to get involved in this span of time and study, you may write for information to: Donald W. Smith, Executive Secretary, Europa Study Unit, 1633 Florida Ave., Johnstown, Pennsylvania 15902.

For information on the EUROPA catalogue: D'Urso EUROPA Catalog, Filatelia D'Urso, Via Della Mercede 11, Rome, Italy.

Sir Rowland Hill.

The World's First Stamp

A bit of paper just large enough to bear a stamp and covered on the back with glutinous wash which the user might, by applying a little moisture, attach to a letter.

Sir Rowland Hill

Sir Rowland Hill conceived of and gave to Great Britain the world's first postage stamp, known as the Penny Black. It was issued May 6, 1840. (See Fig. 1, Plate 7.) He developed what may still be considered the most beautiful stamp in existence. A. G. Rigo de Righi, curator of the National Postal Museum in London, calls the Penny Black "the Mona Lisa of the stamp world."

The center, or vignette, portrays an exquisite profile of young Queen Victoria. The magnificent diadem that adorns her was designed for King George IV. It is set with diamonds and consists of four Maltese crosses alternating with four bouquets made up of roses, shamrocks, daffodils, and thistles above a band of pearls. It is an item of jewelry that has been worn by successive sovereigns or their consorts. Queen Victoria wore the diadem for the main portraits that were painted of her. Today Her Majesty Queen Elizabeth II, great-great-granddaughter of Queen Victoria, wears this diadem at the opening of Parliament.

What Should a Stamp Look Like?

Since no one had an idea of what a stamp should look like, the British Treasury in 1839 had a competition open to artists, scientists, and the public. Two thousand six hundred designs and ideas were submitted. Rowland Hill scrapped the lot of them, prize winners and all, got out

The Diadem.
(By gracious permission of Her
Majesty Queen Elizabeth II)

The Wyon Medal.
(Courtesy of the British Post Office)

his box of watercolors, and painted on a piece of paper his notion of
what an adhesive postage stamp should be like. For his model he chose
as his theme the portrait of the young Queen Victoria from a medal
designed by William Wyon. Henry Corbould, a London artist, was
given the task of making the drawing of the Queen's head.

Rowland Hill made sure that in the engraving and printing of
stamps there would be an "exact uniformity in the whole number
issued." This was further insurance against imitation and forgery. Hill
therefore gave the printing firm of Perkins Bacon & Co. the order to
print the first postage stamps.

The time for the postage stamp was ripe. Rowland Hill, a former
schoolteacher, was the champion of the common people. He proposed
that the government engage in the delivery of letters, including the

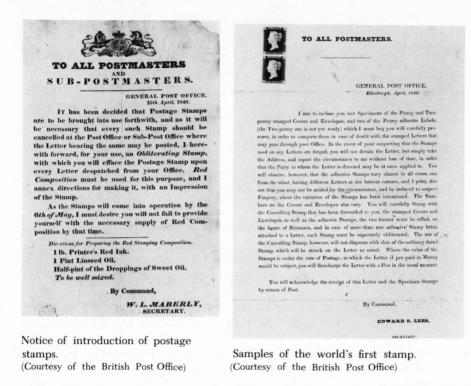

Notice of introduction of postage stamps.
(Courtesy of the British Post Office)

Samples of the world's first stamp.
(Courtesy of the British Post Office)

sale of stamps to be paid for by the sender. Prepaid adhesive postage stamps were a revolutionary innovation. The postage stamps would cost only one penny and would carry a half-ounce letter all over the United Kingdom. These ideas appeared in the now-famous paper of Rowland Hill titled *Post Office Reform, Its Importance and Practicality*.

The Duke of Wellington opposed the idea of cheaper postage and rallied behind him the aristocracy and Parliament, forces who risked losing their franking privileges. The postmaster general, Lord Litchfield, said of the plans set forth by Mr. Hill, ". . . of all the wild and visionary schemes which I have heard of or read, it is the most extravagant."

Rowland Hill had the merchants, businessmen, and public on his side. At that time, Charles Dickens, after writing a letter to a friend living in Elstree, a suburb of London, added a postscript, "A dreadful thought has just occurred to me, that this is a quadruple letter and that Elstree may not be within the two-penny post. Pray heaven my fears are unfounded."

The public needed what Rowland Hill had to offer. In 1839 his concept of a prepaid adhesive post was finally accepted and signed into law by Queen Victoria.

1d black, Plate 2, a present to King George V from Queen Mary.

(By gracious permission of Her Majesty Queen Elizabeth II)

The Machin Head Portrait of H.M. Queen Elizabeth II

In 1967, one hundred twenty-seven years later, a stamp was issued picturing a profile of Her Majesty Queen Elizabeth II wearing the same diadem (see Fig. 2, Plate 7). This portrait was the result of twelve months of work by Arnold Machin. Machin's sculptured bust was modeled on a photograph by the Earl of Snowdon, and it was the first definitive series to be issued without the words "Postage and Revenue." The first value of the series was a 4d, and the olive brown sepia color was selected by the Queen.

Because it was the first nation to use postage stamps, Great Britain is the only country in the world that does not have to put its name on its stamps. The portrait or profile of the monarch stands to identify the nation, as it has since 1840.

A rare cover cancelled on the first Sunday after the date of issue of the Penny Black (May 6, 1840).

(Courtesy of the British Post Office)

The £ 1 "Stamps for Cooks" Book for Housewives

On December 1, 1969, a £ 1 "Stamps for Cooks" booklet was issued by the British Post Office, sponsored by the British Milk Marketing Board. Thirteen cooking recipes including Stuffed Cucumber, Baked Haddock, and a Ham Club Sandwich were printed opposite panes of the Machin Heads. The idea was not popular with housewives at all. Only later were keen collectors aware that 374,904 booklets had been stitched but 10,848 booklets had been *stapled*. One-third of the entire lot remained unused and were returned to the post office and burned. Only 6,000 of the "stapled type" were sold to the public. At the time, friends of mine, who were avid Machin Head collectors, asked me to buy these booklet panes. Even dealers at stamp shows did not take special notice of my successful search for the "stitched types"; the difference was too minuscule then.

In his article in *Stamps* magazine, September 4, 1976, G. I. Barrow stated, "The sale of cookbooks has boomed for one outstanding reason, namely, the se-tenant pane has two vertical strips of three 4d vermillion stamps coated with a single phosphor band. The first strip of 4d has a single phosphor band at its right-hand side and the last strip of 4d has a single phosphor band at its left-hand side."

The normal 4d stamp has a single phosphor band down the center. If you own the stapled panes of this booklet, the price is about $85. The profit, if you bought this at the post office in England, would be $84.40.

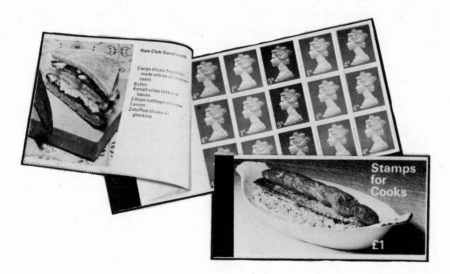

"Stamps for Cooks."
(Courtesy of Abbot Lutz)

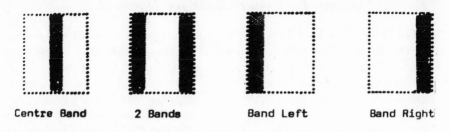

| Centre Band | 2 Bands | Band Left | Band Right |

Illustrations of the four phosphor bands.

Phosphor—The Hidden Side of Stamps

"ALF" STEPS IN

Like the United States, Canada, France, and many other countries, Great Britain has been experimenting over the years with quicker ways to sort and process its mail. In England an Automatic Letter Facer, nicknamed "ALF," sorts the mail with an electric eye. The phosphor bands applied to the stamps in the "Cookbook" (which we call "tagging") trigger the electric eye and because of the placement of the bands, ALF is able to sort the mail by classes: first, second, etc.

France is using phosphor bands, Canada has used tagging and non-tagging, and in the United States a simpler form, overall phosphor coating, is used. The phosphor is sprayed on the continuous sheet of printed stamps as it rolls through the presses, as one would spray paint. There are interesting varieties to be found in this field. In Great Britain, the phosphor bands actually had a plate number and in the United States, if the spray was not turned on in time, a few stamps would come through untagged, but to participate in this part of the hobby, you don't need just a good eye, you need a fluorescent black UV lamp. When turned on, all the problems of phosphor and even paper pop up and dazzle the eye. It is entertaining, growing in popularity, but almost impossible to exhibit—unless by some chance you can attach a UV light above your exhibit. (See the section on printing and paper for more details on this subject.)

The World's Most Valuable Stamp

The phone rang and a voice said, "Meet me at the St. Regis for lunch at 12:30." On the other end was Irwin Weinberg, owner of the most valuable stamp in the world, the 1-cent British Guiana black on magenta of 1856 (see Fig. 3, Plate 7). It was he who paid $280,000 to be its proud owner. To date this is the highest price paid for a single stamp. When the famous auction took place, the bidding contest was between Weinberg and the famous Raymond Weill of New Orleans, owner of the most valuable letter in the world, which he purchased in 1968 for $380,000. Raymond Weill sat in the distinguished audience of millionaires hoping to obtain the great rarity. "I get a special warmth from it. You might say it turns me on," he said.

The British Guiana 1-cent stamp has been the guest of honor at the largest stamp exhibitions throughout the world. It is usually flanked by two severe-looking guards and locked into a bulletproof glass case and has been seen by millions of people.

On the way to meet the person who owned the British Guiana, I thought of a line from the book on the stamp titled *Paper Gold:* "The quantity of rare stamps never varies." I had wondered what Irwin Weinberg would be like and when we met, I found a handsome man in his mid-forties. He is bullish on "conservation of capital." He says, "True investment must have withstood the test of time, have protected its capital consistently in terms of purchasing power and it must be instantly liquid in all major financial centers of the world as well." He says gold, diamonds, and real estate are dangerous spheres of investment while "the great classic stamps are first of all known unchangeable quantities." He might sell his famous stamp for one million dollars now, but in the meantime his fame has made him a proud owner of the stamp. The stamp receives more invitations than any living person in the world and Weinberg has trouble keeping up with all of them.

Damus Petimus que Vicissim

British Guiana, located on the northeast coast of South America, was the first British colony in the Western Hemisphere to issue a stamp. That was in 1850. In 1852, it issued a 1-cent black on magenta surfaced paper and a 4-cent black on blue surfaced paper. These stamps have a picture of a ship, the motto of the colony, "Damus Petimus que Vicissum," meaning "give and we seek in return," the value of the stamp, and the name British Guiana.

In 1856 the regular supply of postage stamps ran out and, although an order had been placed for a new supply of stamps, it did not arrive. The postmaster ordered provisional stamps to be printed until the others came from London. The postmaster awarded the job of printing the stamps to Joseph Brown and William Dallas, publishers of the *Official Gazette*. They had a small hand press, 18 × 12 inches. The postmaster wanted a design similar to the stamps then in use. Since they did not have the design of the exact ship, they used the vessel from the masthead for shipping notes used in the *Gazette*. They printed the 4-cent value on blue surfaced paper and the 1 cent on magenta surfaced paper, both with the motto of the colony. They were put into circulation in February 1856. To prevent forgery, the initials of the postmasters, E. D. W. (Wight), E. T. E. D. (Dalton), C. A. W. (Watson), and W. H. L. (Lortimer) were written on the stamps as they were sold.

The General Post Office, Hincks Street, Georgetown, British Guiana.
(Courtesy of the National Library, Guyana)

Catalog Comparison, 1868–1977

By 1868 *Scott's Catalogue* in twenty-one pages listed stamps available from a little more than one hundred countries. At random, it is fascinating to compare *Scott's* listings of 1868 to the *Scott's Catalogue* of 1977. The former was a selling list while the latter is an estimated value of a stamp's worth. Here are a few examples:

	Scott's 1868	*Scott's* 1977 Unused	Used
British Guiana, 1852, 1 cent magenta	$2	$3,500	$1,500
Cape of Good Hope, 1861, 4p blue	$2	$2,500	$900
Austria, 1851, 6K red, newspaper stamp	$5	$23,000	$27,500
Canada, 1851, 12p violet black	$3 used	$32,500	$20,000
U.S.A., 1847, 5¢ brown	$0.05 used	$800	$225

Catalogues were just beginning to be published in different countries. Stanley Gibbons, J. W. Scott, J. B. Moens, and Mount Brown were some of the leading dealers emerging. By 1874 more than 347 catalogues, albums, and periodicals began to appear in different countries —Denmark, the Netherlands, France, Germany, Italy, Spain, and, of course, England.

Stamp collectors, like bees to honey, were finding stamp dealers and the hunt was underway. Surely Rowland Hill could never have dreamed that from the practical use of the postage stamp would eventually come an avalanche of collectors who would make stamp collecting the number one hobby worldwide. Here was an unexpected and undreamed-of United Nations, a people-to-people program that created the biggest hobby the world has ever known.

To Study Their Stamps

In 1869 in London an indication of the beginnings of stamp collecting took place when a most fascinating group of people met Saturday afternoons to discuss and compare their stamps. Dr. Charles W. Viner, editor of the *Stamp Collector's Magazine* (1863–1867); Frederick A. Philbrick, a lawyer and later a judge (and collector of British Guiana provisionals); Mr. Mount Brown, publisher of *Mount Brown Stamp Catalog;* Henry Haslett; Sir Daniel Cooper, who had been speaker of the General Assembly of New South Wales; Edward L. Pemberton, dealer; and W. Dudley Atlee, noted philatelic writer and stamp dealer, met regularly.

An interesting controversy, which has a familiar sound, arose. Two schools of thought were emerging in relationship to stamp collecting. The English school of thought written in the *Stamp Collector,* March–May 1868, says, "The collection of postage stamps should be nothing

A letterbox and postman in Paris, 1840.
(Courtesy of the Swiss PTT Museum, Bern)

more or less than the accumulation of the printed designs." Today, those of us who are "accumulators" can agree with writers and their followers who say, "I collect for the fun of it." On the other hand, in the beginning of our hobby the opposition was labeled the French school. Mr. Pemberton pointed out that "stamps, apart from their illustrative value, have sufficient interest to justify the study of their specialties and that the history of every design is worth tracing through the various mutations of shade, paper, watermark, and perforations." Pemberton along with Thornton Lewis (1863) wrote a book on forgeries. Yes, the thieves were with us then, only in smaller numbers than today. Pemberton also drew up the first catalogue listings of shades, watermarks, and perforations (1867). Over the years the English school of thought has faded.

The Rolls-Royce of Stamp Clubs

In the May 1869 edition of *The Philatelist*, it was reported that a preliminary meeting was held to form a philatelic society chaired by Sir Daniel Cooper.

At that meeting, Sir Daniel Cooper became chairman of the new society known as The Philatelic Society, London. The objectives of the society were the collection of all possible information respecting postage stamps, the prevention of forgeries, and facilitating the acquisition and exchange of postage stamps among its members. Membership was limited to amateurs.

Collecting of the classics now merited its own society. Standards were set that have never changed. In fact, the standards have only expanded in influence. Atlee proposed that "exhaustive monographs of the issues of all countries should gradually be prepared" as a part of the society's activities. Baron Arthur Rothschild, Judge Philbrick, and Sir Daniel led the way with papers on Great Britain, South America, and South Africa, as well as Mauritius.

Pioneer Lady

In this remarkable early stage of "students of philately" came a Miss A. L. Fenton, who presented a paper to the society on "The Secret Marks on the Stamps of Peru." She used the pseudonyms "Herbert Camoens" and "Fentonia."

Because she wrote so often for *The Philatelist* and the *Stamp Collector* magazines, she presented the society with bound volumes of all the early issues. Thus, the society's library was underway.

The nucleus of a scientific approach to philately now grew to international contacts and exchange. While experts dealt primarily with pioneering papers on a variety of philatelic research, no one could begin to know—as indeed they do not today—the answer to "Who collects?" and "Where are the collectors?"

The Worst Stamp Swap in History

The year is 1873. A young boy by the name of L. Vernon Vaughn, who lived in Georgetown, British Guiana, was a most enthusiastic collector. One stamp he had on an old envelope was a 1-cent black on magenta paper British Guiana. It was shabby-looking and cut octagonally and, although he figured it was not a nice specimen, he soaked it off and placed it in his album, thinking he would replace it with a better one. The stamp had been initialed E. D. W. (Wight) and it was postmarked Demerara, AP4, 1856.

One day Vaughn received approvals—colorful mint stamps—from a dealer in London. He needed $2.50 to buy them. Like all collectors, he knew the top local collector, Mr. N. R. McKennan.

Young Vernon, not caring for his 1-cent black on magenta stamp and sure that he would find another one, went to sell this stamp to Mr. McKennan. At first he was turned down, but the lad explained why he wanted to sell it. McKennan softened and told the boy, "Look here, my lad, I am taking a great risk on paying you so much for this stamp,

Glasgow to London Royal Mail Coach, circa 1845.
(Courtesy of the British Post Office)

two dollars and fifty cents, but I hope you will appreciate my generosity." Vernon went away happy, for he had the money to buy his approvals.

Five years later Mr. McKennan sold his collection to a dealer friend, Mr. Wylie Hill of Glasgow, Scotland, who contacted the well-known London dealer Edward L. Pemberton. Pemberton looked at the collection, but didn't buy it. He had noticed the rare stamp. Mr. Hill contacted Mr. Thomas Ridpath, also a dealer, who didn't have the cash himself but got it from one of his clients, Mr. James Bottley, who loaned him £150 or $1,035. Bottley was not interested in the stamp, but Ridpath knew it was rare but not unique. Ridpath happily sold the stamp to Count Philippe la Renotière von Ferrari in Paris for £120 or $828.

Count Philippe la Renotière von Ferrari

Over a period of fifty-six years, Count von Ferrari amassed the biggest and most valuable stamp collection the world has ever known. The count was born in Paris, January 11, 1848. His father, Raphael Marquis de Ferrari, was a banker known as "the King of Railroads"— he built the first railroad from Paris to the Mediterranean. Pope Pius IV gave him the title "Duke of Galliera." His mother was an Austrian duchess named Maria de Galliera, who was a beautiful and highly intelligent woman. She was the daughter of the Marquis di Brigniola.

Count Philippe de Ferrari.

Philippe, as a boy, was known in the stamp world. He and his mother visited many of the Paris stamp shops, and while he selected the stamps, she paid the bills. As a student this activity continued, and as he grew older, mother simply received the bills. He went rampant and bought everything in sight, including new issues, singles, blocks, and sheets. He bought entire collections, such as the one belonging to Sir Daniel Cooper, for $15,000, which today is worth $500,000. He purchased Baron Nathan Rothschild's collection, and his greatest effort to increase his philatelic holdings was the purchase of the superb collection on Great Britain that Judge Philbrick had developed over the years. Every "classic" stamp that had ever been issued he purchased in singles, pairs, on covers. By the standards of the now highly developed classic collector, he was considered a "crazy" accumulator. Everyone else did the work and he purchased the results.

The count traveled throughout England, Germany, Austria, Switzerland, Holland, and Italy feverishly searching for stamps. He and his mother lived in a mansion in Paris at 57 Rue de Varenne. When she died, she willed the palace to Emperor Franz Joseph of Austria with the proviso that as long as her son lived he would have the use of one wing for his stamps.

Ferrari loved Paris, but not its people, and especially not his French relatives. As a matter of fact, with his stamp purchasing mania, his relatives were convinced that he was crazy or surely mentally retarded. To satisfy them he completed a law degree in five years in France. His doubting relatives simply had to tip their hats to him.

The count was a great linguist, fluent in French, English, German, and Italian, just for starters.

At age twenty-eight, to mark one spot in his philatelic career, he purchased without question the stamp offered to him by Ridpath—the 1-cent black on magenta of British Guiana—for $828. He was delighted to have it. It was the highest price ever paid for a stamp at that time.

Upon the death of his mother, he took the right wing of the palace of Emperor Franz Joseph and set up his entire household to accommodate his passion for stamp collecting. He inherited the entire fortune of his mother and father which ran into millions of dollars. By 1897 he had spent $1,250,000 on stamps, covers, and collections.

He hired a philatelic confidential secretary, Pierre Mahe, a stamp dealer he met in Paris around 1860. A rather fascinating account was written of this scene by Charles J. Phillips of Stanley Gibbons who often visited the count with, no doubt, valuable stamps. Phillips described: "Once inside the courtyard, large enough for twenty coaches and guarded by ferocious dogs which had to be tied up before a visitor could enter, the first floor had three rooms and a small anteroom. Two rooms were for stamps, one just for postage stamps, the other for envelopes. Here Pierre Mahe had his desk. In front of his desk he had a scheme, you might say, every collector's dream. Pierre had a board on the wall and on it a series of sharp, pointed nails. Every Monday morning the Count's treasurer fixed bundles of French banknotes of 20's, 50's, 100's, 500's, and 1,000 franc denominations, totalling $10,-000—Ferrari's weekly allowance to buy stamps."

In 1891 Ferrari joined the giants of philately when he became a member of The Philatelic Society, London. That did not give him the status of being a philatelist in their sense of the word. He was already known as the "insatiable collector of collectors." He already owned the Sir Daniel Cooper Collection, and a year later he purchased Judge Philbrick's collections which included Great Britain, the Confederate States of America, Hawaii (including the complete series of the first issue which catalogs today for $148,500), Mauritius (including both values of the "Post Office" stamps which catalog for $190,000), British Guiana, and the Australian Colonies. Philbrick's collection was considered the finest in the world when Ferrari bought it. Meanwhile, the 1-cent black on magenta had been in Ferrari's possession for fourteen years, stocked up with all the other treasures.

The Earl of Crawford

The study of stamps had become a science. Through the monographs and other writings the hobby had begun to inspire many brilliant minds. One such illustrious person was the twenty-sixth Earl of Crawford (Premier Earl of Scotland), who was distinguished in the fields of astronomy, electricity, engineering, exploration, ornithology, and photography. His collecting interests were the United States, Egypt, and the Italian States (which later formed the basis of the famous Rothschild Collection which Ferrari bought.

He did most of his research on his yacht, the *Valhalla*. He accumulated his philatelic material on land by attending auctions, visiting dealers and friends, then went yachting where he would arrange and write up his findings.

The earl was the father of modern stamp collecting. What he enjoyed was choosing a stamp and analyzing it in minute detail. In his albums he began with essays on the stamps, then color trials as well as proofs in all possible stages. In chronological order he presented every printing of the stamp, all varieties, all different papers, perforations, and varied watermarks. Then he proceeded to present used covers, including every important postmark, and a detailed analysis and description of the postal history of every cover. He put displaying stamps chronologically and beautifully "on the map." His system became the guide to all future collectors. His collection is now in the British Museum. He used to show up at meetings in a kilt or large black-and-white checked trousers. His United States collection is considered unique.

His Royal Highness the Duke of Edinburgh

His Royal Highness the Duke of Edinburgh, second son of Queen Victoria, was keenly interested in philately. The Philatelic Society, London, invited him to open the Jubilee Philatelic Exhibition in London, where he himself was an exhibitor. On December 19, 1890, he became the first honorary president of the society. In later years he sold his collection to his older brother, the Prince of Wales, who became King Edward VII, who in turn presented the collection to his son, His Royal Highness, the Duke of York, the future King George V.

His Royal Highness the Duke of York

On March 10, 1893, it was intimated that His Royal Highness the Duke of York would like to become a member of The Philatelic Society, London. Shortly thereafter he was elected honorary vice-president. That same year he married Princess Victoria Mary of Teck, and as a wedding present, one hundred members gave him a collection of fifteen hundred stamps, including Great Britain and British colonies. "Great care had been taken to ensure that they would be acceptable" to the collection of His Royal Highness.

At the annual dinner, 1896, J. A. Tilleard, honorary secretary of the society (a position he held brilliantly for twenty years), announced that the Duke of York had graciously consented to be nominated as the new president. One can hardly imagine the total joy of the annual meeting, which took place the following day. His Royal Highness was elected by acclamation.

King George V

George V, known as the "Sailor King," was the second son of King Edward VII and Queen Alexandra. Upon the death of his father, he ascended the throne on May 6, 1910.

He began to collect stamps when he was a naval cadet and later as a midshipman on the *Bacchante.* Quite on his own, he began to pick up items of interest to him, here and there. Like the Earl of Crawford, he was both a student of stamps and a perfectionist, and like millions of stamp collectors, he used the Stanley Gibbons catalogue—since Great Britain and her colonies were his specialty. The stamps he "ticked" on a page were the ones he had. This will hearten many collectors using *Scott's, Stanley Gibbons,* or any other catalogue, who mark them with what they have and what they need. Little wonder this fascination of stamp collecting was labeled the "Hobby of Kings" and the "King of Hobbies." George V, of course, was in a unique position to pick up a "royal cover."

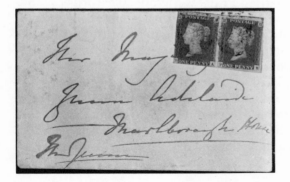

King George V as Duke of York in command of his first ship, H.M.S. *Thrush,* wrote to his mother from Bermuda, 1890. The initial (bottom left) is his.
(By gracious permission of Her Majesty Queen Elizabeth II)

Cover from Queen Victoria to Queen Adelaide, signed "The Queen" (bottom left).
(By gracious permission of Her Majesty Queen Elizabeth II)

King George V checklist from Stanley Gibbons' *Catalogue.* (By gracious permission of Her Majesty Queen Elizabeth II)

"I Wish to Have the Best Collection"

As Duke of York and Prince of Wales, King George V was an extraordinary president of the now "Royal" Philatelic Society, London. He read his outstanding paper, entitled "Notes on the Postal Issues of the United Kingdom during the Present Reign," and he illustrated his lectures with superb essays, proofs, and stamps from his collection. He built the finest collection of Great Britain and Colonies up to that time and was its foremost authority. His letter to Tilleard, whom he appointed "Philatelist to the King," is clearly the hope of all philatelists. In it he wrote: "But remember, I wish to have *the* best collection, not just one of the best collections, in England." This he attained with great distinction.

Charles J. Phillips recorded that when the Duke of Windsor was a boy in his teens, he would buy stamps with his pocket money. "He once said in a gloomy moment that he did not believe he would get anywhere collecting because 'the old man' picked up everything good that came along."

Letter from King George V to J. A. Tilleard, the King's first philatelic advisor.
(By gracious permission of Her Majesty Queen Elizabeth II)

Color Plates

PLATE 1

Fig. 1. Elizabeth of Glamis.
Fig. 2. A rose hybrid.
Fig. 3. Golden Scepter.
Fig. 4. Turkish rose.
Fig. 5. Princess Grace.
Fig. 6. Papa Meilland.
Fig. 7. Josephine Bruce.
Fig. 8. Iceberg.
Fig. 9. Rosa Odorata.
Fig. 10. Rosa Canina.
Fig. 11. Desert Rose.
Fig. 12. Grandpa Dickson.

(British roses copyright, British Post Office)

PLATE 2

Ten Prized Dogs.

(Courtesy of the Directorate General of Posts, Republic of China)

PLATES 3, 4, and 5

Fig. 1. Lascaux cave painting, from France.
Fig. 2. Hercules wrestling Antaeus on Athenian vessel, from Greece.
Fig. 3. Etruscan tomb painting, *The Musicians*, from San Marino.
Fig. 4. From *The Miniature Book of Kells*, from Ireland.
Fig. 5. *Pietà* fresco, from Yugoslavia.
Fig. 6. *Portrait of Lady Talbot* by Petrus Christus, from Belgium.
Fig. 7. Departure for the Hunt, from France.
Fig. 8. *Adoration of the Child* by Fra Felippo Lippi, from the Central African Republic.
Fig. 9. *The Battle of San Romano*, Paolo Uccello, fifteenth century, from San Marino.
Fig. 10. *The Anatomy Lesson* by Rembrandt, from Togo.
Fig. 11. *Grandfather and Son* by Ghirlandaio, from the Republic of the Congo.
Fig. 12. *The Creation*, by Michelangelo, from India.
Fig. 13. Detail from *The Virgin of the Rocks* by Leonardo da Vinci, from Argentina.
Fig. 14. *St. Paul* by El Greco, from Greece.
Fig. 15. *Monks in Abbey Workshop*, miniature, circa 1040, from Luxembourg.
Fig. 16. *The Good Shepherd* by Murillo, from Spain.
Fig. 17. *The Singing Boy* by Frans Hals, from Rwanda.
Fig. 18. *Prince Balthazar* by Velazquez, from Spain.
Fig. 19. *Madonna and Child* by Rogier van der Weyden, from Belgium.
Fig. 20. *Crossing the Alps* by David, from Grenada.
Fig. 21. *The Boating Party* by Mary Cassatt, from the United States.
Fig. 22. *The Beer Drinkers* by Manet, from Togo.
Fig. 23. *Merriment* by Paul Gauguin, from France.
Fig. 24. *Dancer with Bouquet* by Degas, from France.
Fig. 25. *The Hay Wain* by John Constable, 1821, from Great Britain.
Fig. 26. *The Blue Nudes* by Matisse, from France.
Fig. 27. *Guernica* by Picasso, from Czechoslovakia.
Fig. 28. *The Honeymooners of the Eiffel Tower* by Chagall, from France.
Fig. 29. *The Joy of Life* by R. Delauney, from France.

(From the collection of Irwin Rosen)

PLATE 6

Fig. 1. Tile stove.
Fig. 2. Byzantine goblet.
Fig. 3. Lapp spoon.
Fig. 4. Sevres porcelain plate.
Fig. 5. Wooden bowl.
Fig. 6. Decorated pitcher.
Fig. 7. Delftware bowl.
Fig. 8. Pocket watch.
Fig. 9. Florentine jug.
Fig. 10. Tassilo cup.
Fig. 11. Soup tureen.
Fig. 12. Bishop bowl.
Fig. 13. Ceramic plate.
Fig. 14. Knife, sheath, and belt.
Fig. 15. Silver plate.

(From the collection of Melvin Garabrant)

PLATE 7

Fig. 1. The world's first stamp, 1840.
       (Courtesy of Robert P. Odenweller)
Fig. 2. The Machin head design.
       (Courtesy of H. R. Holland)
Fig. 3. The world's most valuable stamp, 1856.
       (Courtesy of Irwin Weinberg)
Fig. 4. The world's most valuable cover, 1847.
       (Courtesy of Raymond H. Weill, Co.)

PLATE 8

New Zealand.
(From the collection of Robert P. Odenweller)

Fig. 1

Fig. 2

Fig. 3

Fig. 4

Fig. 5

Fig. 6

Fig. 7

Fig. 8

Fig. 9

Fig. 10

Fig. 11

Fig. 12

Plate 1

Plate 2

Fig. 1

Fig. 2

Fig. 3

Fig. 5

1. 12. 1972

Fig. 8

Fig. 4

Fig. 6

Fig. 7

Fig. 9

Fig. 10

Plate 3

15.2.1968

Fig. 11

Fig. 12

Fig. 13

Fig. 14

Fig. 15

Fig. 16

Fig. 17

Fig. 18

Fig. 19

Plate 4

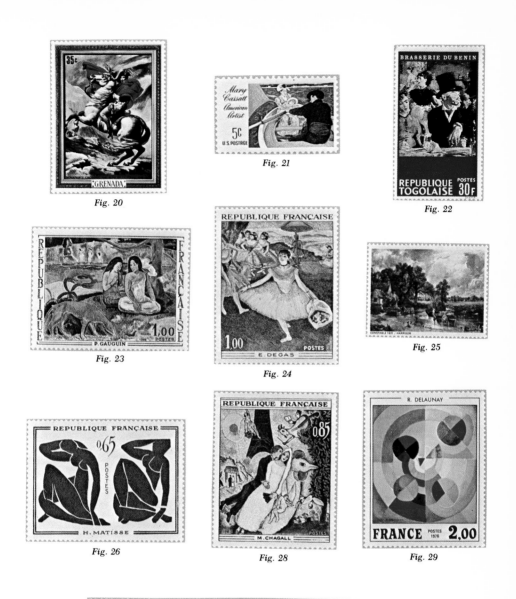

Fig. 20

Fig. 21

Fig. 22

Fig. 23

Fig. 24

Fig. 25

Fig. 26

Fig. 28

Fig. 29

Fig. 27

Plate 5

Fig. 1

Fig. 2

Fig. 3

Fig. 4

Fig. 5

Fig. 7

Fig. 6

Fig. 8

Fig. 9

Fig. 10

Fig. 11

Fig. 12

Fig. 13

Fig. 14

Fig. 15

Plate 6

Fig. 1

Fig. 2

Fig. 3

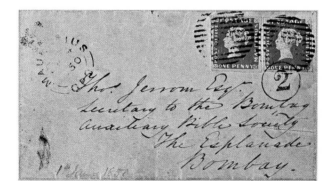

Fig. 4

Plate 7

Imperforate   1858 – 61   Unwatermarked White Paper

Unused

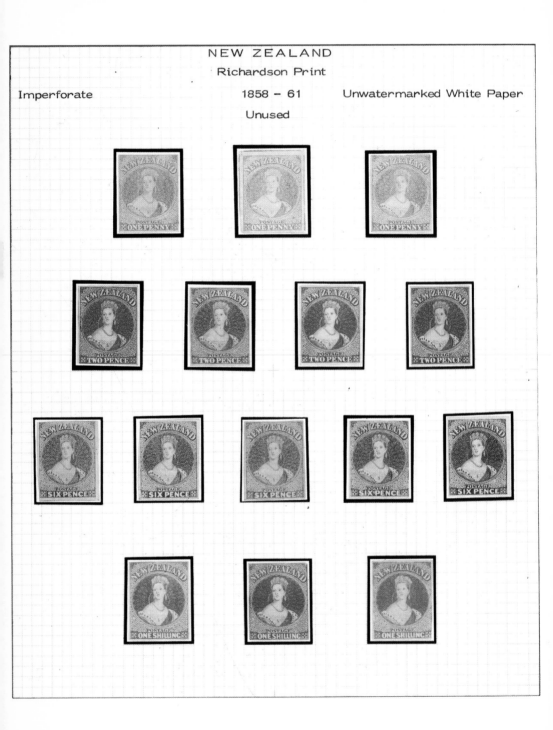

Plate 8

Art Nouveau

When he became King, George V was already a distinguished philatelist. He was deeply involved with the plans of the design and production of the stamps of his new reign.

Art Nouveau was a novel concept whose proponents sought to integrate art with the everyday things one lives with and looks at. The

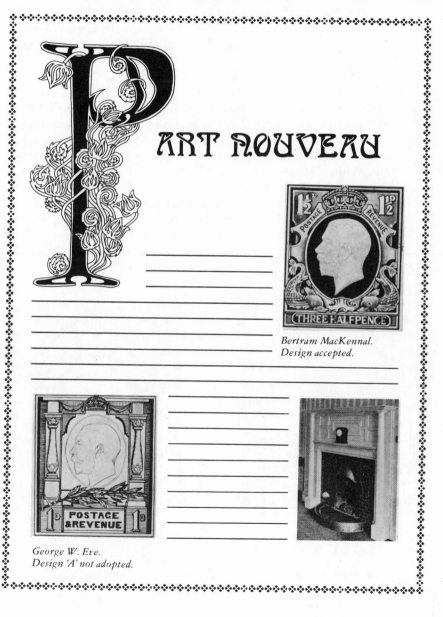

Bertram MacKennal.
Design accepted.

George W. Eve.
Design 'A' not adopted.

British postmaster general approached the Royal Academy of Art, suggesting that the frames of the stamps be made by members of the Art Workers' Guild. Two of the members approached were Garth Jones and G. W. Eve, both noted for their book plates. Eve also was an expert in heraldic work, whose books are classics on the subject. Finally, Eve's pillar and wreath designs were accepted. At the suggestion of the king, Sir Bertram MacKennal designed the portrait.

Today the spirit of Art Nouveau is popular around the world. In France it is called Le Style Moderne, Sezessian in Austria, Stile Liberty in Italy, Modernista in Spain, and, like England, Art Nouveau in the United States.

About the time the Duke of York was president of The Philatelic Society, London, across the Atlantic Ocean in the United States, a young boy whose mother as a girl had collected the Penny Black of 1840 and the first issues of the United States of 1847 was becoming a stamp enthusiast. The boy was young Franklin D. Roosevelt, who would one day become president of the United States, and bring with him to the White House a greater recognition of the hobby, just as King George V did in England.

On November 28, 1906, King Edward VII had signified that henceforth The Philatelic Society, London, would be called the "Royal Philatelic Society, London." From that day, the "Royal" has been considered the elite of students and scientists in the art of philately.

A rejected design by Bertram MacKennal for the George V issue.
(Courtesy of the British National Postal Museum)

A rejected design by George W. Eve for the George V issue.
(Courtesy of the British National Postal Museum)

George W. Eve's accepted design for the George V issue.
(Courtesy of the British National Postal Museum)

Bertram MacKennal's accepted design.
(Courtesy of the British National Postal Museum)

The Royal Philatelic Society, London.
(Courtesy of Royal Philatelic Society, London)

The Ferrari Auctions

"By 1910," wrote Mauritz Hallgren in his most interesting book on philately, "Ferrari had carried his dislike of the French to the point of becoming a Swiss citizen. When World War I came, the French considered Ferrari an Austrian because at his mother's death, he was adopted by an Austrian officer." Ferrari died May 20, 1917, and in his will he left his entire collection to the Reichpost Museum in Berlin. The French government announced at the end of the war that Ferrari's collection would be sold as part of German war reparations.

From June 30, 1920, to November 24, 1925, fourteen auctions were held of the superb holdings of this insatiable collector. Although up to this point the leaders in philately repeatedly said that Ferrari contributed little or nothing to the hobby, no greater gathering of philatelists and their agents ever appeared at a series of auctions. The highlight of them all was the auction of the unique and famous 1-cent black on magenta British Guiana. Ferrari had held the stamp labeled as the world's most valuable scrap of paper for forty-four years. This stamp was the dazzling star of the fourteen auctions, and the philatelic wealth of the world was there to try and become its owner. Arthur Hind, a textile millionaire from Utica, New York, was determined to be the owner of the rarest stamp in the world. He counted on the worldwide publicity of his purchase to bring him offers of rare stamps wherever they might be.

Hind had a philatelic secretary, William C. Kennett, and together they traveled around the world buying stamps at post offices and visiting dealers. Often they entered weird attics and combed through trunks in search of amazing surprises. At some point in their philatelic career they landed in Samoa and caught up with a group of gorgeous Samoan girls, all claiming to be princesses of royal blood. The two eager stamp hunters followed this lead to find themselves at the home of Robert Louis Stevenson. All they met there was a caretaker who would not let them in, and who declared there were no letters in the house at all.

Like Ferrari, Hind took advice from no one at all. He must have been the last of the clan who attempted to collect all aspects of philately.

The sale of the British Guiana took place on April 5 and 6, 1921. Some of the distinguished people eagerly bidding were King Carol of Romania, Maurice Burrus, the tobacco millionaire, and King George V through a representative. The king had put in a bid but dropped out. Burrus became the runnerup, but Arthur Hind gave his agent the signal to bid up to $60,000 if necessary. The hammer went down, "Sold for $33,000 . . . to Arthur Hind." Remember, the stamp had cost

Ferrari only $828 and now it had become a worldwide conversation piece. The owner was famous overnight, for never had so much money been paid for a single stamp. King Alphonso of Spain lost out on a Spanish error that Hind picked up for $20,000. But the story of the British Guiana moves on to greater riches.

The Duplicate 1-Cent British Guiana

It seems an American seaman, a cabin boy, was also a stamp collector. He began to collect during his youthful days on a tramp steamer. Among his many ports of call was Georgetown, British Guiana, where he had made the acquaintance of an old man, a rather vague stamp collector. They became friends. On one trip, the boy found out from the old man's son that the father had died, but the son, knowing that the boy collected stamps, handed him a book of stamps which he would have otherwise thrown away. When the boy grew up he read an article in the *Virginia Philatelist* and caught up with the editor who was now with another magazine. He decided to write his story to Mr. Dietz. "I am torn between the desire to tell you one of the most unusual experiences of my life and keeping a secret with Mr. Arthur Hind," he wrote.

Our cabin boy, now a man, had read about Arthur Hind's purchase of the 1-cent unique British Guiana. He looked at his old envelope he had brought from British Guiana, and although he had the twin, he knew that two should not exist. In 1928 he went to Utica, New York, to see Hind. He showed Hind his album, which included his 1-cent British Guiana. "Well," said Hind, "one of us has to own both." Hind offered him $100,000 in cash on the basis that no one would ever know of the transaction. When he returned the next day, Hind had the money. "He compared my stamp to his. He gave me the money, and offered me a cigar. I put it in my pocket. He lighted his cigar, looked at my stamp again, and then held the stamp to the burning match. 'Now ashes,' Mr. Hind said, 'there is only one magenta stamp now.'" Ending his letter, our former cabin boy said, "I am still shaking after ten years just remembering this event."

In 1921 Hind paid $33,000 at the auction, astounding the world, and seven years later, he paid $100,000 to put the duplicate to rest.

Hind, a passionate owner of this unique stamp, was most generous in lending the stamp for view at stamp shows. He often sent it by registered mail to different parts of the world, and it was sent back to him through the post as well.

The British Guiana Lost . . . and Found!

In 1935 when Hind died there was a legal battle over who owned the stamp. His wife claimed that he had given the stamp to her as a personal gift. But during the battle something out of the ordinary happened. No one could find the stamp! One day in cleaning the house, Mrs. Hind found it in a registered envelope from a stamp show, behind a filing cabinet. Mrs. Hind won her case and was awarded the famous stamp.

In 1940 Finbar Kenny bought the stamp for $45,000 for Frederick T. "Poss" Small, an Australian living in the United States and an executive of the Celanese Corp. The deal was concluded quietly. Mrs. Hind only wanted the money, not the stamp.

In 1970 when the sale of the famed British Guiana was announced with the firm of Siegel and Co., the stamp world was again aglow. When the gavel finally fell, the stamp had sold for $280,000 to Irwin Weinberg. You can figure the investment value from Vernon Vaughn who was paid $2.50 by McKennan who thought he was taking a risk. Some stamps do have fascinating careers.

President Franklin D. Roosevelt

I commend stamp collecting to you because I started a stamp collection when I was about ten years old and have kept it up ever since. In addition to the fun of it, it has kept up my interest in history and geography, past and present. I really believe that stamp collecting makes one a better citizen.

Franklin D. Roosevelt

A beginner can identify with the story of FDR's stamp collecting. At about ten years of age, his mother gave him an album of stamps from around the world. What gripped FDR from the very start were the designs of the stamps and the study of them. As time went on, his stamps became an increased source of information about countries and the people who lived in them.

In the philatelic world, FDR was known as an accumulator who collected everything. He was not particularly concerned with "condition-itis," and it made little difference to him whether a stamp was valued at 2¢ or $200. He had a compulsion to try to fill every blank spot on each and every one of his album pages. When he moved into the White House, his albums moved right in with him. As a matter of fact, he planned his stamp fun time just as he did his three meals a day. He set aside a half hour before bedtime, propping himself up with pillows to study his stamps as a nightly routine. Eleanor Roosevelt once remarked, "He got a relaxation absolutely unknown to most people. It refreshed him like nothing else from the day's work."

Franklin D. Roosevelt, the United States'
most distinguished collector.
(Courtesy of the Franklin D. Roosevelt
Philatelic Society)

Franklin D. Roosevelt as a
boy.
(Courtesy of the Franklin D.
Roosevelt Library)

Letter to Aunt Doe with first-day cancellation.

"Because I Am a Stamp Collector"

All of FDR's life he was enchanted with the navy and ships at sea. He was a map flyspecker, learning from his stamps about many odd places around the world, especially little islands that related to his naval-trained mind.

About a year after Pearl Harbor, at a meeting of the Allied War Council, the president met with leading representatives of the nations at war with Japan. The New Zealand deputy prime minister proposed that our forces occupy a certain island as a stepping stone in the drive to win. "That would be all right," President Roosevelt said, "but Mangareva would be better." The New Zealand deputy prime minister was embarrassed to admit that he wasn't acquainted with Mangareva, which is in the Tuamotu Archipelago under the postal administration of Tahiti. "Oh, it's a few thousand miles from New Zealand," the president told him. "I know the place because I am a stamp collector." It wasn't long after this episode that the forces moved into Mangareva.

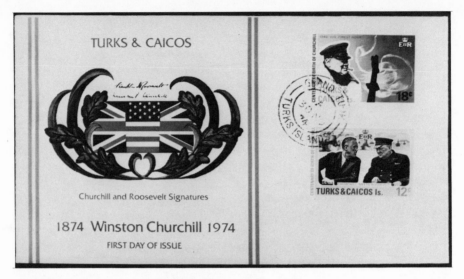

Franklin D. Roosevelt with his friend Winston Churchill.
(Courtesy of Commemorative Heritage Ltd., New York)

At the Big Three Conference

When FDR prepared to go to the Big Three Conference at Casablanca, he told his valet to pack several albums, even if it was necessary to leave some clothes that might be needed for the warm climate. When FDR and Winston Churchill found that they were obliged to wait around for a few days because of de Gaulle's and Giraud's differences, an official in the party visited FDR in his quarters to find him looking at an Argentine stamp. The president smiled, "Look . . . [the stamp design had a pair of clasping hands, symbolizing peace and friendship] I suspect that we have the operation for Giraud and de Gaulle." The next day the two Frenchmen met and were shaking hands.

During his presidency FDR approved 225 new stamp designs. He often made corrections and suggestions. On the NRA (National Recovery Act) stamp that was issued in 1933, he removed the silk hat worn by the man on the original sketch because he felt wealth should not be the message while people were selling apples on the street corners.

When the proof of the Byrd Antarctic stamp was put before him, he pointed to a line indicating New York to Ver Sur Mer, saying, "He landed further north than that." He redesigned the entire stamp before the finished drawing was made by an artist.

When FDR was shown the 25-cent stamp to be issued for the first trans-Pacific airmail service, he noticed that the Yankee clipper ship in the lower part of the design had only two masts instead of three. This was corrected.

FDR had his mother to thank for introducing him to stamp collecting. His favorite classic collecting was Hong Kong, perhaps because he read his grandfather's letters written to his mother from Hong Kong.

He designed the original sketch for the Mothers of America stamp, which he gave to his famous friend and postmaster general at the time, James A. Farley, and the stamp caused an uproar. The painting of Whistler's mother, now in the Louvre in Paris, was altered by the stamp's creators, who chopped off her feet and added a bouquet of flowers. Someone said, "The vase was a cheap one." All this caused a larger press and more sales, and Farley went so far as to urge every American "who had a living mother" to buy and use the stamp on a card or letter to her.

The controversial Mother's Day stamp was issued May 2, 1934, and FDR's mother gave him a block of six, printing in her own hand,

Roosevelt's original design for the Mother's Day stamp.
(Courtesy of the Franklin D. Roosevelt Library)

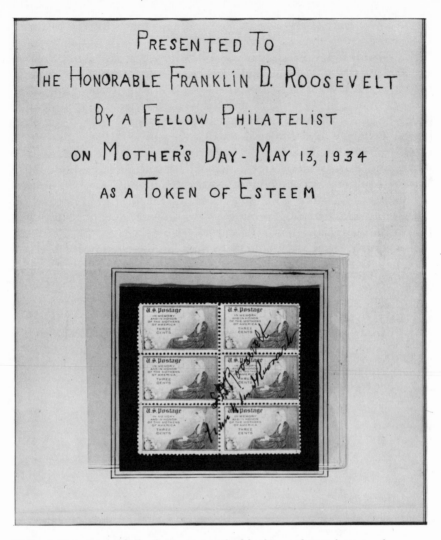

PRESENTED TO

THE HONORABLE FRANKLIN D. ROOSEVELT

BY A FELLOW PHILATELIST

ON MOTHER'S DAY - MAY 13, 1934

AS A TOKEN OF ESTEEM

Mother's Day stamp, block of six, autographed by his mother to her son, the president, Franklin D. Roosevelt.
(Courtesy of Harmers International, Inc.)

"Presented to the Honorable Franklin D. Roosevelt by a fellow philatelist on Mother's Day, 1934, as a token of her esteem."

Postmaster General Farley and the president were good friends. Together, they came up with some novel ideas that created more interest than ever in stamp collecting. When Farley took office, annual sales to philatelists were about $300,000, but by the time Roosevelt died, sales were $2 million a year. The number of stamp collectors increased, according to Farley, from two million to nine million. At FDR's suggestion, philatelic windows were opened in various post offices around the country. It was his feeling that although one could order a stamp from Washington at the Philatelic Sales Office, most people liked to see what they were getting for their money.

In April 1933, the new postmaster general was asked to see the first run of the Bureau of Engraving and Printing's rotary press. The press was stopped for a short moment and the postmaster general was asked to approve the sheet. This he did, and the sheet was cut out of the roll and would have been destroyed except that it was offered to Farley upon the payment of the value of the sheet, $12. He also purchased another sheet for FDR, and thereafter picked up imperforate sheets of the next nineteen issues for himself, the president, and other government friends. In about two years' time some of these imperforate stamps showed up on the market at very high prices. Because Farley was criticized by collectors, he ordered what have become known as "Farley's Follies," a reprint of all the issues from the same plates in order to allow any collector who wanted them to have them. Postal Bulletin #70782 read that these stamps would be "issued for a limited time in full sheets as printed and in blocks thereof, to meet the requirements of collectors and others who may be interested." They were on sale from March 15 to June 15, 1935, and the sales to collectors amounted to $1,663,717. In 1940, the Post Office offered to gum full sheets of these stamps (they were sold without gum), and many people took advantage of the offer.

Farley introduced another custom which continues to this day: the first day of issue ceremony—really the birthday party of a stamp.

John Steinway tells the story of the day he and his father went to Hyde Park to get the official approval for the White House Steinway piano. Everyone was amazed how swiftly he signed his approval. "Actually FDR was more anxious to talk stamps with my father than analyze a piano," says John. FDR and Theodore Steinway spent hours in the stamp room and kept Eleanor waiting one hour for lunch.

"Someday I'll Get Around to It"

Like many collectors before and after FDR, the president looked forward to the day when he would retire and just enjoy his hobby. FDR, unlike many famous collectors, never had a philatelic secretary, nor did he allow anyone to touch his albums. Once when Ernest Kehr, a contributing editor of the *Collectors Club Philatelist*, showed FDR a few of his pages on Egypt, FDR remarked, "I wish I had time to mount my stamps like you. Someday I'll get around to it." When Ernie offered to mount FDR's stamps for him, his answer was from the heart of a true collector: "Thanks, but working on the stamps myself provides all the fun of the hobby, so why should I let someone else do it for me?"

Toward United Nations

Of all the conferences FDR looked forward to attending, it was the first meeting of the United Nations Organizing Conference, which was to take place in San Francisco on April 25, 1945, that excited him the most.

FDR had given much thought to the stamp that would be issued in its honor. By telephone from Warm Springs he spoke to Postmaster General Frank C. Walker. He suggested the design be simple, with the wording "Toward United Nations," and added instructions to "make the border plain." He approved of the idea of a small olive branch at the bottom of the stamp as the only detail. When sketches drawn by the Bureau of Engraving and Printing were flown to Warm Springs, he initialed the drawing he thought would be most inspirational to the conference destined to have profound influence on the people of the world. FDR even paid attention to the value of the stamp—5¢, the then-current rate for foreign mail.

On April 17, 1945, FDR again spoke to the postmaster general and agreed to purchase the first stamp issued for the momentous occasion. Aware of the demands that would be made on him while in San Francisco, he settled the matter as a directive. "By this action it would bring to the world the high hopes of working towards a United Nations." It was to be his last directive—half an hour later he was stricken.

Eleanor Roosevelt said: "Everything my husband did, everywhere he went and every position he held, served the purpose of increasing his collection, since he never forgot this hobby of his which filled a great many leisure hours."

The Collectors Club

The Collectors Club of
New York.
(Courtesy of the Collectors
Club)

The Collectors Club of New York was founded in New York City in 1896. Like the "Royal," a small but brilliant group of philatelists felt a responsibility and need "to promote, encourage and contribute to the advancement of the science and practice of philately in all its branches." John W. Scott of *Scott's Catalogue* became its first treasurer. Gilbert A. Jones, one of the owners of *The New York Times*, and H. J. Duveen, noted art dealer, were two of the original group. From the start, the early great names both in American and British philately were enjoying friendship on a visiting transatlantic basis. King George V entertained Alfred H. Caspary, Arthur Hind, and Alfred Lichtenstein at Buckingham Palace in his stamp room where he delighted in poring over his albums pointing out both unique and interesting items.

The Collectors Club Library

The Collectors Club Library has one of the very largest collections in the world of material devoted to philately. It was Mr. Steinway who was responsible for building the library. His outstanding contribution was the presentation of the Victor Suppantschitsch Collection, which embraced almost everything that had been printed on stamps and stamp collecting during the nineteenth century. Today there are more than 150,000 items in the library and with the exception of certain unique periodicals and rare limited editions, all material is available on loan to members and students of philately worldwide.

The Collectors Club Philatelist

The *Collectors Club Philatelist* is a bi-monthly periodical published for members of the club.

One of the aims of the publication has been stated by the club itself: "Primarily the *Collectors Club Philatelist* is for the benefit of Club members. We are not conscious of any mission or expectation of bettering results obtained over and over again elsewhere. The primary aim is to give our members an opportunity for publishing the results of their studies, if they so desire, and to increase, if we may, such influence as we may have in the service of philately."

Study Groups

Because of the growing specialization in stamp collecting and the need for specialist organizations to exchange ideas and information, many associations have their study groups meet at the club.

Philatelists who comprise these groups are not required to be members of the Collectors Club, but it is requested that one person from the study group join to act in matters pertaining to the Collectors Club.

To give you some idea of the variety of groups that meet here, a typical schedule follows:

American Airmail Society with the Metropolitan Air Post Society
American First Day Cover Society
American Revenue Society
American Topical Association
American Philatelic Society
Austria Philatelic Society
British Empire Study Circle
Essay-Proof Society
Fine Arts Philatelists
France and Colonies Philatelic Society
Hellenic Philatelic Society
Germany Philatelic Society
International Society for Japanese Philately
Italia Philatelic Society
Junior Study Group of the Collectors Club with Junior Ambassadors
Judaica Historical Philatelic Society with the Society of Israel Philatelists
Masonic Stamp Club of New York
Netherlands and Colonies Philatelists

Postal History Society
Rossica Society
South Slavic Philatelic Society
United Nations Study Unit—Turtle Bay Philatelic Society
United Postal Stationery Society

Collectors Club Meetings

The scheduled meetings are the most popular function of the club. It is at these meetings that members and their guests can hear fine lectures of leading philatelists and see outstanding exhibits of material.

An Encounter

The unknown has always intrigued Harrison D. S. Haverbeck, past president of the Collectors Club. He formed a collection on the circular stamp of Jammu and Kashmir. In 1937 he became interested in collecting Indian states. Few knew or cared about these stamps, and for $25 he purchased a mass of material that included stamps from Tibet, Nepal, Moroccan locals, and Turkish revenues, all lumped together, gathering from this that no one had attempted to study the postal history of Nepal and Tibet.

Over the years his collecting interests have included Mongolia, Arabian states, Yemen, Saudi Arabia, Siam, China, Thailand, Hejaz, Nejd, China Treaty Ports, and, of course, Tibet—considered one of the finest ever assembled.

He struck up a friendship with a retired Indian civil service officer who was on loan to the kingdom of Nepal and traded United States mint commemoratives for material his friend had gathered from the Nepalese treasury. He also visited Nepal and became friendly with His Holiness, the 14th Dalai Lama. Presently he is collecting Bhutan. This seed of interest was planted in his vivid imagination when he became acquainted with King Jigme Wanchuck, father of the present king of Bhutan, while the father was a student at the Lhasa house of Tsarong Sharp, member of the governing council of Tibet. King Jigme was a photography fiend. Haverbeck sent him cameras and film. In return he got all sorts of stamps and covers, which interested him. His original research became handbooks. *The Postage Stamps and Postal History of Tibet* and *The Postage Stamps and Postal History of Nepal* are but two examples.

His judging and exhibiting have taken him around the world from Bombay to Scandinavia.

While serving as president of the club, he encouraged a change in the bylaws that allowed associate members ranging in age from eigh-

Cover from Bhutan via Yatung, China, to Kalimpong, India, with pair of 1-anna Indian stamps and Shee Lok cancel on Bhutan stamp.
(From the collection of Harrison D. S. Haverbeck)

Cover from Bhutan via Yatung, China, to Kalimpong, India, with China stamp and Bhutan stamp with Shee Lok cancel.
(From the collection of Harrison D. S. Haverbeck)

teen to twenty-one. Once the gates were opened to this group, a junior study group was launched for young collectors, ages nine to seventeen.

What makes Mr. Haverbeck unique is that he did not buy someone else's collection; he built his own, doing original research and making breakthroughs via his own talents. He was concentrating upon areas unknown to the formal collector and built his collection with unusual inquisitiveness and timing in parts of the world with which today's new collectors are most intrigued.

The American Philatelic Society

The American Philatelic Society, known as the APS, is the largest stamp society in the United States, with a membership of 44,000. The activities of the APS are many and for the minimal cost of the membership, a host of advantages are yours. You will find your membership card a top reference when you need identification with a dealer or auction house.

SALES DIVISION

One of the most popular of APS services is its Sales Division. Here you can sell your duplicate stamps to your fellow members. They have "circuit books" which have had purchases amounting to $842,522. With 35,000 circuit books in circulation, the APS Sales Division has an inventory of $2 million worth of stamps.

PUBLICATION

Included in your membership is the *American Philatelist,* the official journal of the society. It is full of useful and interesting information. For instance, in reporting on the APS Sales Division of the "circuit books," they list the priority needs of members. In a recent issue they placed the following "We Need" item: Australia, Baltic states, Benelux, British North America, British Oceania, China, Denmark, Hong Kong, Ethiopia, Finland, German Colonies, Greenland, Iceland, Ireland, Israel, Italian Colonies, Jamaica, Liechtenstein, Luxembourg, Monaco, Netherlands Colonies, Norway, Portuguese Colonies, San Marino, Siam, South Africa, Sweden, Vatican, Yugoslavia, United States (except plate blocks).

Let us say you collect Jamaica and you have many duplicates. You could write to the Sales Division for a circuit book. Upon receiving it, you could mount your stamps and covers and then you would be en route to making your sales, since you set your own price. In reverse, if you are looking for stamps that are of special interest to you, then you can receive a specific circuit book from which to select. The "need" list shows what is in demand at the moment.

The jumbo-size issue of the *American Philatelist* that lists every member, his or her address, his or her collecting interest is worth more than double the membership. It is like a superb telephone directory where you can locate all your collecting friends. Its uses are many. Let us say you collect Singapore. Under Singapore the journal lists the members that collect just that country. This, of course, enables you to contact fellow members with the same collecting interests for swap, trade, and sharing of knowledge. Besides this excellent listing, there is a section of names of dealers who are members with a list of the items they carry. In a sense having this membership directory is like having 44,000 friends to whom you can turn for advice on your collecting.

The monthly *APS Journal* lists new issues of stamps worldwide, and has excellent book reviews that keep you up to date on new literature. Handbooks of various types can be purchased directly from the APS. Included are learned articles which cover special areas of collecting or new finds.

INSURANCE

The APS has both an insurance committee and a stamp theft committee which offer practical advice and service. Added to this is an expertizing service which provides evaluations of the authenticity of stamps. The rates for such expert opinions run from $6 to $11 per stamp for members and $8 to $15 per stamp for nonmembers.

LIBRARY

The American Philatelic Research Library is the speediest, most efficient library I've ever encountered. Available is a vast array of literature that can be of great help to you in understanding your collection.

The APS Writer's Unit #30, a chapter of the APS, is an excellent investment for those who like to write or have journalistic responsibilities. The cost per year is only $1.

The APS has many chapter organizations which run from specialty groups to local stamp clubs. It is easy to find a club in your area by consulting that list.

The APS sponsors both a spring and a fall exhibition. The *APS Journal* lists all the stamp shows for the year so that you can make plans to enter or attend.

Information on these and the many other activities of the APS can be had by writing to: American Philatelic Society, Box 800, State College, Pa. 16801.

Black Blots

In 1962 the American Philatelic Society launched a program of black blotting spurious stamps. This has become a most constructive and useful evaluation program of warning of what to watch out for in the new issues of the world. Black blots are a guide to any newcomer, young or of any age, regarding questionable stamps. This includes warnings to avoid mass production of canceled-to-order material, useless souvenir sheets, and imperforates made to order only for the gullible, uninformed collector.

Rip-offs

The rip-offs in the world of philately need their story told; this by itself would occupy several volumes. A few examples to beware of are:

Expensive first-day covers with only part of a set of stamps. When you go to dealers to sell them, they will generally ask, "Where is the other cover with the complete set?" Try to get a complete set, when one is issued.

Countries that don't exist. Pretty stamps come and go from countries that do not exist. Nagaland, a province of India, as an example, does not have its own stamps, but you may find some Nagaland issues at a show that are bright and pretty and not very expensive. Just remember that they are labels.

Another gimmick for the unaware is a series of stamps in "gold" or "silver." Usually these are a gold paste or gold leaf sold at inflated prices in a pretty box or album but from a place where they could never be used for postage. I can think of one such place, which is uninhabited in the winter, except by goats, a few tourists and the laird of the island off the coast of Scotland in the summer. All these items are tempting, pretty, and usually expensive. *Caveat emptor!*

The Aristocrats of Philately

The aristocrats of philately symbolize the greatest philatelic items in the world. In almost all countries there are
certain pieces which stand head and shoulders above the
rest in terms of philatelic significance.

Dr. Norman S. Hubbard

The aristocrats of philately—the greatest philatelic rarities of the
world—were first brought together for ANPHILEX '71, commemorating the seventy-fifth anniversary of the Collectors Club of
New York, which was held in the Waldorf Astoria. So spectacular was
this exhibit that in 1976, for the Bicentennial exhibition in Philadelphia known as INTERPHIL, the aristocrats were again assembled.

Dr. Hubbard, who accomplished the almost impossible task of bringing together philatelic rarities with a value of $3 million, said, "It will
be many years, if ever again, before such an array of the finest in
philately will be seen in one place."

The history of the "aristocrats" runs a gamut ranging from a discovery in an old cigar box, a single direct visit to a post office, survival of
a cover about to be burned for trash, to a find in a Paris flea market,
a fortune found in an Indian bazaar, a discovery in an old desk of a
furniture dealer, and a search through old files in a business office. The
door never closes. Anyone anywhere has the potential to find a rarity
in stampdom. That is the allure. Here are a dozen "aristocrats" valued
in the millions, all small enough to put in your pocket.

The Most Valuable Cover in the World—for £50!

The most valuable cover in the world (see Fig. 4, Plate 7) was found
in 1887 in an Indian bazaar in Bombay, fifty years after the stamps had
been issued. Albert Howard of London, a world traveler and avid

philatelist, was always on the lookout for an unusual stamp or cover wherever he went.

On one of his visits to Bombay he paid his usual visit to an Indian merchant who sold mostly coins and antiques. Delighted to see his potential buyer, the Indian asked him, "Do you collect old envelopes?" and produced an envelope he had never seen before. After much haggling he paid £50, but he knew he had purchased a great rarity. He was now the owner of what was to become the most famous cover in the world.

The Mauritius cover, the most celebrated item in philately.
(Courtesy of Raymond H. Weill Co.)

1: The "Post Office" Mauritius

Lady Gomm was busy preparing for her annual fancy dress ball to be held at the Governor's House on September 30, 1847. This was the most-talked-of social event of Port Louis and all of Mauritius. Her husband, Sir W. Maynard Gomm, was governor of this tiny speck of land in the Indian Ocean near Madagascar.

She had everything organized for the gala event, but like all dynamic hostesses, she wanted something different and very special. Mail had been coming from London with stamps portraying young Queen Victoria. While looking at these unique English stamps, Lady Gomm decided to adorn the envelopes containing her invitations with an unusual, decorative stamp. She went straight to the governor and as soon as he took her idea to the council, things began to happen.

Mr. J. Barnard, the local jeweler and watchmaker, was the only person who could produce the stamp despite the fact that he had poor eyesight. Called to the Governor's House, he listened to the request, bowed politely, and promised to do his best in producing the stamp. Upon his departure, Lady Gomm said, "Don't forget the ball is September 30."

The almost sightless jeweler took a copper plate back to his shop and engraved two copies of the English stamps—a penny stamp and a two-penny stamp. On the right side he added "Mauritius" and on the left side "Post Office." He printed five hundred copies each of the orange red penny and the deep blue two-penny. Each stamp was printed separately as there was only one plate.

Lady Gomm was ecstatic. She made certain that the stamps were carefully affixed to the envelopes of her invitations sent to the "Who's Who" of Mauritius. No one paid the slightest attention or even noticed the fact that Mr. Barnard had engraved "Post Office" instead of "Post Paid." None of the invitations survived, but a few of the stamps were left over in the Post Office and the few that were purchased went out on mail to Europe and Bombay. Mr. Barnard corrected the next batch of stamps with the inscription "Post Paid." These stamps are also rare, but the "Post Office" Mauritius cover has become the greatest legend in philately.

Mr. Howard sold his cover one year later (1888) to a London dealer for £1,600, making a profit of £1,550. In 1906 the Mauritius cover was purchased by an American collector named George Worthington for £2,200; it remained in his collection for eleven years. Then in 1917 the famous Alfred F. Lichtenstein bought the major portion of the Worthington collection, which included the "Post Office" Mauritius cover.

Upon his death, Alfred F. Lichtenstein left his collection to his daughter, Louise Boyd Dale, who had the same love and knowledge of stamps as her father. She was to become the most distinguished woman philatelist of the twentieth century.

A PHILATELIC HAPPENING

On Monday evening, October 21, 1968, the illustrious auction house of H. R. Harmer, Inc., held the first of ten auctions of the Louise Boyd Dale and Alfred F. Lichtenstein collections. The prices realized for the ten auctions in New York totaled $3,455,574, the largest amount of money ever obtained by one auctioneer for one collection to date.

The auction house was packed to the hilt! For the overflow, a closed-circuit TV was installed from the auction room to the exhibition room. Television cameras, photographers, and reporters were all set to catch the moment when the highest bidder would become the owner of the most valuable cover in the world. When the gavel struck and the auctioneer cried "Sold," the story would be headline news around the world.

Seated in the back of the room next to one another were Roger and Raymond Weill. David Small, in an article in *The New Yorker* entitled, "The Weills Deal in the World's Rarest Stamps," wrote, "There is something about the Weill brothers' life-style which is strongly reminiscent of Sherlock Holmes and Dr. Watson and the lodgings on Baker

Street. Raymond with his clipped speech and manner of precision is
the Holmes to the affable and faintly bemused Roger's Dr. Watson."

The long-awaited moment had arrived. From the back of the room,
Roger did the bidding for Lot #1. It got up to $280,000. Down came
the gavel: "Sold" . . . when the signal of A. L. Michael, chairman of
Stanley Gibbons, Ltd., was missed by Bernard Harmer. Amid Mr.
Harmer's chagrin, the auction continued. The Weills began to jump
in $20,000 bids until the final bid of $380,000—only $100,000 more
than when the gavel fell the first time. The cameras and reporters
huddled around the victorious Weill brothers. When questioned on
the excess $100,000, Raymond replied, "Oh, well, we don't mind
paying for nice stamps."

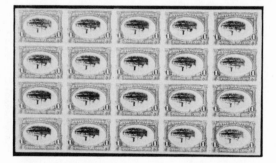

United States 1-cent inverted
centers of 1901. Estimated
value: $100,000.
(Courtesy of Raymond H. Weill
Co.)

#2: U.S. 1-Cent Inverted Center, 1901

This block of twenty of the 1-cent inverted center 1901 issue of the
U.S.A. was issued for the Pan American Exposition. It was in a collection built by Warren H. Colson, a dealer, for one of his clients. According to Dr. Norman Hubbard, the owner died in 1951. The block stayed
in a bank vault in Boston until 1976 when it was acquired by Raymond
H. Weill Co.

Confederate States of America, Mt. Lebanon provisional of 1861. Estimated value: $50,000.
(Courtesy of the owner)

3: Confederate States of America

Use of United States stamps in the Confederate States stopped on June 1, 1861, when the southern states seceded from the Union. It was not until October 16, 1861, that the first Confederate stamps were issued. As a result, some of the local postmasters produced their own stamps, which in many cases are quite rare.

One of the rarest provisionals was used in Mt. Lebanon, Louisiana. The 5-cent stamp was made from a woodcut which you see in reverse image. This cover was in the collection of Count Ferrari, then in the Alfred H. Caspary Collection, but later sold in the Caspary auction by H. R. Harmer in 1957. It is now in a great Confederate collection.

Cape of Good Hope 4p red color error of 1861. Estimated value: $150,000.
(Courtesy of the Anne Boyd Lichtenstein Foundation)

4: The Cape of Good Hope

Among the rare classic stamps in existence, the triangular stamps of the Cape of Good Hope are considered the classic imperforate issues of the world.

"The rarest," wrote Dr. Hubbard, "are the one penny and the four penny blue. These were typographed locally in February, 1861. They are known as 'woodblocks,' although printed from metal stereos made from dies engraved in steel. The second printing of the four penny and the first printing of the one penny were each in sheets of 128 stamps, two panes of 64 clichés. In putting together the 64 clichés for each denomination, a cliché of the one penny was erroneously inserted in the printing frame of the four penny, and a cliché of the four penny erroneously inserted in the printing frame of the one penny, producing the rare color errors, one penny blue and four penny red."

Dr. Hubbard continued, "The most significant and important piece showing the color error is the block of four with three one penny red and one four penny red on the above cover." This is considered one of the top covers in philately. It was the highlight of the Alfred F. Lichtenstein Cape Collection, passed to his daughter, Louise Boyd Dale, and is now owned by the Anne Boyd Lichtenstein Foundation.

Hawaiian 2-cent of 1851. Estimated value: $275,000. (Courtesy of the *Honolulu Advertiser*)

#5: Hawaii

The "Missionary" stamps of Hawaii, the first four stamps issued 1851 to 1852, are ranked among the world's greatest rarities. The rarest of these is the 2-cent blue. Only fifteen have survived.

Dr. Hubbard wrote about this item: "There is absolutely no question that the incomparable cover bearing the 2 cent and 5 cent Hawaiian missionaries in combination with the 3 cent pair, 1851, is by far the greatest Hawaiian item and one of the greatest covers in the world."

The cover was found in 1903 among papers to be burned in New Bedford, Massachusetts. It was acquired by Alfred H. Caspary and sold in the Caspary auction by H. R. Harmer, Inc., in 1957. There it was purchased by Raymond H. Weill Co., and is now the crowning item in the greatest collection of Hawaii ever assembled, owned by the *Honolulu Advertiser*.

Newfoundland 2p scarlet vermilion of 1857. Estimated value: $150,000.
(Courtesy of Harmers International)

6: Newfoundland

The most important piece in Newfoundland, Dr. Hubbard writes, ". . . is the unique cover bearing a strip of three of the two pence scarlet vermillion addressed to England."

It was found in a desk in Devonshire by a used furniture dealer in 1935. Soon after, this unique multiple on cover was acquired by Alfred H. Caspary. At the Caspary auction by H. R. Harmer in New York in 1956, it was purchased by W. E. Lea, a British dealer, for Lars Amundsen, a collector. It was finally bought by Raymond H. Weill Co., who sold it to Ralph A. Hart.

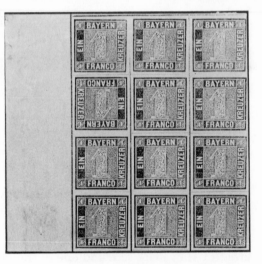

Bavaria. 1Kr. tête-bêche of 1849. Estimated value: $175,-000.
(Courtesy of the Anne Boyd Lichtenstein Foundation)

7: Bavaria

This stunning block of twelve tête-bêche variety was in the Ferrari auction. It was sold in the Ferrari sale of 1923 and acquired by Alfred F. Lichtenstein. It was inherited by his daughter, Louise Boyd Dale, and is now owned by the Anne Boyd Lichtenstein Foundation.

8: United States 24-Cent Inverted Airplane

The famous United States rarity of the 24-cent, 1918 inverted airmail that was purchased by W. T. Robey at a post office in Washington, D.C., was noted in the first chapter of this book.

After a Philadelphia dealer purchased this from Mr. Robey, the entire sheet of one hundred was acquired by Colonel Edward Howland Robinson Green, who was the son of the Wall Street financial wizard Hetty Green. It is said that he was as extravagant as his mother was stingy. He bought a four-foot diameter magnifying glass for $20,-000. When the colonel broke up the sheet of one hundred, "he kept the best for himself," writes Dr. Hubbard.

In 1976 it was sold by H. R. Harmer to Raymond H. Weill Co.

Chile. 5-cent lithograph of 1854. Estimated value: $100,-000.
(From the collection of Dr. Norman Hubbard)

9: Chile

This magnificent multiple of fourteen stamps of the classic imperforate of Chile was issued from 1853 to 1865. Some were printed in London and some in Santiago. Other than this the scarcest is the 5 centavos printed by lithography, rather than engraved. The stamp is virtually unobtainable in any multiple larger than a strip of five. The most important piece in Chilean philately is the cover seen bearing a block of fourteen of the 5 centavos lithographed. Because of its condition and rarity, it is considered one of the top covers in philately.

After World War II, it was discovered in a Paris flea market. It was acquired by John F. Rider and ultimately sold to Dr. Norman Hubbard.

Uruguay. 120c tête-bêche of
1858. Estimated value: $25,-
000.
(Courtesy of Harmers International)

10: Uruguay

Dr. Norman Hubbard writes, "One is in the Tapling Collection of
the British Museum, another is in the Hoffman Collection of Uruguay,
and the third is shown here."

The pair was in the Ferrari Collection of Uruguay which was purchased by Alfred F. Lichtenstein at the first Ferrari sale in Paris on
June 23, 1921. It remained with his daughter, Louise Boyd Dale, until
the Dale-Lichtenstein auction sale by H. R. Harmer, Inc., on May 7,
1970, when it was purchased by "Mr. L."

Mauritius. 1p and 2p of 1847.
Estimated value: $300,000.
(Courtesy of Hiroyuki Kanai)

11: Mauritius

Here is a remarkable cover of the 1-penny and 2-penny "Post
Office" stamps that were the errors of Mr. J. Barnard. Dr. Hubbard
writes that these "are two of the rarest and most important stamps in
philately."

This cover ranks among the top five covers in philately. Originally
this great find was discovered in 1902 by a French boy searching the
files of a Bordeaux wine merchant who had received it. In 1922 Arthur
Hind bought the cover, and at the Hind sale of H. R. Harmer in
London in 1934, it was acquired by Maurice Burrus. When the cover

was sold in 1963 at the Burrus auction by Robson Lowe in London, it was purchased by Raymond H. Weill Co. In 1970, it was acquired by Hiroyuki Kanai, who has put together the greatest collection of Mauritius ever assembled.

United States of America, Alexandria blue postmaster provisional, 1846. Estimated value: $125,000.
(Courtesy of Raymond H. Weill Co.)

#12: United States of America

About the United States Alexandria Blue, Dr. Hubbard writes: "The provisional Alexandria, Virginia, was very simple: the words 'Alexandria Post Office' in a circle with 'Paid 5' in the center. A few of the stamps have been found on buff paper, apparently the usual paper. A single copy is known on blue paper. This stamp, the Alexandria Blue, is on a cover addressed to Richmond, Virginia, and is considered the greatest postmaster provisional."

There is a romantic story involving this exquisite cover. In 1847 Jannett Brown of Richmond, Virginia, received a letter with a proposal of marriage. Her daughter found this letter tied in with a bundle of love letters. An envelope had a curious stamp inscribed with the name "Alexandria." After talking to friends a Boston dealer was recommended to her. She sent the letter and envelope to him. In turn he wrote to her suggesting that the stamp on the envelope, cancelled with the date August 25, 1846, a year before the United States issued a postage stamp, might be worth a few dollars. He explained that this was an Alexandria Postmaster Provisional on a 5-cent bluish stamp. She sold it for a handsome profit. In 1907, soon after its discovery, it was acquired by George H. Worthington and then by Alfred H. Caspary. At the Caspary auction sale by H. R. Harmer it was purchased by Josiah K. Lilly and sold again in 1967 by Robert A. Siegel.

#13: British Guiana

Of course one of the most famous aristocrats of all is the British Guiana 1-cent black on magenta, which we have already presented.

Classic
Country
Collecting

Scott's Catalogue lists in their five volumes some quarter of a million stamps. Classic stamp collecting has always consisted of country collections. More and more collectors not only choose a specific country to collect but often specialize in a specific area within the country. The classics are usually the first sets (nineteenth century), such as USA, Scott numbers 1 and 2. If you follow the "aristocrats" you have a pretty good idea of the best of the "classic" material.

One excellent way to view a classic country collection is to visit a stamp exhibition. At first one's reaction in seeing a fine exhibit is "How did he or she ever do it?" One of the large gold medals was awarded to the beautiful exhibit at INTERPHIL by Robert P. Odenweller, entitled "New Zealand, 1855–1874." It showed the early issues of the Chalons, famed delicate stamps portraying the young Queen Victoria by the Royal Artist Alfred Chalon.

To demonstrate how a classic collection is created, I asked the exhibitor of the Chalons, Robert P. Odenweller, to tell his own story with the hope that it will inspire you to follow in his footsteps.

CREATING A CLASSIC COLLECTION
Robert P. Odenweller

Creating a classic collection is a process that has many levels, and it is rarely ever completed, due to the revisions of the goals set by the collector. My collection of New Zealand saw its start when I was seven years old, and I paid the princely sum of two dollars for a single New Zealand stamp. I remember feeling that with that much capital invested in New Zealand, I was committed to it for life. Little did I realize how difficult many regarded it to collect. (It really isn't, but that's all a matter of perspective.) At the same

Robert P. Odenweller: fellow of the Royal Philatelic Society, London; fellow of the Royal Philatelic Society of New Zealand; trustee of The Philatelic Foundation; and governor of the Collectors Club of New York.
(Courtesy of Jane Odenweller)

time, I received sage words of advice from a real "old-timer" (at least triple my age—all of, say, twenty-one). His words, which have guided me ever since, were: "If you want to be a success in philately you have to pick a country you like, learn everything you can about it, get all you can from it, and, in short, become an expert." I took his advice to heart and have thought of his words many times since then.

How does one start a classic collection? When I first began collecting New Zealand I really didn't think I'd ever manage to get even one of the earliest New Zealand issues, often called the Chalon Heads. They were much too expensive and only the stuff of dreams. By the time my years had doubled from those first days, however, I got my chance. In a small office of a building on Nassau Street in New York City, I saw a Chalon with a price that I could afford. I'm sure I was unable to conceal the eagerness with which I extracted the stamp from the book and pushed my money across the counter. I didn't know it then, but I had taken the major first step toward my classic collection. The commitment was made, even though I may have considered it a logical expansion of my collecting area at the time.

The stages in forming a classic collection are much like those of a collection of other areas. First you must decide on a goal. Though it's not necessary to limit it to a modest level, consideration of how realistic it is with regard to the power of your pocketbook will avoid many frustrations. After all, it can, and usually will, be revised upward as goals are approached and means increase. The goal, as set, must describe a coherent selection of stamps and covers if it is to have true significance philatelically. My feelings on this have been greatly colored by prejudices developed through close association with many top philatelists in London and Europe, as well as in the United States. Though there are a number of approaches to classic collecting, I consider the approach usually connected with the British as "the classic of the classics," and the one I try to follow. It is, simply stated, to collect all issues unused, used, and on cover. There is more to it than that, of course, but that gives the basic idea.

Perhaps the easiest way to demonstrate how to develop a collection of classics is to show the stages I passed through in the process of developing my own collection.

Upon obtaining my first Chalon Head, I prepared individual album pages for all the Chalons, with a separate page for each catalogue number. Though I realized that many pages would remain empty for quite some time, I also knew that the blank pages would serve to remind me of what was yet to be done. In forming a classic collection, I believe that the selection of a classic area in which to specialize is perhaps the most difficult task of all unless you are of unlimited means. An area should be selected such that reasonable acquisitions of the better material might strain but never break your budget. It is a sad but unavoidable fact that a true classic area will never be cheap, especially if anything decent is to be found therein. I will freely admit, however, that although New Zealand Chalons were well outside my means when I started collecting them, my ability to purchase better material coincided with the need and desire to do so.

After having purchased a number of single Chalons and having thus whetted my appetite for them, I was introduced to auctions. Robson Lowe's auctions in London were a particularly rich source of Chalons so I overextended myself to acquire as much material as possible to sort through, often in the form of collections or accumulations. This I would consider to be a desirable though not necessarily an essential phase of forming a classic collection—that is, the opportunity to handle a large quantity of the stamps to develop a feel for what patterns to expect from them. At the same time I purchased volumes I through IV of *The Postage Stamps of New Zealand,* published by the Royal Philatelic Society of New Zealand, and considered to be among the finest specialized reference sources in the world. I read and became intimately familiar with all the references to the Chalons, not to mention the later issues. A deep knowledge of the basic references in any area must be considered vital to one who collects it.

The pages of my collection filled out and soon the third stage was reached—to eliminate any second-grade material and to

The Postage Stamps of New Zealand catalogue.

pinpoint areas for specific improvement. This requires a heavier financial commitment and is often the phase that can make or break a classic collection. My approach is to ask myself two questions: "Can the material needed be found?" and "Can it be afforded?"

Often, when a major collection comes up for sale, it will be necessary for a collector to choose how best to exploit his limited means to acquire what is needed. I would recommend always going for the basic items in top quality, saving those lesser varieties which are of an ancillary nature or of lesser quality for later. On the other hand, however, I must mention one very important factor which has been most significant in the building of my own collection. When a major sale of essential material comes along, particularly if the material is the best extant of all known copies, it is necessary to search any and every means of making the purchase. I have done this many times and have never regretted it. As a matter of fact, the most talked-about items are as with fishermen, the ones that got away.

The process of filling in the quality "holes" is often a slow one. (And be thankful for that—the super sale can be most heartbreaking if everything that you need, and really can't afford, comes all at once. You may not live long enough to see "the ones that got away" a second time.) As a goal is neared, the rate of new acquisition usually slows down, as much from a dearth of available material as anything. To keep a high level of activity, often the specialist will turn to side pursuits which can take many forms, some of these peculiar to the country or area of specialty. In many countries reconstruction of a sheet of stamps is an active sideline. This involves careful observation of each stamp, particularly those in blocks or larger multiples, to seek out minute differences in the design which will identify the specific position on the sheet from which they came. By matching up different shaped pieces, a full sheet can eventually be reconstructed.

In some cases this will present the collector with an obvious "impossibility"—for example, the top left stamp from a sheet as identified by the large margins on those sides may have very different characteristics from another which also comes from the top left. If this happens, there are usually two possible explanations. First, there could have been more than one plate from which the stamps were printed. If this happens to be the case, the collector becomes involved in "plating" while carrying on the reconstruction, that is, he has to identify which plate the stamp came from as well as where on the sheet.

The second possibility is one illustrated by a page from my collection. This page, which introduces three pages of reconstructions, shows that there were different states of damage on a portion of the plate which had to be retouched to restore it to something like its original appearance. As reprint sheets show us the final state of the plate, reconstructions can be relatively easy. On the other hand, however, in my collection there were stamps that did not show retouching and yet had marks that should have made them easy to locate. Unfortunately this was not the case. After looking carefully for possible clues to their existence, I suddenly realized that some had a close resemblance to some of the retouched stamps and then all became clear. These were stamps from the damaged but not yet retouched plate. Knowing this made the rest a lot easier.

Other sidelines can keep the activity level going when supplies start to dry up. Essays, proofs, and reprints add by providing the "before" and "after" of the stamps you happen to collect. Covers mailed to your country during the time period you collect can show markings you might see only rarely on your own covers. Trying to develop a full showing of the primary cancellations in use in your country can be most challenging. Assembling a selection of covers showing each rate, particularly if a stamp was intended for that rate, and unusual combinations of stamps to create a rate which was normally paid in a different way are very popular. These last few are all covered with the postal history aspect of your specialty which cannot be ignored if you are a true specialist.

A cover which illustrates some of these ideas is shown on another page from my collection. The rate and early use of the 6d stamp are explained in the write-up on the page. If this had been intended as a postal history exhibit page rather than one from a

The three stamps above correspond to the three pages in this row, each being a copy from Row 17, No. 9, which was retouched after being damaged. Over half of the positions to be later retouched on Plate II are represented at the left. All 36 positions, with exception of one with a negligible retouch, are shown in the blue reconstruction on the right, and that position is covered in the vermilion.

Row 18, No. 2

Row 19, No. 1

As no guide is known for the appearance of stamps from the damaged lower portion of Plate II prior to retouching, it is necessary to use a bit of imagination when viewing stamps with a worn or damaged portion of the design. If the stamp has marks which are common with those of the retouched plate and the worn area is retouched on the retouched plate, a correlation can be made and identification may be confirmed. Above are stamps from identified positions, with the one at the right probably from the left hand portion of Row 18.

(Courtesy of Robert P. Odenweller)

classic exhibit, it would have had even more information presented, somewhat differently.

Another page illustrates how unusual cancellations (in this case from the Maori Wars) as well as unusual rates can be shown along with the normal stamps of an issue. Although this page is intended to show the forms that the used 1d issue of 1862 can take, the rates and markings add depth and interest to the showing.

The final stage of forming a classic collection involves learning as much about the area as is possible. Then, through handling and speculating on unusual anomalies, one may come up with new research, new ideas, and new findings. Some may challenge the

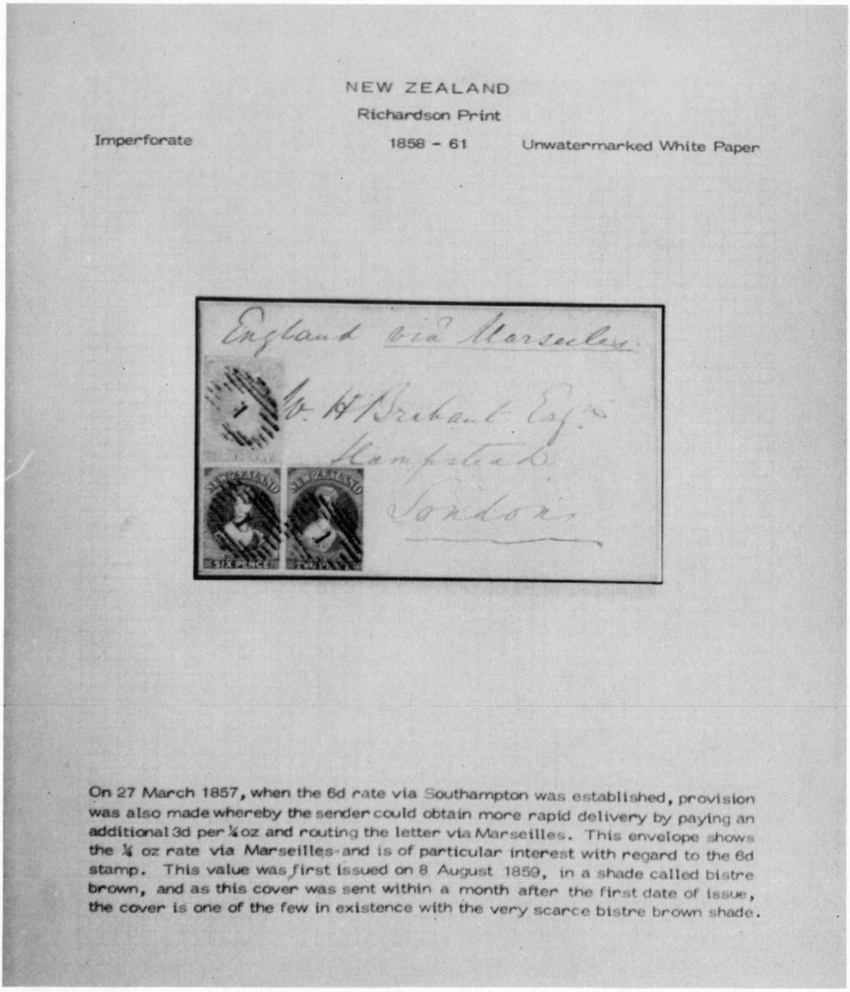

NEW ZEALAND

Richardson Print

Imperforate   1858 – 61   Unwatermarked White Paper

On 27 March 1857, when the 6d rate via Southampton was established, provision was also made whereby the sender could obtain more rapid delivery by paying an additional 3d per ¼oz and routing the letter via Marseilles. This envelope shows the ¼ oz rate via Marseilles and is of particular interest with regard to the 6d stamp. This value was first issued on 8 August 1859, in a shade called bistre brown, and as this cover was sent within a month after the first date of issue, the cover is one of the few in existence with the very scarce bistre brown shade.

(Courtesy of Robert P. Odenweller)

findings which have long been established by the earliest researchers. This final stage, however, carries with it a tacit necessity to publish your findings, for they are relatively useless if you keep them to yourself.

In a similar fashion one must learn about the postal history—the rates, routes, and markings—of the area to be collected. In New Zealand, I gleaned as much as I could from all the standard writings and set them down in bar graph form with all the changes easily delineated. This simplified depiction was adopted by Campbell Paterson of Auckland in his outstanding *Catalogue of New Zealand Stamps.* In achieving this final level of doing original

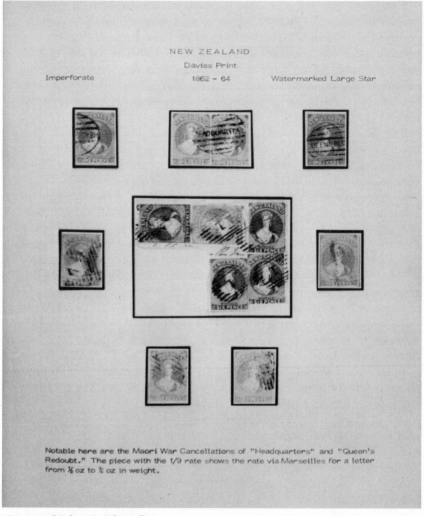

research one must always bear in mind a basic concept: what has previously appeared in print, however venerable the study and student, findings must be regarded with a certain amount of suspicion until proven correct. I must hasten to say, however, that this is advice to the few who would aspire to research an area and have the ability to do so convincingly. For most collectors the standard reference sources are and should remain relatively unquestioned, lest the whole problem develop into an unresolvable frustration built from an urge to question and a lack of ability to disprove what is said (see Plate 8).

Similar to original research, expertization represents a deep involvement in the higher forms of philately. Philatelic experts come in almost unlimited variety. Most have formed highly specialized collections, often of classics, but this is not of itself sufficient to make an expert. One of my first memories of expertization came with the creation of the rate sheet mentioned earlier. It enabled me to help prove false a cover which otherwise looked perfect.

The essence of expertization lies in the ability to evaluate the genuineness of a stamp or cover with an open mind, aided by personal knowledge and an adequate reference collection. Though that may sound simple, the catch phrase is "personal knowledge." This encompasses a wide range of experience—experience in knowing how to test for repairs or other treating of stamps that might be done to enhance their value, experience in knowing what features to expect on a genuine stamp or cover of the sort being considered, experience in knowing where to look for the answers: the books, catalogs, clippings, and other reference sources besides the reference collection of the stamps themselves. A great number of experts agree that there is an undefinable "smell" to a bad item —something that cannot at once be identified. It is amazing how accurate this sense can be when the final results are in. It is developed only by experience.

Relatively few collectors aspire to become experts, but many use the services of expert committees as insurance against possible expensive mistakes of their own when buying choice but costly items in their area of interest. Others, such as would-be speculators and investors, substitute expert certificates for their own lack of knowledge or laziness, or to insure more ready salability when it comes time to sell. Often it comes to a combination of the three. Whatever the reason, services of expert committees the world over are coming more and more into demand. Philatelic fakery, particularly in "created" covers, is spreading. Much of the work is very difficult to detect, especially by individual collectors who lack the constant contact with such items, and as a result are unable to tell the difference. As long as philately continues there will be a need for new experts. If my musings serve to generate only a small handful of collectors to take up the challenge, I shall be happy that this vital function is being rejuvenated.

I have found over the years that the work on my classic collection has provided many rewards, but somehow when all is said and done, the collection has less total meaning to me than the friends I have made in the process of building it.

The Philatelic Foundation

One of the points made was in the discussion of detecting fakes, forgeries, and other "gems" apt to deceive the unsuspecting collector. It is here that some note must be made about one organization whose sole duty it is to discover, detect, and make known such hoaxes before much harm is done to the collector—The Philatelic Foundation.

The Philatelic Foundation is the major expertizing center in the United States. It is here that stamps and covers are carefully examined to determine whether or not they are genuine. It has two primary functions in the philatelic world: education and expertization. Founded on March 16, 1945, by some of the United States' most eminent philatelists, some of whom we have encountered earlier, including Alfred F. Lichtenstein, Theodore E. Steinway, and Harry L. Lindquist, the foundation received a unique charter as an educational institution from the University of the State of New York. This small band of philatelists believed in the future of philately and were prepared to do something about it.

EDUCATION

Two basic audio-visual programs are seen annually by thousands of collectors all over the country: "The Romance of Stamp Collecting" and "The Drama of Postage Stamp Creation," available without charge to organized groups and schools, and include slides, tapes, and a manual. Starting with the basics of stamp collecting in "Romance" and following with information on how stamps are produced in "Drama," the two are an ideal introductory program for beginners, young and old. "One Giant Step," made by Juniors, is also available.

For more advanced collectors, there are fourteen shows available which deal with various aspects of early United States philately. These shows were originally produced by the U.S. Philatelic Classics Society and are enjoyed by sizeable audiences each year.

The foundation also offers a philatelic workshop course which is held at the Collectors Club in weekly sessions over a period of six weeks. This course makes use of the foundation's popular reference and textbook, *Foundations of Philately,* by Winthrop S. Boggs.

Reference materials and a philatelic library are available to students and researchers. The photographic files of the over 60,000 stamps that have been sent in for expertization are an irreplaceable source of information for research study. In a single visit a student can see how many genuine and less then genuine stamps of a specific catalogue number have passed through the Expert Committee's hands since 1945.

EXPERTIZATION

The education and expertization functions of The Philatelic Foundation are closely linked together. Members receive "counterfeit leaflets" and bulletins on a regular basis with the knowledge of how to tell genuine from not genuine or analyses of the problems and frequency of genuineness of popular issues.

Expertization, as such, is like a consumer protection agency for philately. The Expert Committee is a group of amateur philatelists who donate their time and expertise to evaluate the authenticity of some 750 stamps each month. The committee is ably assisted by a fine group of consultants—dealers who give freely of their time and knowledge to help in these determinations. By use of the usual techniques of comparison with known genuine stamps, ultraviolet light, watermarking fluid, magnification, and knowledge, as well as less usual techniques including microscopic and photographic examination as well as occasional spectrophotometry, the opinions are entered on a worksheet by each expert. The chairman of the Expert Committee then evaluates the opinions to reach a decision on how the final opinion will read. The initial examination is done by permanent curators.

The opinion (and it is not a guarantee) is entered on a certificate along with a photograph of the stamp or cover. It states whether or not the stamp is genuine as well as whether it has been altered by regumming, reperforating, repairing, overprint or cancellation, faked, or any of a wide range of other possibilities. Though not a guarantee, the foundation's opinion is so universally respected that most auction firms state, "In the case of United States stamps the 'mutually acceptable authority' (for authentication) shall normally be The Philatelic Foundation of New York."

The fees for these certificates range from $15 to as much as $500, depending on the catalogue value of the items submitted. Members who donate $50 or more annually are entitled to three free certificates. Members contributing $25 receive one free certificate annually. Contributions are deductible from federal and state income taxes. For information write to: The Philatelic Foundation, Inc., 270 Madison Ave., New York, N.Y. 10016.

The Stamp Auction

Domenico Facci, noted contemporary sculptor and president of the Italia Philatelic Society, says, "I'm too emotional to go to a stamp auction. Why do I send for an auction catalogue? When I find myself in the auction room, before anything begins, I've promised myself, let's say, not to spend more than $500 for an item I can't live without."

He continues, "Whatever chemistry starts within me, I can't account for . . . but suddenly any bid that's flying through the air sends me into a rage of competition. Of course, I go home victorious!" He then moved to pick out an album from his voluminous and brilliant Italian collection. He turned to a page. "Here it is! I've always wanted it. Now it's mine! Auctions are really exciting, aren't they?"

Today collectors have come to know that to move out of "average" collecting and into the better material area, it's the auction house that becomes the major source. Not all items are in the thousand-dollar range. You can often get a lovely item for far less than you planned. A catalogue listing can be $100 and the successful bid can be $40 or lower!

Selling Your Collection

Whether you have a stamp collection, assembled over a period of time, valued in the thousands of dollars, or maybe only a few items to sell in order to purchase new material, you can benefit from auctions. Big or small, you can take your collection to an auction house to get an evaluation. You may even walk out with a cash advance if you like.

You can also get the disappointment of a lifetime if, on the other hand, you bring into the auction house sheet after sheet of mint United States stamps of the last twenty years or so only to find that they aren't even worth their face value. That's why what you collect and the condition that your material is in makes it so necessary from the start to know what you are doing. If you simply want to be amused, there is no problem, but why not have the same good time and come out with a profit? Knowledgeable buying results in successful selling. Here is where the phrase of King George V has meaning: "I don't want a good collection; I want the best collection." To be demanding when you buy means that you can be commanding when you sell.

Every step involved with collecting develops into a repeated pattern, one that separates the men from the boys. If your early collection habits become firmly placed with direction and comprehension, your ABC's on "how to" will develop your ability and increase your pleasure. You avoid gimmicks and shifty bargains of "classics" for small amounts of cash. Learning through your new associations in stamp clubs, attending shows, reading the philatelic press, counseling and asking advice from auction houses will contribute to the further enjoyment of your collecting.

The Big Six

Today's collecting is sophisticated and the auction house can be an important guide and ally. Which auction house you choose is of enormous importance. Six of the most distinguished auction houses in the world are H. R. Harmer, New York, San Francisco, London, and Sydney; Robson Lowe, London; Edgar Mohrman, Hamburg; Stanley Gibbons, Ltd., London, Frankfurt; Corinphila, Zurich; and Robert Siegel, New York.

H. R. Harmer International

One of the world's major auction houses was started in London just after World War I by Henry Revell Harmer, when the Penny Black was celebrating its seventy-eighth birthday. The hobby of philately was beginning to reap rewards for the swiftly growing public of stamp collectors throughout the world. The more advanced collectors needed a center point of contact to buy the best and the rarest stamps available, and at this point some stupendous collections began to appear on the market. It was at this time that Henry Revell Harmer opened his auction house at 6, 7, and 8 Old Bond Street, London. It was above the famous Embassy Club where the Prince of Wales, who became King Edward VIII and then Duke of Windsor, was taking guitar lessons while his father, King George V, was building the greatest British collection ever formed.

The Man and All the Kings

Henry Revell Harmer was hobnobbing with the then-passionate collectors among royalty including King Alphonso XIII of Spain, King George V and King George VI of Britain, King Carol of Romania, King Fuad and his son Farouk of Egypt, and the Maharaja of Bahawalpur. The "commoners" included the insatiable collector from the United States, Arthur Hind, and the rich Alsatian tobacco magnate, Maurice Burrus. When kings began to go into exile, King Carol of Romania talked to Mr. Harmer, took his advice, and fled with his stamps. Less attentive was King Farouk, who left his collection behind (which the Egyptian government sold for a healthy sum through Harmer's London office).

The Tradition Goes On

The saying goes that the apple doesn't fall far from the tree. Thus it is only natural that both Cyril and Bernard Harmer, sons of the founder, who grew up within a philatelic ambiance, inherited the appreciation of the art of philately. Indeed, they enhanced it.

Cyril, the elder son, headed the London office and became known as the dean of British philately. His book, *Newfoundland Airmails, 1919–1939,* is now a classic reference. Airmail collectors were then wrapped up with the "flying crates that flew the Atlantic."

While Cyril maintained the continuity of the London office, along came the bright and peppery organizer Bernard. In 1940 Harmers opened the United States branch and at the end of World War II, he took over from his father and made philatelic history. So much has passed through this house of stamps, including the major part of the Hind collection that sold for $2,895,146, the Dale-Lichtenstein auction that realized over $3 million, and the famed, so-called junk sale of Franklin Roosevelt's collection that brought $250,000.

Bernard Harmer, chairman of the board of H. R. Harmer International, seems to have a good time with his global operation. It's a family affair, and it is also big business.

The Stamp Auction

Mr. Bernard Harmer, when interviewed, said, "The dealer makes the collector; we steal them." What he really means is that sooner or later if you have spent $100 on your stamp interests, you are ready to send for an auction catalogue. That's the first step. The major magazines and newspapers that make up the philatelic press such as *Linn's Stamp News, Stamps, Stamp Collector, Mekeel's, Scott's Journal, Min-*

Bernard D. Harmer, chairman of the
board of Harmers International.

kus Monthly Journal, APS Journal, SPA Journal, and the publications
of other clubs, organizations, and groups, both here and abroad, constantly keep you abreast of what auctions are coming up and where.

The stamp auction catalogue is an education in itself. At first it may
be a bit difficult to figure out, but once you've spotted an item that
interests you, the learning process is quite simple. In order to be exact,
I have quoted from a pamphlet which is free from H. R. Harmer:
"How to Buy at Auction" (courtesy H. R. Harmer, Inc.).

During the last five decades the development of Auction Sales has become
one of the marked features of philately. Even so, there must be some collectors who have not yet taken up this most economical method of acquiring
stamps because of a mistaken idea that auction-buying is reserved for the
advanced philatelist only.

On the contrary, we have many a buyer who spends quite a modest sum in
the course of a year, and as he grows in philatelic and financial stature we
certainly can continue to help him.

The advanced philatelist has obviously learned that if he wishes to make his
collection something more than ordinary, the quickest, safest and most economical method is via the Auction Room.

CATALOGUES

Probably you have already seen our catalogues; all are illustrated (some in
color) and you may be a regular subscriber. If not, you can receive twelve
months' catalogues (about 20) for a nominal $6 or, followed by Lists of Prices
Realized, for $13.50. There are reduced subscriptions for specialists, and rates
for long-distance mailings by first-class mail and air mail. The application form
is available on request. The catalogues are mailed well ahead of the auction
date, giving ample time for viewing requests and for sending in your bids. The
Lists of Prices Realized are mailed some seven days after the auction. As a

guide to market values these records can save you many times their annual cost on the purchase of a single stamp. An unknowledgeably high bid on your part will not normally result in an excessive realization, BUT . . . if there is another unrealistic bid on the same lot then someone will get hurt!

VIEWING

Lots may usually be viewed on the Tuesday, Wednesday, Thursday, and Friday preceding days of Sale, and on the days of Sale. Days and times of viewing are given in each catalogue. Under special circumstances, subject to 24 hours notice, limited groups may be viewed at other times. Lots of convenient size and value are sent for postal viewing to clients in the United States and Canada on payment of postage, insurance, plus a small handling charge.

References are requested from collectors unknown to us. Lots sent for postal viewing are insured while in transit to and from the viewing client, but are the client's responsibility while in his possession.

BIDDING

You will notice that many of the lots have an estimated market valuation noted thus: "Est. Cash Val. $100." Alternatively where a figure without this notation is printed it indicates the value as listed in the Scott catalogues. If you wish to have further advice on values, note the lots of interest and we will give you our ideas of market value. Please enclose a stamped addressed envelope or card.

If time or distance prevents you attending our auctions, you can bid by post and you will find the necessary bid-form with each catalogue. Fill in the lot number and maximum price you are prepared to pay. Do not forget your full name and address, adding references (or the appropriate deposit) if this formality has not been taken care of previously.

Professional agents will also be pleased to act for you for a small charge, supplying more detailed information regarding lots where necessary.

We do *not* accept "Buy" bids. There must be a figure at which you would drop out if you were in the room, and that is exactly the price you should bid. You can also limit your *total* expenditure in any one sale. Although you may wish your total purchases not to exceed, say $500, this does not prevent you from entering bids for more than this amount. If and when your $500 is exhausted all later bids will be cancelled. All you have to do is to note the limit in the space provided on the bid form.

Where similar lots occur you may make "alternative" bids if you wish to buy one only. These should be entered as follows:—

256	...	...	...	...	$35
or					
257	...	...	...	...	$35

(It is often a good idea to bid a little more on the second lot, since, if this offer has to be used it will obviously be because your previous limit has been exceeded.)

THE AUCTION

This is always interesting and often exciting. If you come to 48th Street almost any alternate Tuesday to Thursday during the season (September to July) you can be sure of an intriguing experience—interesting enough at times to have been featured on both radio and television programs. Please sign your name and address on request. This will help the auctioneer when you buy. If you bid by post your offer will have been recorded in the auctioneer's catalogue and bidding will commence at one bid above the second highest offer "on the book."

An actual example best explains how this works. For, say, Lot 104, the auctioneer has recorded three bids—(1) $30, (2) $32.50 and *your* bid of $45.

The auctioneer will start on your behalf at $35 and if room competition develops, he will bid up to $45 for you. If there is further room-bidding you will lose this lot. If the initial bid of $35 is unchallenged the lot is yours at that figure. If you are unlucky, do not be discouraged—raise the level if the Prices Realized indicate your bidding is too modest—and remember, there are some 30,000 worthwhile lots sold every year. The normal bidding increases are by 5% and odd-amount bids are reduced to the normal bidding level.

GREAT AND SMALL COLLECTIONS

But, the cynic may ask, can he (or she—for we have many lady clients) be sure of finding just the stamps required? If you are looking for some very minor variety of a group seldom on the market, the answer is clearly that you may have to wait—but you stand a better chance at 48th Street.

However, for 90% of philatelists we can reasonably claim that they are indeed unlucky if they cannot buy a few coveted items in the great and small collections annually realizing a total of around $3,000,000.

FINALLY

We suggest you study each Catalogue—some are better described as Philatelic Handbooks—come to the sale or send your bids and become one of the thousands of satisfied clients in many parts of the globe who are buying regularly in our New York, London and Sydney Auctions.

Pay serious attention to condition. The controversy of hinged versus never-hinged still rages. Although you don't exhibit the back of a stamp, nevertheless, it does affect its value, and a hinged stamp usually sells for less than an unhinged one. Remember, though, that when you talk of really old and rare stamps, the chances are that they have all been hinged—as that was the normal way.

Original gum is important with regard to old or valuable stamps. Care must be taken to see that the gum is original and not "regummed." Regumming is noted, as a rule, when known.

KEY TO CATALOGUING

SYMBOLS

★	Unused.	○	Used.	▲	On piece.	✉	On entire.
✈	Air Post.	⊞	Block of four.	⌷	Block larger than four.	S	Specimen.
DE	Die Essay.	PE	Plate Essay.	DP	Die Proof.	PP	Plate Proof.

MAJOR ABBREVIATIONS

SE = Straight Edge; s.l. = straight-line; c.d.s. = Circular Date Stamp;
c.t.o. = Cancelled to Order; F.D.C. = First Day Cover;

CONDITION

The various gradings of stamps are, in order:
superb; extremely fine; very fine; fine; fair
A lot described as "fair" is so listed either by reason of general appearance or more often because of a small fault or faults, such as a crease, thin spot, short or missing perf, perforated into, cut into, etc.
In the case of sets, large blocks, sheets, etc., the condition quoted represents the average and quality above and below this standard can be expected.

GUM

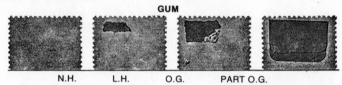

N.H.   L.H.   O.G.   PART O.G.

Shaded portion can represent an actual hinge or the area disturbed by a hinge.

n. h.	=	Never hinged — unused with original gum in Post Office state and unmounted.
l. h.	=	Lightly hinged — unused with full original gum showing some evidence of a previous hinge, which may be present in part or entirely removed.
o. g.	=	Original gum — unused with original gum somewhat disturbed by previous hinging which may still be present.
Part o. g.	=	Part original gum, as issued.
Ungummed	=	Unused without gum, as issued.
Unused	=	Unused without gum (unless gum is mentioned).

BLOCKS OR SHEETS AND THEIR GUM

Minor separations are the rule, rather than the exception, in the case of blocks or sheets of any size. A few separations—around two perfs per row—do not affect the value of a block or sheet and are not grounds for the return of a lot.

Blocks of four that have two stamps o.g. and two stamps n.h. are described "n.h./o.g."

PAIRS

All pairs are horizontal, unless otherwise mentioned.

CATALOGUE NUMBERS

The catalogue numbers of the contents of the lots are given in parentheses immediately following the descriptions, but in bulky lots, only the range of issues is shown.

CATALOGUE VALUES

The final column shows the catalogue value of the lot. This is shown in parentheses where, in the opinion of the auctioneer, the market value exceeds this figure.

ESTIMATED VALUES

If an estimated cash value is given, it is shown in the description and always indicated by the abbreviation "Est. Cash Val." It is used where the lot is large or where the actual value has little relation to the catalogue price.

It represents the auctioneer's appraisal of the true MARKET value of a lot and the figure is invariably close to the actual realization. It is useless for mail bidders to list any bids that are only a low proportion of such estimates.

CATALOGUES USED IN LISTING

Scott U.S. Specialized Catalogue (1977)
American Air Mail Catalogue (1970)   ———
and others as noted in the description   A.A.M.

In most auction houses of good repute, a viewing time is set aside a few days before the auction. For those who can walk in and look at a specific auction, it is an experience. You may have checked one item that you really want, but the "eyeful" of all the material you see can be overwhelming. The word "distinguished" comes to mind. But if you attend the auction that has what you want, don't let the fish get out of the net, if what you see is material that you will never see again.

Also, through viewing comes your chance to ascertain that the condition of the material is suitable for your collection needs, and that the lot is described correctly.

ATTENDING THE AUCTION

Attending an auction is, of course, a marvelous experience. It's better if you don't spot a competitor who wants just what you do. Some collectors have agents to whom they give instructions on what to look for in the viewing and what their top bid is. The atmosphere is friendly, and when the auctioneer starts auctioning off the lots described, the auction begins. It is also interesting and exciting for the newcomer to discover that often he or she can purchase material for less than he or she had ever imagined.

Louis Grunin

He received one of the three major international awards at INTER-PHIL '76, the Grand Prix National. His nine-frame exhibit started out with the U.S. 5- and 10-cent stamps of 1847, and continued through some of the rare varieties of the 1851–1857 issues. His collection was hailed as one of the great assemblages of United States stamps.

Louis Grunin began collecting at the age of ten. He collected "everything I could get my hands on, used and unused, from all over the world." He continued, "Since I was poor, all I could get were the commonest, which, incidentally, I enjoyed immensely."

In an interview with him he said, "I stopped collecting until I completed college and I resumed my collecting when I got married. I always was interested in becoming a serious collector, but I realized that important collecting means important money." Not limited to the classics, he once built a serious twentieth-century collection, which he subsequently sold. He reflected, "I wanted to work my way into a sort of the dessert of a good dinner." Grunin acquired material from all directions, large and small. He sold his duplicates as fast as he could. Winning at INTERPHIL '76 was the climax of forty years of work in

Louis Grunin, winner of the
Grand Prix National Award,
INTERPHIL '76.
(Courtesy of *Linn's Stamp News*)

building his collection. When asked how he could part with his prize-winning collection, he replied, "I believe in collecting for fun. I do not consider possession of stamps fun. One of the reasons I sell completed collections after I lose the kick of exhibiting them is that I feel there is little left for further expansion." Though Mr. Grunin started out poor, he now says, "Stamps have not been just a source of relaxation, but also they have been a damned good investment." He ended, "They've kept me better than one step ahead of inflation."

The Catalogue—A Study

The auction catalogue of Grunin's collection is in itself a collector's item for anyone interested in United States classics. In Grunin's own words, "Give a man a million dollars and he won't necessarily build a good collection." He continued, "To build that collection, you have to do a lot of studying to know what pieces are known. You have to be familiar with old collections and auction catalogues."

I have chosen a few items from the H. R. Harmer auction catalogue of Mr. Grunin's collection to give you an idea of the look of a catalogue, description of lots, and prices realized. Actually, an in-depth analysis of the items chosen is an enormous and interesting study in itself. This embraces the most important era of United States philately. The main point to remember is you have to make a start somewhere. If United

States classics appeal to you, follow Louis Grunin's route and choose pieces as you can and with comprehension. You could dare to pick up the challenge that brought Mr. Grunin his fame.

Lot #2006: This is a spectacular 5-cent deep red brown block of eight of the first stamp that was issued in the United States in 1847. At the Harmer auction of the Caspary Collection in 1956, this multiple sold for $2,700. At the Grunin auction, as you can see, the catalogue price was $18,000 plus, and the price realized was $24,000. The percentage in profit from 1956 to 1976 was 788 percent. (Did you bother to take your magnifying glass to find the dot in the "S" in the third and seventh stamps? If so, you have what it takes to make a serious collector.)

Lot #2081: This used block is the second United States stamp issued in 1847, bearing the portrait of George Washington. Did you check the "Key to Cataloguing"? Otherwise you wouldn't know that this was a used block. The catalogue listing was $14,000. Why then did it sell for $7,750? In the first place, the cancellation was made with a pen, which in most cases is philatelically unattractive. Secondly, note the absence of a margin at the bottom. This is mentioned only to suggest the incredibly minute detail that comes with knowledge that can give you the acute ability to understand the way an important multiple is calculated to make the final realized price.

In the classic issues of the United States, details of cancels and postmarks are of extreme interest and importance. To enjoy this area of research, the finest reference books are essential to possess or certainly to read.

Lot #2016: Grid Cancel. This stamp of U.S.A. #1 bears a beautiful example of a Grid Cancel. The catalogue value listed $200 and the price realized was $900. This is an increase of 350 percent. The reasons that this brought such a fine price are its "full small black cancel," its clarity, its full margins.

Lot #2035: Pinwheel Cancel. This fancy cancellation known as a striking pinwheel cancel is unique because it was used in Paris, Kentucky. The catalogue price was $185 and the price realized was $2,-100. The increase was 1,035 percent. Obviously the cancel is valuable and scarce.

Lot #2175: Numeral Cancel. The bold numeral "5" is a beauty. You can begin to see how intriguing it could be to collect the different types of postmarks on the early stamps. This is the 1851–56 imperforate. The catalogue value is $42.50. The price realized was $130, a 206 percent increase.

Lot #2234: Town Cancel. This 3-cent dull red is tied to piece by a stunning, vivid cancellation. It realized $70.

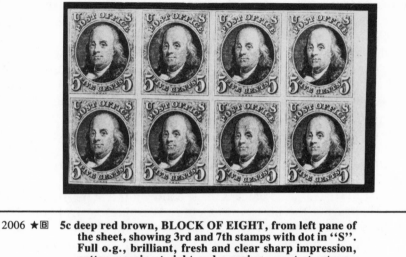

2006 ★▣　5c deep red brown, BLOCK OF EIGHT, from left pane of
　　　　　the sheet, showing 3rd and 7th stamps with dot in "S".
　　　　　Full o.g., brilliant, fresh and clear sharp impression,
　　　　　gutter margin at right and margins except at extreme
　　　　　bottom right. There is a crease in the 3rd row and a
　　　　　slight corner crease at bottom left. This glorious block
　　　　　is one of the gems of classic United States Philately.
　　　　　Catalogued as two ordinary blks of 4. Ex. Caspary
　　　　　...(1)　　(18,000+)

(Courtesy of Harmers of New York)

2081 ○⊞　10c deep black, BLOCK OF FOUR, margins except cut
　　　　　into at bottom, faded and barely imperceptable pen
　　　　　cancel, faulty but very fresh and fine unused appear-
　　　　　ance. A very desirable and scarce multiple. Very few
　　　　　blocks exist ....(2) 14,000.00

(Courtesy of Harmers of New York)

Lot #2412: Multiple. This 1-cent blue in an unbelievable block of nine was the "star" of the Grunin auction. In 1956, when it was last auctioned, this unique prize from the Caspary Collection sold for $8,250. At the Grunin auction, a joyful bidder purchased this dazzling item for $65,000. The increase in value over the last twenty years has been 688 percent.

This is a slim analysis indeed, but it gives you an idea of the investigation aspects of what is considered the best. It took Grunin forty years to get his collection together.

2016 ○ **5c dark brown,** large margins and very sharp impression, full small **black** cancel., superb ....(1a) (200.00)

2035 ○ **5c dark brown,** rich true color and very sharp impression, extremely fine, cancd. by **red Pin Wheel of Paris, Ky.**...........................(1a)(185.00+)

2175 ○ **1c blue, recut top,** cancd. by bold numeral 5, negligible tiny imperfections, striking cancel ....(9)   42.50+

(Courtesy of Harmers of New York)

2234 ▲   **3c dull red,** very fine, tied on piece by **Suspension Bridge, N.Y. Apr. 23, 1857** pmk. ....(11)

2412 ★ Ⓑ   **1c deep blue, A FANTASTIC BLOCK OF NINE FROM THE BOTTOM RIGHT CORNER OF THE RIGHT PANE OF PLATE TWO. The center stamp of bottom row the finest example of type III, THE FAMOUS 99RII (78-80 to 98-100RII). Full bottom sheet margin. Pos. 89 showing double transfer. Brilliant fresh and full original gum, rich color and clear sharp impression. Few negligible imperfections, but the rare type III is perfect. One of the rarest United States stamps unused and unpriced thus. This piece, the prize of this great collection is probably unique and one of the most beautiful showpieces extant. Ex. Caspary ......(21, 20)**   unpr.

Mail Bid Auctions

There are many types of auctions. Some auction houses specialize in specific areas. In California there is the Sun Philatelic Centre which specializes in Japanese material and related items such as the Ryukyu Islands.

J. Millard Williams in Columbia, Maryland, specializes in China. Theo. Van Dam, an outstanding postal historian, specializes in postal history worldwide. Where mail bid auctions differ from other auctions is that you must rely totally on the description of the writeup in the catalogue sent to you. As Jake Williams says in his auction pamphlet, "A public philatelic auction differs from a 'mail sale' in that the closing and final bidding is open to the public for participation."

This is a very big difference. Buying by mail bid sale can be a "gray area," because you can't see what you are getting. If you know the house with whom you are dealing, you can call up and ask for more detailed information. Some fine items come out of mail bid sales, but it is quite necessary to know with whom you are dealing. In all areas that are specialized, by the nature of what you are collecting, you should try to find both the dealer and the mail bid auction that serve you best.

The gray area comes in when you are dealing with a post office box number. If what you bought was described inaccurately, you are stuck, usually. In short, don't bid in a blind alley. You are in safe hands with reputable dealers. Always be aware of what and from whom you are buying, and then bidding by direct mail can give you enjoyment and peace of mind.

Investing in Stamps

Viewing the aristocrats and studying the percentage increase of gain from the Grunin auction can mislead you concerning the glories of investment in stamps. What you see are the great rarities and in the case of the Grunin auction, you viewed material that in some cases took the collector forty years to accumulate.

If you don't know your stamps, contact a reputable auction house, a top stamp dealer, or a leading collector who can suggest what direction you might take—but at best, since no one is infallible, it is much wiser to develop into a philatelist yourself, whereby you can have sound judgment of your own.

C. Ellis Millbury in his book, *So You Want to Invest in Stamps*, wrote, "To be a successful investing collector is to be a dyed-in-the-wool pessimist. All stamps of value, however genuine they may seem, must be held in relentless suspicion until proven guiltless." He continues, "It is rather well known that some of our American millionaires are notoriously adept at acquiring spurious works of art and such, but in the matter of acquiring creations in phony stamps, the American buyer has no equal as a twenty-four-carat sucker. Seek the counsel of those of undisputed repute who really know stamps."

I have yet to meet a superb collector who will admit he ever considered his stamp collecting as an investment. Yet, one after another, as their collections come up for auction, their profits are stunning. One must realize that money is just a fraction of the total effort. Inquisitiveness, inquiry, research, study, and knowledge over a period of years are always part of the fabric of abilities that make a good collector who in turn creates a top-notch collection.

Harrison Haverbeck of the Collectors Club says, "Searching for good material, making friends, writing about discoveries are all part of the development of the serious philatelist. After that, the profits take care of themselves." There you have the heart of the hobby: "Do it yourself." That is the basic reason the great collectors never discuss the hobby as a program of investment.

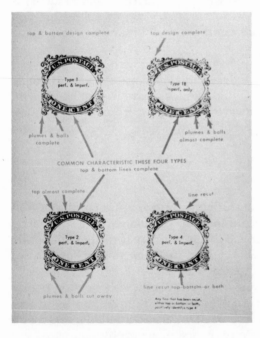

1851 1-cent "Blueboy" Graphi-Guide.
(Courtesy of VONCORP, Dunedin, Florida)

Comprehending Innovators

To become involved with the early stamps of the United States is to be concerned with those that are usually the "blank" spaces in one's albums, the stamps Louis Grunin wanted most when he was poor and got when he was rich. It is not just a matter of money with these issues; it is a matter of comprehending.

Along has come a "wave maker," Donna von Stein, who has created what she calls "Voncorp's Philatelic Educational Tools." Basically, she has blown up the United States classics to a size much larger than their originals so that you can easily see the differences. By becoming aware of the details of the stamp you can comprehend these involved issues. She calls these "Graphi-guides for U.S. Stamps." Here is a page of her 1851 1-cent "Blueboy."

She has also created beautiful philatelic educational folders in full color of early United States rarities that include detailed information on the history of the issue. Furthermore, she presents a series of precision, millimeter gauges to help you measure your stamps with accuracy. One that is especially useful is the "Grill-a-Vu," which outlines nine of the major grill varieties of United States stamps. By matching the stamp against these grill outlines, you can instantly identify the grill. She issues a journal, *Strictly U.S.*, "An independent bi-monthly magazine, by, about, and for U.S. philatelists."

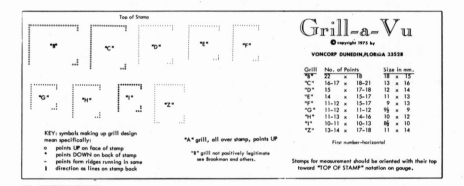

Grill-a-Vu for deciphering the U.S. grilled stamp issues.
(Courtesy of VONCORP, Dunedin, Florida)

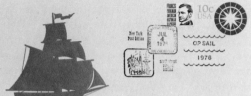

The
Bicentennial

On February 23, 1976, the United States Postal Service issued a pane of fifty stamps depicting the fifty state flags, se-tenant, arranged in order of each state's admission to the Union. On the Tennessee flag the stars were incorrectly placed. The Tennessee Legislature passed a resolution suggesting that the USPS correct the stamp. The proportion of red and blue in the flag of Iowa was also incorrect. Otherwise, all went well.

The first day of issue coincided with the plenary session of the midwinter meeting of the National Conference of Governors. Aside from the first-day cancel out of Washington, D.C., a second cancel was announced for the same date. One could get the cancel from every state by sending a cover with the stamp affixed of that state's flag to the postmaster of each state capital.

Honor R. Holland, president of the ATOZ Stamp Club, being British, felt that to acquire a first-day cancel from each state would provide an interesting souvenir of America's two-hundredth birthday. She not only proceeded to send the postmasters of the fifty state capitals covers to cancel first day of issue but also went one step further. Having gathered her fifty cancelled covers, she wrote to the governors of the fifty states, asked for an autograph from each, and asked them to affix the official state seal on the left of the envelope.

Each day for months, she awaited a response, and she began to receive her autographed covers, one by one. The first to come through was from Governor Wallace of Alabama. Alas, he autographed her FDC, but remailed it, thereby getting a second cancel dated April 8, 1976.

By the time she had received forty-nine autographs, it seemed certain the fiftieth would never arrive. Without the fiftieth signature, her collection would be incomplete. Months went by, but finally she got it! Governor Jerry Brown of California was back home after trying for

Sheet of fifty state flag stamps. (Courtesy U.S. Postal Service)

the 1976 Democratic nomination for president, and found the time to sign the cover.

From the first woman governor, Ella Grasso of Connecticut, she received a lovely letter: "I am honored to be included in your collection." Governor Bennett of Kansas said, "Thank you for your interest in my administration." But Governor Jerry Apadaca of New Mexico was the most cooperative from Miss Holland's point of view. He wrote, "It is my pleasure to autograph the first-day cover you enclosed. I have also had the State Seal affixed to the cover. Your project is most appropriate for the Bicentennial year and I am honored to be included in your collection."

She became more and more interested in her "governors." She was happy when Governor Arch Moore of West Virginia was found innocent of an extortion conspiracy. During the Democratic and Republican conventions, she was truly excited to see some of the governors on TV whom she now considered to be her friends.

From the postmaster of Cheyenne, Wyoming, came this message: "Your fifty flag commemorative was inadvertently cancelled with the wrong die. We regret that this happened and have tried to correct the error to the best of our ability. If you are not satisfied with what we have done and wish to submit another envelope for cancellation, we would be delighted to cancel it for you." Did she send for the corrected cancel? Of course, because she needed both for the collection.

The next step was recognizing that all the cancellations were not the same. Type I had a box cancel, Type II had a double line top and bottom, and Type III, only seen from South Dakota, had four lines.

Finally, she noticed that there were differences in the circular date stamp. Some had no postal zone markings, such as Richmond, Virginia. On some the time was above or below the date, such as Pierre, South Dakota.

Governors sent her maps, tourist brochures, and fact sheets on their states' major industries. The governor of Maryland sent a pamphlet on *The Mountains, the Bay, the Ocean,* and even a photo of the Baltimore Checker Spot Butterfly. The heart of this story is the time and interest the governors took to please an admiring British friend of the United States.

Governors 100 Percent Philatelically Correct and Plus

The governors whose covers were cancelled clearly, autographed, and affixed with their official gold state seals were:

1. Alaska	Governor Jay S. Hammond
2. Colorado	Governor Richard D. Lamm
3. Georgia	Governor George Busbee
4. Idaho	Governor Cecil D. Andrus
5. Indiana	Governor Dr. Otis R. Bowen
6. Maryland	Governor Marvin Mandel
7. Michigan	Governor William G. Milliken
8. Minnesota	Governor Wendell R. Anderson
9. New Hampshire	Governor Meldrim Thomson, Jr.
10. New Mexico	Governor Jerry Apadaca
11. North Carolina	Governor James E. Holshouser, Jr.
12. Oklahoma	Governor David L. Boren

13. Oregon	Governor Robert W. Straub
14. Texas	Governor Dolph Briscoe
15. Utah	Governor Calvin L. Rampton
16. Vermont	Governor Thomas P. Salmon
17. Virginia	Governor Mills E. Godwin, Jr.
18. Wisconsin	Governor Patrick J. Lucey
19. Wyoming	Governor Ed Herschler

It is reported that a Type IV exists . . . so Miss Holland is in search of her missing type. Now for her fifty-flag collection, she picks up first-flight covers, used stamps on piece, multiples or pairs, zip numbers, plate numbers, and Fourth of July cancels. The pursuit is never-ending.

Type I box cancel.
(From the collection of H. R. Holland)

Type II double-line cancel.
(From the collection of H. R. Holland)

Type III four-line cancel.
(From the collection of H. R. Holland)

Colonial
America

The earliest first-day cover in America.

The Earliest First-Day Cover in American History

One of the fifty flag Bicentennial covers cancelled first day of issue, February 23, 1976, is signed by Governor Hugh Carey of New York.

The earliest first-day cover in American history was January 22, 1673, when the governor, Francis Lovelace, of New York, scribbled "Post Payd" on a letter that he handed over to post rider Lord John Archer for delivery to Governor Trumbull of Hartford, Connecticut. Calvet Hahn, noted postal historian, explained this cover in an article, "The Colonial Period in America." On Lord Archer, he wrote, "Archer was apparently somewhat overwhelmed by the first day of issue ceremonies. It is reported that he stopped in the tavern in Harlem for refreshments before braving the unmarked wintry forests. For two weeks, he ducked the Indians and blazed the trees along the route to Hartford and Boston, thus marking what we now know as the old Boston Post Road. Eighty years later, Ben Franklin arranged to have milestones placed on this route, a few of which can be found today."

The Earliest Postmark

Calvet Hahn in his *Postal History Primer* (a must to own if postal history of the colonial period is of interest to you) writes, "Collecting postal history is more complex than stamp collecting. Material is harder to locate, reference works are far less extensive and much less pioneering work has been done. Nevertheless it offers pleasure in the study of the postmarks, rates, routes and practices of the postal service that are an unending challenge."

The above earliest reported example of a United States postmark is a letter from Newburyport, Massachusetts, which, explained Calvet, was postmarked at Cambridge. The American post office for Boston, which at the time was occupied by British troops, was besieged by General George Washington. It reached New York on the way to Philadelphia on August 24 and was given a lovely blue handstamp postmark, "N.York.Au.24," the first handstamp to have been applied to mail carried under the authority of the Act of Congress of the United States. The dateline in the letter was Newburyport, August 11, 1775. It discusses "the capture of an American flour ship by British cruisers off Cape Cod." It is postmarked with a manuscript "CAMB" and a manuscript "⅛." (Cambridge, 1 shilling eight pence—the postage rate.)

Earliest known United States postmark.
(From the collection of Calvet Hahn)

Two Postmasters, Two Eras

Free frank from A. Lincoln, Postmaster, New Salem, Illinois.
(Courtesy of Seymour Kaplan)

Abraham Lincoln

The most famous postmaster in American history was Abraham Lincoln. At the age of twenty-four (1833), he still had no specific vocation. He was assigned the task of postmaster in New Salem, Illinois. Of this job, Lincoln said, "The office was too insignificant to make my politics an objection." Although the post office was in Lincoln's store, most of the time he carried letters in his hat, delivering them at the appropriate time. He often read letters for those who couldn't read. Groups of friends would, when a newspaper arrived, ask him to read it out loud and give his comments on the news.

He made little money as postmaster. He was forced to eke out his living by helping out in other stores in the village, by splitting rails, working in the mill, and finally, taking up surveying.

The First American Postmaster General

One hundred years before Abe Lincoln, another twenty-four-year-old youth owned his own printing office and was publishing the *Pennsylvania Gazette*. In 1737 he became postmaster of Philadelphia. This young man was Benjamin Franklin. In his autobiography he wrote, "For tho the salary was small, it facilitated the correspondence that inform'd my newspaper, increas'd the number demanded as well as the advertisements inserted, so that it came to afford me a comfortable income."

In an article entitled "Ben Franklin," Beatrice Hessen wrote, "Since no one else had undertaken to improve the postal system, Franklin decided that he would do so."

He wanted the job of "Joint Deputy Postmaster General for the Colonies" and he got it along with a William Hunter.

In Carl Van Doren's biography on Franklin, he wrote, "During 1754, Franklin visited all the post offices in the northern colonies and during 1755–1756 those in Maryland and Virginia, becoming acquainted with the postmasters, systemizing their accounts, studying their special difficulties, surveying roads, fords and ferries." By 1761, Franklin made the Postal Service solvent and was able to send profits to London. The Treasury commented, "This is the first remittance of its kind ever made." On January 30, 1774, Franklin was dismissed because of his activities in the cause of American independence. "By then the profits of the post office had reached some £3,000 a year."

Special "B Free Franklin" postmark.
(From the collection of R. E. Beresford)

Letter of August 10, 1753, appointing Benjamin Franklin as Deputy Postmaster for North America. (Courtesy of the British Post Office)

Letter of January 31, 1774, dismissing Benjamin Franklin from his post. (Courtesy of the British Post Office)

This is what Benjamin Franklin had to say upon his dismissal: "Before I was dismissed by a freak of the moment, we had brought it (the Post Office) to yield 3 times as much clear revenue to the Crown as the post office in Ireland. Since that impudent transaction, they have received from it not one farthing." This actually put an end to British control of the postal system in the Colonies.

Three months after the American Revolution began, the Continental Congress named Benjamin Franklin its first postmaster general on July 6, 1775.

Free Franking

In establishing postal rates, the First Continental Congress inaugurated the practice of free franking, November 8, 1775. The word "free" and the signature of the writer was necessary on the front of the envelope.

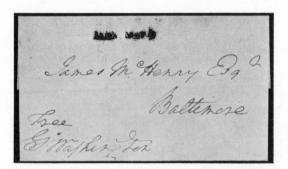

George Washington had free franking as president of the United States.
(Courtesy of Seymour Kaplan)

As a signer of the Declaration of Independence, John Hancock had free franking.
(Courtesy of Seymour Kaplan)

Confederate Philately

Brian Green in the uniform of his grandfather, General Green, for the annual cotillion of the Sons of Confederate Veterans Ball.
(Courtesy of Brian Green)

Brian Green, assistant curator of the Philatelic Foundation, is an ardent collector, historian, and student of Confederate philately. One of the aspects of stamp collecting that holds enchantment is the human interest of a subject that brings living meaning to the past. For Brian it was a patriotic tie to his own heritage.

On his mother's side was General Pierre Gustave Toutant Beauregard, hero of the Battle of the First Manassas, or, as he said to me, "To you Yankees, the Battle of Bull Run." There was also a sporting dandy, General John Bankhead Magruder, known as "Prince John," who served champagne on the battlefield.

On his father's side, General Martin Green was killed by a sniper at Vicksburg, and General Thomas Green was killed by a cannonball at Red River Landing.

From General Robert E. Lee

At the end of the Civil War, General Robert E. Lee wrote, "All my records were needlessly destroyed by the clerk's having them in charge on retreat from Petersburg, and such as have forwarded to the War Department in Richmond, were either destroyed in the conflagration or capture in an attempt to save them."

The story behind this marvelous cover from General Robert E. Lee to Mrs. Hetty Pegram began with a wedding invitation. Hetty Cary,

Wedding invitation of General John Pegram and Miss Hetty Cary.
(From the collection of Brian Green)

Cover from General Lee to Mrs. Hetty Pegram, February 11, 1865.
(From the collection of Brian Green)

known for her beauty, was a belle of the South. (Her sister married Burton Harrison, who was private secretary to Jefferson Davis.) Hetty's most ardent suitor, General John Pegram, pursued her for four years, and finally the wedding date was set for January 19, 1865. The ceremony was to take place at the church Jefferson Davis attended, St. Paul's Episcopal Church.

On her wedding day, while putting on her makeup, Miss Hetty's hand mirror fell to the floor and cracked. President Jefferson Davis sent his personal carriage and horses to take the young couple to the church, but on the way, the horses bolted, forcing the young couple to change carriages. On her way down the aisle, the bride tripped and tore the train of her wedding gown.

The couple spent their honeymoon outside Richmond, Virginia, close to General Pegram's army headquarters. Proud of his wife's beauty, he took her to his headquarters so that his troops could see the most beautiful belle of the South. Again, in his own carriage, the horses galloped into the camp, hurting a few soldiers. The omen from the wedding day held a haunting cloud over the young couple. Three weeks after the day of the wedding, the young general was killed at Hatcher's Run, February 6, 1865, dying of a chest wound.

That very same day, according to Brian Green, General Lee was given command of all the armies of the Confederacy.

General Lee sent his condolences to Mrs. Pegram via army courier:

I cannot find words to express my deep sympathy in your affliction, my sorrow at your loss as dear as your husband was to you, as necessary apparently to his country and as important to his friends, I feel assured it was best for him to go at the moment he died. His purity of character, his services to his country, and his devotion to lead prepared him for the peace and rest he now enjoys.

Truly and affectionately your friend,

R. E. Lee

Petersburg, 11 Feb '65

This cover is known as a Lee Field Letter. General Lee always put his signature at the upper right-hand corner of the envelope. Brian Green found this remarkable cover from a dealer. He located the letter by searching through the dusty archives of the Historical Society in Richmond, only three blocks from his home. The Pegram family donated the letter to the society. When Brian Green found the letter, he proceeded to meet the Pegram family and piece together the history of this cover and letter. Furthermore, he also checked a number of books on the history of that specific part of the Civil War, including *A Diary from Dixie, The Autographed Field Letters of General Robert E. Lee,* and *I Rode with Stonewall.*

Green reports that while most of the Lee Field Covers known today are in the Library of Congress, some are located in historical societies or museums, and a very few are in private hands.

An example of a Confederate patriotic cover. Patriotic covers were popular on both sides. Hand stamped "PAID 5" (from an altered U.S. 3-cent handstamp) and Lewisburg, Virginia (West Virginia) dated August 13 (1861).
(From the collection of Brian Green)

Issued by the postmaster (W. B. Payne) of Danville, Virginia, from a cut used for boot and shoe advertising.
(Courtesy of Brian Green)

Postmasters created provisional stamps until the first Confederate stamp, a 5¢ green imperforate was issued October 16, 1861, bearing the portrait of President Jefferson Davis.

From 1861 to 1862 the Confederate states issued eleven stamps. The plates of the final stamp issued in 1862 were dumped into the Congaree River by the printers Keating and Ball, who remained loyal to the South to the end.

If Confederate collecting appeals to you, you might consider joining the Confederate Stamp Alliance. Membership is $10 for the first year and $8 per year thereafter. A bimonthly journal, *The Confederate Philatelist,* comes with the membership. In addition, you become a colonel in the Confederate Stamp Alliance. This type of stamp club is highly specialized, numerically small, but most distinctive. The collecting of Confederate states is not only interesting but also rewarding, for history can come alive at your fingertips. For further details you may write to: Brian Green, c/o The Philatelic Foundation, 270 Madison Ave., New York, NY 10016.

The first stamp of the Confederacy.

A cover from the office of President Jefferson Davis, the Southern "White House."
(From the collection of Brian Green)

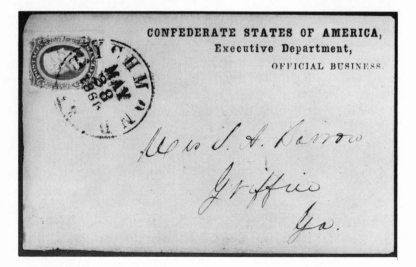

The Society of Philatelic Americans

The Southern Philatelic Association was founded February 1, 1894, by ardent young supporters of the ill-fated Confederacy who resented what they thought to be Yankee domination of organized philately. As the organization grew with members nationwide, they changed the "Southern" to "Society" and at the end of World War I, became the Society of Philatelic Americans. The only Southern hangover that remains, and makes this stamp organization most enjoyable, is that it is still small enough (about 10,000) to be "friendly." Membership includes branch chapters throughout the United States and in many foreign countries.

SERVICES OF THE SOCIETY

In addition to its annual conventions, the SPA also has an Expertizing Service, as well as a membership directory including the names and addresses of members wishing to be listed.

Also offered by the SPA is an Estate Advising Service designed to aid relatives who wish to have the best possible advice concerning the disposal of philatelic holdings. This is most important, for too often families of collectors haven't the foggiest idea of the value of a collection and, as a result, don't know where to turn without being "clipped."

Like the APS, the SPA also offers circuit books for sale through their branch chapters.

At intervals the Sales Division has a *Better Values* bulletin which features individual stamps, sets, and covers that have a retail value of $25 or more. This is a fine way to obtain the more elusive and better-valued items at good prices. It is also a top-notch way to dispose of high-valued duplicates you don't need.

SPA offers a Philatelic Photography Service because of the rapid advances in closeup photography techniques. This is a new and interesting innovation.

TAPE SLIDE PROGRAM

SPA Tape Slide programs are vast. Some seventy-eight different programs listed include "Stop Thief," "Basketball," "One Frame Exhibits," "Specialized Album Pages," "What Police Should Know About Stamps," and "Historical U.S. Material."

HANDBOOKS

The Association offers a host of handbooks, among which are *The Fournier Album of Philatelic Forgeries, Ryukyu Postal Stationery,* by M. H. Schoberlin, and *The United States One Cent Issue of 1851–1857,* by W. V. Kenwall.

SUPPLIES FOR MEMBERS ONLY

Also offered are binders for the *SPA Journal,* and supplies such as philatelic arrows which are handy for marking an important point on a stamp in your album or exhibit and are often hard to find. Quality albums and extra pages for albums are also available.

INSURANCE

The SPA also offers an insurance service with reasonable rates through the prestigious firm of Lloyd's of London.

The SPA gives you your money's worth and always greets you warmly at stamp shows or at a visit to one of its branch chapters. For details, you may write to the Society of Philatelic Americans, P.O. Box 9041, Wilmington, Delaware 19809.

The
Pony
Express

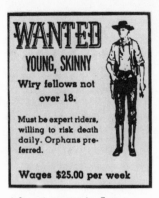

Advertisement in *San Francisco Press*, 1860.

Washington, D.C., January 27, 1860:

Have determined to establish a Pony Express to Sacramento, California commencing the 3rd of April. Time ten days.

Wm. H. Russell
(Founder of the Pony Express)

A little more than one hundred years ago, William H. Russell sent the above message to his son, John W. Russell. The freight firm of Russell, Majors & Waddell, owners of the Central Overland, California, and Pike's Peak Express, financed the Pony Express "which produced the swiftest and most daring company of post riders the world has ever known."

Mauritz Hallgren, in *All About Stamps*, wrote: "It was hoped that the Pony Express could run successfully through the plains country, over South Pass to Salt Lake City, Utah, and on to California, demonstrating the practicality of the Central route for year-round travel. This way, the owners could obtain an enlarged government mail contract and open the way for a transcontinental railway."

The Gold Rush

Once it was "Pike's Peak or Bust" (1858), the post office was not equipped to handle the huge amounts of mail that had sprung up with the development of the great western spaces. Few or no gold dust packages were carried overland by the transcontinental companies up to this time.

Until the Pony Express, regular communications to California were by way of steamer around Cape Horn. After 1885, when the railroad was completed across the Isthmus of Panama, schedules improved to the extent of a twenty-two-day service.

Express companies developed out of public demand. Workers and gold seekers were miles beyond post offices and postal routes. Furthermore, the miners needed a safe means of transporting gold. By 1859, the postmaster general produced statistics that showed it cost the post office $2,185,000 per year—producing $340,000 in postal receipts, 90 percent of which came from the steamer mail. In 1849 there was one post office in San Francisco and one in Sacramento!

One Charles P. Kimball from Bangor, Maine, had a stationery store in San Francisco. He was nicknamed "Noisy Carrier" as it was his loud, deep voice that informed all who would listen that they could give him letters destined for the East. "He forwarded letters for his clients who worked in the mining camps and charged $1.00 which he accepted in gold dust. His fee was one ounce of gold for every letter delivered, and he served more than 2,000 customers daily, clearing $1,000 per day!" said Ray S. Bloss in his book *Pony Express—The Great Gamble.*

Enterprise in a Fast Age

On February 6, 1860, a St. Louis newsletter wrote, "The horse express and riders are being placed on line for this new enterprise in this 'fast age.' "

First Pony Express Rider Out

In *The Overland Mail,* LeRoy R. Hafen describes the event that would be the beginning of a saga of "the pick of the frontier." Young men were selected for their nerve, courage, light weight, and daring. On April 3, 1860, darkness was settling down upon the little town of St. Joseph. Hafen writes, "The roar of a cannon from the express office announced the arrival of the train (The Hannibal & St. Joseph) and the inauguration of the Pony Express. Lots had been cast among the young men employed to ride the express to determine who should take the first ride. Number one fell to a young lad, 'Billy' Richardson. The bright bay mare was ready, Billy leaped into his saddle, and was off!

"The approach of the West-bound Pony Express was telegraphed ahead from Genoa, Nevada, and expectant crowds gathered to receive the first arrival."

The *Sacramento Bulletin* of April 16, 1860, reported, "It took seventy-five ponies to make one trip in 10½ days, but the last one—the little fellow who came down in the Sacramento boat this morning—had the vicarious glory of them all. He shoved a continent behind his hoofs so easily, who snuffed up sandy plains, sent lakes and mountains, prairies and forests whizzing behind him, like one great river rushing Eastwards. The bands played as though their cheeks would crack, the crowds cheered until their throats were sore. One lady tore the ribbons off her bonnet and tied them around the pony's neck. Pony Express riders made history."

The Route of the First Pony Express

Left St. Joseph	6:30 P.M.	April 3
Arrived at:		
Salt Lake City	6:30 P.M.	April 9
Carson City	2:30 P.M.	April 12
Placerville	2:00 P.M.	April 13
Sacramento	5:30 P.M.	April 13
San Francisco	1:00 P.M.	April 14

Pony Express riders made record time delivering government mail marked "rush." President Lincoln's inaugural address reached California in seven days and seventeen hours from St. Joseph, Missouri, covering the last ten miles in thirty-one minutes.

The rate per letter was $5 per half ounce. The only interruption

Fish Springs Station in Utah.
(Courtesy of Ray S. Bloss)

Pony Express cover addressed to Abraham Lincoln. Left San Francisco on August 18, 1860, and arrived at St. Joseph, Missouri, August 30.
(Courtesy of the Collectors Club of New York)

PONY EXPRESS SADDLE · MADE BY ISRAEL LANDIS' FAMOUS SADDLERY · ST JOSEPH · MISSOURI · A MODIFIED DESIGN OF THE REGULAR STOCK SADDLE USED IN THE WEST·

MOCHILA
MAIL POUCHES WERE NEVER IN USE ON THE *OVERLAND PONY EXPRESS·* TO AVOID DELAY IN CHANGING MOUNTS, A LEATHER MOCHILA WITH FOUR HARD LEATHER CANTINAS OR MAIL BOXES FASTENED TO THE SKIRT WAS THROWN OVER THE SADDLE ·· THE CANTINAS WERE LOCKED WITH SMALL PADLOCKS · THUS THE RIDER COULD CHANGE THE MOCHILA FROM ONE SADDLE TO THE OTHER AND BE AWAY WITHIN THE ALLOTTED TWO MINUTES·

MODIFIED STOCK SADDLE STRIPPED

GEORGE FRAY

The Pony Express saddle and mochila. It should be noted that the same mochila made the entire trip, being transferred from horse to horse and rider to rider. The letters were wrapped in oiled silk to protect them from moisture. (Courtesy of the Collectors Club of New York)

Facsimile of the Pony Express letter which carried the news of Abraham Lincoln's election. (Courtesy of the Collectors Club of New York)

during their glorious nineteen months in service was due to Indian uprisings. The Pony Express riders received $400 per year plus board. They carried two revolvers, a bowie knife, and a rifle. The revolvers were Navy Colts, 1851 model. This huge pistol was a five-shot, percussion-fired .36 caliber weapon, with an octagonal-shaped barrel, with the loading level omitted.

Two of the most famous riders were Buffalo Bill (Bill Cody) and Wild Bill Hickok. Bill Cody began riding when he was fifteen years old. Once, after covering a run, he found that his next relay had been killed, so he rode the 85-mile route of his dead friend and completed 322 miles without one stop.

In the main lobby of the post office in Denver, Colorado, are carved in stone the names of ten well-known Pony Express riders: Rand, Cody, Kelley, Keetley, Beatley, Haslam, James, Rising, Boulton, and Baughn. Five Pony Express riders are known to be buried in Colorado, and in the Library of the State Historical Society is one of the very rare Bibles carried by the pony riders. All of the riders received a Bible and were required to sign an oath promising that they would not drink intoxicating liquors, nor fight or quarrel with any other members of the firm. They were also required to pledge loyalty to the Union.

Ray Bloss wrote, "The Pony Express was of immense service in holding California for the Union. Messages from the State Department, from the Secretary of War, and General Scott in Washington to Governor Downey of California or General Sumner in command of troops in San Francisco bear the routing 'By telegraph to outer station, thence Pony Express.' For seventeen months this was one of the most important lines of communication."

By October 24, 1861, telegraph lines were completed between Omaha and California. Railroad mail distribution had begun, as had the Civil War, putting the remarkable Pony Express on the sidelines. The Express was a financial failure whose founders lost $200,000 on the experiment.

Yet the Pony Express opened the way for the transcontinental railway, linking East and West, and it remains a landmark in the history of the postal development of the United States. It was finally taken over by Wells, Fargo & Co., thus closing one chapter and opening another romantic saga of the fabulous Old West.

A Pony Express rider and the route.
(Courtesy of the U.S. Postal Service)

A mounted pigeon with a message tied to its leg. (From the collection of William H. Miller, Jr.)

Winged Mail Carriers

> The pigeons which convey letters are a miracle of God's almightiness which deserves to be admired and praised by us.
>
> Abul Kasim Mansur

Perhaps the first winged mail carrier was the dove Noah sent out during the Flood to see if the land was drying, for it returned with a sprig of green in its beak. The pigeon was used to convey messages by the Greeks and Romans. The photo on page 230 is from a classic Chinese painting of Soo Wu, who made use of wild geese to carry letters. Richard the Lion-Hearted used pigeons for communication with Sultan Saladin during the Siege of Acre. One of the Egyptian sultans during the twelfth century had two thousand pigeons in his messenger service.

In the nineteenth century, the powerful banker Nathan Rothschild, head of the London branch of the famous banking family, used pigeons to relay the latest stock prices for the capitals of Europe. He took great pride in purchasing birds famed for speed. It is said he received the vital news that the French were defeated at Waterloo via pigeon post. He pretended that it had been a British defeat, thereby making a killing on the stock exchange! In 1846, England used pigeon posts to carry news of her biggest racing events. The birds took 25 minutes from the Derby grounds to London. Julius Reuter, founder of the well-known *Reuter's Press*, used pigeons on his first press line.

The Great Barrier Island Pigeon Post

The Great Barrier Island pigeon post came into being as a result of the wreck in 1894 of the S.S. *Wairarapa,* a vessel bound from Sydney, Australia, to Auckland, New Zealand. There were 135 lives lost. Only

Geese carrying letters.
(Courtesy of the Directorate General of Posts, Republic of China)

a few favored envelopes, hand-stamped "saved from the wreck of the *Wairarapa,*" remained.

A year after the wreck, an excursion was organized to enable relatives to visit the graves of the *Wairarapa* dead. Auckland's *New Zealand Herald* had the problem of getting the report of the excursion for the following day's issue, and the newspaper employed pigeons to fly the news to the home office.

Mr. Walter Fricker, a pigeon fancier in Auckland, provided the pigeon post service. Ariel, a sturdy bird, carried five sheets of letter-size paper (three tissue and two ordinary sheets) from the island. Ariel thus became the forerunner of the world's most famous pigeon post.

THE MESSAGE

"Many and varied were the messages that the pigeons carried—of sadness, of gladness, or danger, of anxiety, and mere business . . ."

Who can actually comprehend an entire flight which any one of the birds made? One can only imagine the difficulties of flying through a

The wreck cover from the
ship *Wairarapa*.
(From the collection of William H.
Miller, Jr.)

blinding storm. Tossed at times almost into the surging seas of the gulf, the pigeon battled on with its precious message. Only the bird's condition as it dropped exhausted into the loft three hours later, and the fact that the other one with duplicate message did not arrive until the following day, told of its heroic determination.

Aerophilately

WILLIAM H. MILLER, JR.

You might think that to collect eight stamps issued for the pigeon post 1898–1899 would be a simple affair. Actually, it was not simple at all.

Although there are thousands of collectors attracted to airmail post, there are a select few that have attempted to collect this unusual pigeon post that lasted only a year.

One such person is William H. Miller, Jr., who has won many distinguished awards with his collection. Here are six pages from his collection of "The Great Barrier Pigeon Post."

He began collecting stamps from all over the world when he was ten. His dentist, who, too, was a collector, gave Bill a subscription to *Stamps* magazine, which Bill says he has subscribed to ever since. He found that of all the stamps, he became fond of the U.S. airmail (Scott #C–3) 24-cent Jenny. A friend gave him a cover with the Jenny. It was his first cover and one that he still keeps. This proved to be Miller's introduction to "airmail collecting" or aerophilatelists.

In high school, he did some stamp trading. He started making "want lists" before visiting dealers. While attending Harvard and Harvard Law School, he spent little time on his stamps. "Every six months or

VERTICAL PAIR
SUB-TYPES A + B

MARGINAL BLOCK OF FOUR
SUB-TYPES C + A
POSITIONS 8,9,11,12

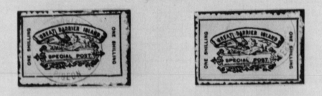

USED EXAMPLES

CANCELLATION APPEARING ON THESE
STAMPS. THE FIRST TO BE EMPLOYED,
AND USED ONLY ON THIS ISSUE.

(From the collection of William H. Miller, Jr.)

THE THIRD ISSUE
MAY 1899 PROVISIONAL

ONE SHILLING   BLUISH-GREEN
OVERPRINTED "PIGEONGRAM" IN
BLACK.   960 ISSUED.

OWING TO POST OFFICE OBJECTIONS TO THE USE OF "POST"
IN THE PRIOR ISSUES, 40 SHEETS OF THE SECOND ISSUE WERE
OVERPRINTED "PIGEONGRAM" TO CANCEL THE ORIGINAL WORDING.

CANCELLED COPY OF THE THIRD
ISSUE ON PORTION OF A FLOWN
PIGEON FORM WITH A PART OF
THE MESSAGE ON THE REVERSE.

CANCELLATION USED
ON THE STAMP ABOVE.
TYPE 3.

(From the collection of William H. Miller, Jr.)

ISSUES OF THE "ORIGINAL GREAT BARRIER
PIGEONGRAM SERVICE" FOR USE FROM MAROTIRI

PROVISIONAL ISSUE OF
AUGUST 1899

ONE SHILLING   PALE BLUE
240 ISSUED   SHEETS OF 12 (3×4)

RIGHT SHEET MARGIN COPY,
POSITION NUMBER 6 ON THE
SECOND ISSUE PRINTING.

OVERPRINT HIGHER THAN NORMAL.

THIS OVERPRINT APPEARS ON POSITION 2
(DENT IN TOP FRAMELINE AT LEFT). SINCE
THE SHEETS BEARING THIS OVERPRINT
CONSISTED OF ONLY 3 HORIZONTAL STAMPS,
IT IS BELIEVED THAT THE STEREOS OF
THE BASIC STAMPS WERE RE-ARRANGED
BEFORE THIS SPECIAL PRINTING WAS
MADE. THE OVERPRINT WAS SUBSEQUENTLY
APPLIED TO THE NEW PRINTING.

(From the collection of William H. Miller, Jr.)

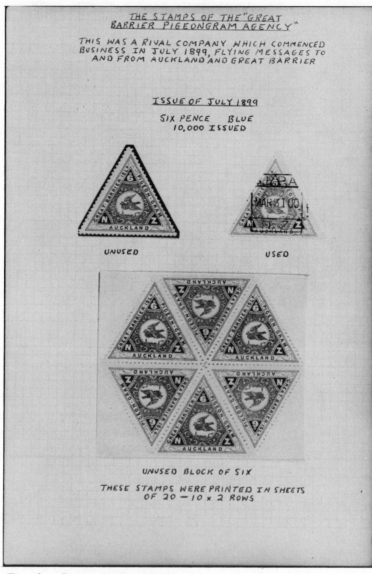

THE STAMPS OF THE "GREAT
BARRIER PIGEONGRAM AGENCY"

THIS WAS A RIVAL COMPANY WHICH COMMENCED
BUSINESS IN JULY 1899, FLYING MESSAGES TO
AND FROM AUCKLAND AND GREAT BARRIER

ISSUE OF JULY 1899

SIX PENCE   BLUE
10,000 ISSUED

UNUSED   USED

UNUSED BLOCK OF SIX

THESE STAMPS WERE PRINTED IN SHEETS
OF 20 — 10 x 2 ROWS

(From the collection of William H. Miller, Jr.)

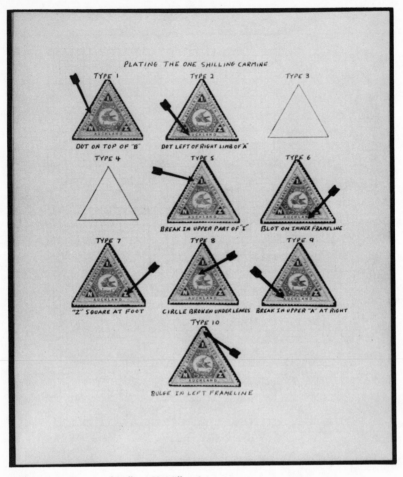

PLATING THE ONE SHILLING CARMINE

TYPE 1 — DOT ON TOP OF "B"
TYPE 2 — DOT LEFT OF RIGHT LIMB OF "A"
TYPE 3
TYPE 4
TYPE 5 — BREAK IN UPPER PART OF "I"
TYPE 6 — BLOT ON INNER FRAMELINE
TYPE 7 — "Z" SQUARE AT FOOT
TYPE 8 — CIRCLE BROKEN UNDER LEAVES
TYPE 9 — BREAK IN UPPER "A" AT RIGHT
TYPE 10 — BULGE IN LEFT FRAMELINE

(From the collection of William H. Miller, Jr.)

so, I would look at my albums. I was historically oriented. My thesis at school was on 'Legal History,' so it was only natural to apply these traits to my stamp collecting."

In 1960, while attending a stamp show, Bill met another aerophilatelist, who invited him to a meeting of the Collectors Club. He was impressed with what he heard at the meeting but felt that what he was doing was just "kid stuff" compared to the giants. Then suddenly he got "hooked," as he says, while tackling a nineteenth-century area of philately. That is how he began his elusive "Great Barrier Pigeon Post" collection.

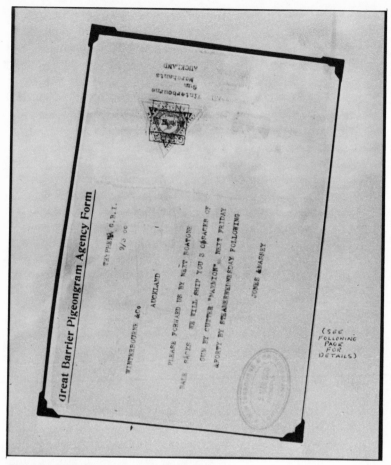

(From the collection of William H. Miller, Jr.)

William H. Miller, Jr., with young collectors at the Junior Study Unit of the Collectors Club of New York.
(Courtesy of LeRoy Wollney)

During the Franco-Prussian War, 1870–1871, the world's first airlift came into being. By the time the armistice was signed at Versailles,

Balloon Garibaldi.
(Courtesy of E. Herbert Mayer)

January 28, 1871, bringing the Siege of Paris to an end, sixty-six balloons carried 110 passengers and over 2.5 million letters out of Paris. No balloon succeeded in making the return flight. Incoming mail depended upon pigeons.

AN AERONAUT—1870

A balloon of 20 meters diameter was piloted by aeronaut M. Iglesia, and had M. Jouvencel as a passenger. The balloon ascended from the Tuileries Gardens at 11:30 A.M. on October 22, 1870, carrying 990 pounds of mail. The day was cloudy and a fast flight was made. The landing was at Quincy-Segy in occupied territory 40 kilometers from Paris at 1:30 P.M. The mail was smuggled to Provence and then forwarded. The balloon itself was smuggled to Auxerre and then shipped to Tours. The cover is addressed to "Monsieur Kobell, Lieutenant of the 36th Regiment of the Line in captivity at Königsberg, Prussia." The stamps used for prepaying this balloon letter were a pair of 20 centimes, part of a set often called the "Siege of Paris Issue."

THE SIEGE OF PARIS PIGEON POSTS

During the siege it was very difficult to get mail into Paris. The city was often without word from the outside for more than a week, and its areas were too small for balloons to float into. Because pigeons could carry a load of only about one-thirtieth of an ounce, microfilm and photomicrography provided a solution to the communication problem. These tiny microfilms were called "Pellicles." One pigeon released January 21, 1871, carried twenty-one microfilms, a total of about 60,000 dispatches. Legend says Crown Prince Frederick Charles, one of the German commanders, found one captured pigeon so beautiful that he sent it home to his mother as a pet. The bird escaped four years later and flew back to France.

A photographed newspaper transmitted by pigeon.
(Courtesy of Herbert Rosen)

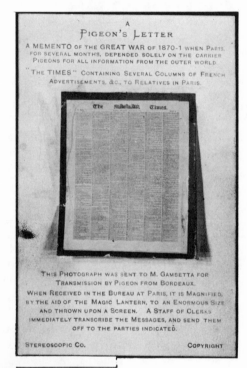

A pigeongram pellicule.
(Courtesy of Herbert Rosen)

Zeppelins

Graf Ferdinand von Zeppelin, affectionately known as "the crazy old Count," was born in Constance at the eastern tip of Baden, Germany, in 1838. When the American Civil War began, the twenty-three-year-old Graf sailed to New York. He arrived in Washington, D.C., with his own horses and a letter of introduction to President Lincoln.

When he told Lincoln that his family had been counts for generations, Lincoln replied, "No one would object to that as long as he fought well and minded his manners." Zeppelin joined the Union Army as an observer. He didn't have to use his second letter, which was an introduction to General Robert E. Lee. When he became bored with the army, he joined an expedition consisting of two Indians and two Russians to investigate the source of the Mississippi.

A few years later, it was in St. Paul, Minnesota, that Count Zeppelin took his first ride in a balloon where "it seemed to him that if the big thing could be steered and propelled somehow, it might make a better scouting device than a platoon of horses." Upon returning to Europe, he served in the Franco-Prussian War. His interest in the success of balloon flights increased so much that he began to draw up plans for a dirigible—using the idea he got from his balloon flight in St. Louis, Missouri.

The Graf Zeppelin Airmails

"The *Graf Zeppelin* was to become a legend in transportation. The awesome size of this most beautifully designed 750-foot-long airship truly was the 'King of the Airways,' " wrote Arthur Falk, author of *Hindenburg Crash Mail,* and philatelic student on zeppelin mails.

The airship was also exceedingly reliable and safe. It made thousands of scheduled flights and hundreds of ocean crossings. On its first flight to the United States in October 1928, it carried 65,714 pieces of

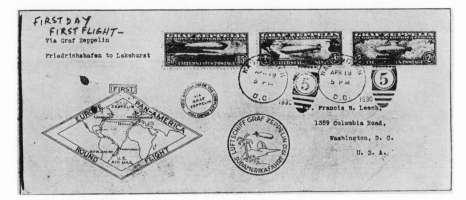

First flight and first day of issue cover—the *Graf Zeppelin*.
(Courtesy of Myron Kaller)

mail and on its return flight to Germany it brought 49,745 letters and 51,938 postal cards. It was probably the greatest mail carrier ever known. Philatelists paid more than a million dollars for zeppelin covers, thereby supporting the great airship. In 1930, the U.S. Post Office issued the now-famous U.S.A. Zeppelin airmail set. The sets were issued for use on the first European–Pan American round trip flight of the *Graf Zeppelin* in April 1930 and withdrawn from sale on June 30 of that year.

If you had walked into the post office during the month of May 1930 and purchased a set of the three values, you would have paid $4.55 for a single set. This at the time was too expensive for most people. Today all zeppelin stamps and covers are twentieth-century classics. Here are the 1977 *Scott Catalogue* values:

Scott #C–13

Single	Mint $185.	Used $110
	On cover $120	
	First-Day Cover $350	
	Block of four mint $760	Used $450

The original cost of the single stamp was 65 cents.

Scott #C–14

Single	Mint $350	Used $175
	On Cover $185	
	First-Day Cover $400	
	Block of four mint $1,450	Used $725

The original cost of the single stamp was $1.30.

Scott #C-15

Single   Mint $525   Used $285
              On cover $300
              First-Day Cover $500

All three stamps on first-day cover: $5,500.
The original cost of the stamp was $2.60.

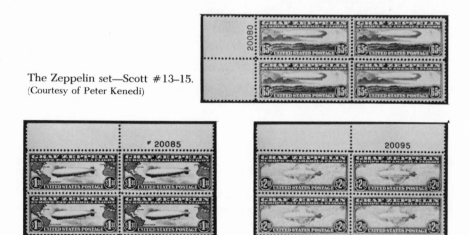

The Zeppelin set—Scott #13–15.
(Courtesy of Peter Kenedi)

Airship Drop Mail

The *Graf Zeppelin* dropped mail in many different German cities. One distinguished American zeppelin cover collector managed to obtain covers of every type from every mailbag dropped by all the zeppelins that flew over Europe. Today, "drop" cards and "drop mail" are rarities.

Cover from Moscow to Lugano, via Berlin by airmail, then to Friedrichshafen onto the London *Graf Zeppelin* flight. This is the only Russian cover known on this English flight with special English flight cachet.
(Courtesy of Ray Hofmann)

Moscow to Chicago cover.
(Courtesy of Ray Hofmann)

This Russian zeppelin cover went on the *Graf Zeppelin* to the Century of Progress Exposition in Chicago, Illinois. Ray Hofmann, its owner, in an article titled, "Flown Mail from and to the USSR," explained his prize cover: "This particular card went all the way to Chicago as endorsed by the German inscription at the top, 'Mit Luftschiff Graf Zeppelin.'" Franked with very high Russian postage of 5 rubles 75 kopecks (Scott #406, #C-20, #25, #29, and #34), it also left Moscow Post Office number 7 (11 October), passing through Berlin (12 October), making connections with Friedrichshafen for the special Chicago flight cachet, and arriving in Chicago 26 October 1933. This card is the only example known to the writer that went to the World's Fair with Russian postage.

When I asked Ray how did he ever get into specializing in Russian zeppelin and Russian airmails, he laughingly replied, "I wanted to specialize in something different and inexpensive." Since then, he has amassed one of the finest collections known in the field of Russian zeppelins and Russian airmails. He is a member of an outstanding club called the Rossica Society of Russian Philately. It embraces all phases of philately related to Russia, and has a fascinating membership, including a number of scientists, educators, and musicians.

Zeppelin collecting, especially covers, has become the "in" collecting of the seventies. Zeppelin material prices are high, but that doesn't seem to discourage this popular aspect of collecting.

From 1908 to 1910 the pioneer flights of early zeppelins dropped mail and cards in various cities. During one phase of zeppelin drop mail, a young American named John V. P. Heinmuller was a student in Switzerland. He received a souvenir card that had been carried on one of the zeppelin short flights in Germany and got "hooked."

As time went on his zeal grew. He became president of the Longines-Wittnauer Watch Co. He was to write the catalogue for all zeppelin covers, compiling a list of dates and routes. As a result of his accuracy, he came to know Count von Zeppelin, and after the count's death, Dr. Hugo Eckner and his entire crew. "When the *Graf Zeppelin* and the *Hindenburg* made their regular trips to Lakehurst, Mr. Heinmuller almost always was on hand to greet the stocky, goateed Captain Eckner. And, stepping from the gondola, Dr. Eckner invariably would ask Mr. Heinmuller first for a cigar, which evidently he had missed during the trip, and then about any new information that his watchmaker friend had discovered about Zeppelin history."

The Hindenburg

The giant zeppelin *Hindenburg* was completed in 1936. "It was designed to be the fastest and most important luxurious airship of all time," wrote Arthur Falk. "Its length of 810 feet and its volume, 8,200,000 cubic meters, gave it nearly twice the diameter of the *Graf Zeppelin*. It could fly 9,000 miles without refueling, could reach a speed of 90 miles per hour, and could hold 42,000 pounds of cargo. However, the *Hindenburg* was not filled with the desirable helium gas, but with hydrogen." The *Hindenburg* was a flying hotel.

The First North American flight, visiting the Third International Philatelic Exhibition in New York, May 9–17, 1936, was planned to coincide with the Philatelic Exhibition at the Grand Central Palace, of which Alfred Lichtenstein was chairman. He had already arranged the introduction of the "Court of Honor," obtaining exhibition frames from King George VI. This trip was most important because it was the first airmail service via zeppelin trans-Atlantic.

The dramatic end of the *Hindenburg* has been written about often. The weather was unusual the day the *Hindenburg* arrived, and many ideas of why it blew up have been advanced, most notably that static electricity caused the hydrogen to ignite.

This cover was on the fifth North American flight, sent by Alfred Lichtenstein from Basel, Switzerland, routed via the *Hindenburg* to his daughter.
(Courtesy of the Anne Boyd Lichtenstein Foundation)

The U.S. Post Office established a section for the New York Post Office unit in the airdrome of American Airlines to process incoming and outgoing mail on the *Hindenburg*. Foreman Henry J. Calsetta, who was detailed to Lakehurst for this activity, wrote a report on what happened: "Around 7 P.M. the *Hindenburg* proceeded to the field to land and about 7:20 P.M. I heard a terrible noise which shook the airdrome where I was stationed. I stepped outside of my section and to my great surprise I saw the *Hindenburg* afire.... After a short while I went to the field to see about the incoming mail but no information could be had as the heat was so intense that no one was allowed nearer than 200 feet. It appeared to me that all baggage freight and mail was burned as it was a mass of flames."

The crash of the *Hindenburg* brought to an end the development of the zeppelins. Advances in aviation made them outmoded. According to Arthur Falk, "Although the LZ130 made a few short flights before World War II, the *Hindenburg* disaster closed the final chapter on Count Graf Zeppelin's invention."

You may think such covers are unattractive, but in his listings, Mr. Falk gives covers such as the one here a value of $3,500.

A "Crash Cover," one of the 357 pieces of mail saved from the *Hindenburg* on May 6, 1937. (Courtesy of Arthur Falk)

Conquest of
the Air

Woodcut, 1482.
(Courtesy of Herbert Rosen)

The oldest known drawing of an airship, of which only a few copies survive, was published by university students in Strasbourg, 1482, only twenty-six years after Gutenberg printed his Bible.

The woodcut portrays a gondola-type vessel in which several individuals are crowded. The original size is 3½ × 5 inches and is entitled "Monopolium et societas vulgo Des liechtschiffs."

In the Beginning

The Wright Brothers, Orville and Wilbur, made the first successful airplane flight in history at Kitty Hawk, North Carolina, on Kill Devil's Hill. On December 14, 1903, Wilbur Wright rose from the earth for 3½ seconds. Today the Concorde is capable of traveling 6,600 feet in three seconds.

Sandwiched between these two amazing flight records is the history of airmail and its development in the early part of the twentieth century.

The Lone Eagle

The most spectacular flight that electrified the entire world was made by Charles A. Lindbergh across the Atlantic in a solo flight, nonstop from New York to Paris in 33 hours and 28 minutes.

At the age of twenty-four, "Lucky Lindy" was one of the young American fliers who flew the mail for the United States government.

Not many people paid much attention to those early flights, but one person who did was John P. Heinmuller. Who could have guessed that

Map of the famous Lindbergh solo flight from New York to Paris in May 1927.

Covers carried by Lindbergh on the first of his airmail flights. Author's Collection.

Lindbergh flies the mails.
(From the collection of the late John P. V. Heinmuller)

the classics of the twentieth century would be the early airmails? Heinmuller was one of the few people interested enough in Lindbergh's flight to go to Paris to be there when Lindy arrived. Lindbergh's luggage was scanty. He carried only a ham sandwich and two covers. The cover, a rarity, shown here, is one of them. It was addressed to G. J. Brandeweide who helped Lindbergh to finance the *Spirit of St. Louis*. He had also been a co-owner with Lindbergh of an airmail service.

This cover was enclosed in an outer envelope which was sent from the American Embassy where he stayed, and went by "pouch" to Mr. Brandeweide. Lindbergh was shy and did not talk much. The letter enclosed to his friend suggests that he didn't write much either.

One of the two covers Lindbergh carried on his solo flight, New York to Paris.
It is signed in the lower left corner.
(Courtesy of Al Zimmerman)

Like the few other Americans in Paris awaiting Lindbergh's arrival,
John Heinmuller went to the popular *New York Herald* office. On the
window was a notice: "4 P.M. No further word from Lindbergh. No
news from any radio station. Please do not inquire or telephone."

On the board of the French newspaper *Matin* at 6:00 P.M. was
"Airplane sighted over Kirkwall. Unidentified. Possibly Lindbergh."

By the time Heinmuller got to Le Bourget Airport, he had to walk
the last mile because the traffic was totally jammed. One hundred
thousand Frenchmen were there to witness this historic event.

"At exactly 10:21," said John Heinmuller, "I clocked the appearance
of a white plane which circled over the airfield twice." Later on Lindbergh told Heinmuller "the only reason for circling the field twice was
the many automobile lights near the landing field," which disturbed
Lindy. On the other hand, the automobile lights did give him an
indication of his altitude and that, of course, was an aid in landing
properly.

Lindbergh was more stunned than anyone at the reception of thousands of French people screaming, "He made it!" He called his plane
the *Spirit of St. Louis* and himself "we." This, too, won the hearts of
the people. He represented everyone's idea of a young American. He
had no place to stay and no baggage. Of course he stayed at the
American Embassy as a guest of the ambassador, Mr. Herrick. For a
few days, he appeared in a borrowed suit. When he returned to New
York, he received a hero's welcome that was overwhelming. He was
showered by a Wall Street ticker tape parade and greeted by thousands of admirers. On June 11, 1927, he received the Distinguished
Flying Cross.

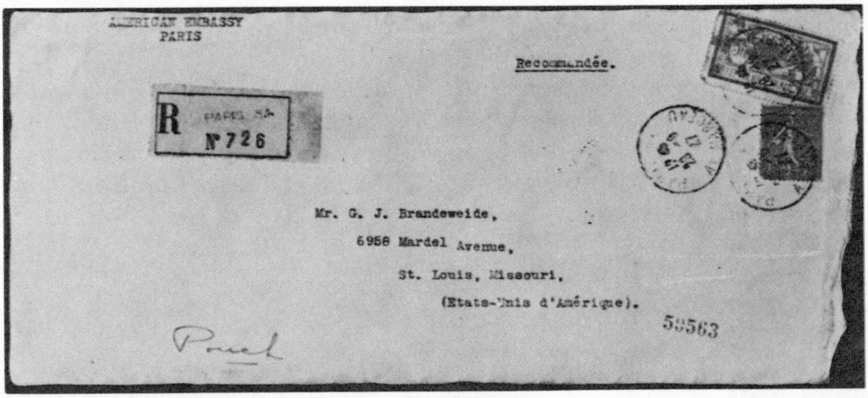

AMERICAN EMBASSY
PARIS

Recommandée.

R PARIS ..
N° 726

Mr. G. J. Brandeweide,

6958 Mardel Avenue,

St. Louis, Missouri,

(Etats-Unis d'Amérique).

59563

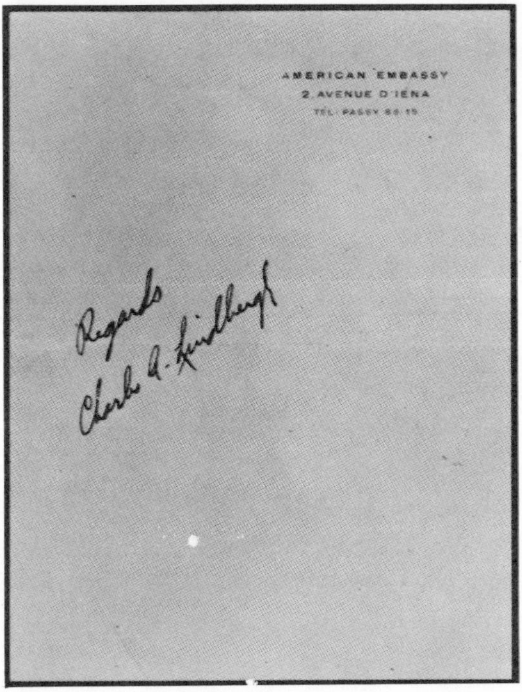

Posod

AMERICAN EMBASSY
2 AVENUE D'IÉNA
TEL. PASSY 80 15

Regards
Charles A. Lindbergh

(Cover and letter courtesy
of Al Zimmerman)

The Alcock-Brown Flight: Trans-Atlantic Air Post

Captain John Alcock and Lt. Arthur Whitten Brown in their Vickers-Vimy machine, equipped with 375-hp Rolls-Royce engines, became the first men in history to cross the Atlantic.

They left Lester's Field, St. Johns, Newfoundland, June 14, 1919, and arrived at Clifden, Ireland, June 15. They flew 1,960 miles in 16 hours, 12 minutes and won the *Daily Mail* prize of £10,000. On June

17, Capt. Alcock took the mailbag which they had carried onboard to London. The contents were postmarked June 17, 1919.

Six days later at Windsor Castle, Capt. Alcock and Lt. Brown presented King George V with the cover shown here. In addition, the king had the two heroes autograph a piece of his personal stationery. Capt. Alcock signed in the lower right the takeoff date, June 14, 1919. Under "Windsor Castle," the king wrote the date of their visit, June 21, 1919.

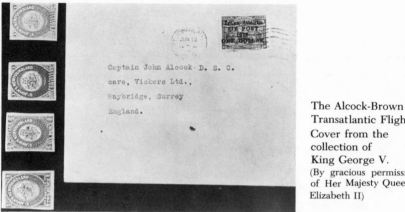

The Alcock-Brown Transatlantic Flight Cover from the collection of King George V.
(By gracious permission of Her Majesty Queen Elizabeth II)

Autographed card.
(By gracious permission of Her Majesty Queen Elizabeth II)

THE AIRMAIL STAMPS

The postmaster general of Newfoundland made arrangements so that the general mail could be carried on this trans-Atlantic flight. The total weight was limited to three pounds.

Ten thousand copies of the 15-cent Cabot issue were surcharged in four lines which read, "Trans-Atlantic Air Post, 1919, One Dollar." No person could send more than two letters. Capt. Alcock and Lt. Brown had sixty-three covers assigned to them for their use.

Amelia Earhart

Amelia Earhart, born in Atchison, Kansas, was the first woman to fly solo nonstop across the Atlantic.

This autographed cover is one of fifty she carried on her trans-Atlantic flight. She left Harbor Grace, Newfoundland, May 20, 1932, and landed the next day in Londonderry, Northern Ireland. The diamond-shaped cancel shows that she carried fifty covers on the flight, of which this is No. 37. It is addressed to one of the world's leading aviators, Bernt Balchen, who helped her organize the trip and went with her as far as Newfoundland, where she took off solo.

For a long time Amelia Earhart worked at Denison House, Boston, as a social worker. She had already taken flying lessons in California. On her days off and after hours, she would go to Squantum Field and fly. It was during this period she flew from Newfoundland to Wales in the *Friendship* to become the first woman to cross the Atlantic, June 17, 1928, with Wilmer Stutz and Lou Gordon as pilot and mechanic.

When she returned to the States, Amelia Earhart became aviation editor of a national publication. When she signed up to write a book on flying, she met and soon married the well-known publisher George Palmer Putnam.

Amelia Earhart cover.
(From the collection of the late J. P. V. Heinmuller)

Amelia Earhart.
(From the collection of the late
J. P. V. Heinmuller)

Throughout her entire career, she used her maiden name. On January 11, 1935, Amelia, now well known throughout the world, flew solo from Havana to California in 18¼ hours.

She received great honors around the world. In France, she was given the Legion of Honor, as well as receiving decorations from Belgium and Romania. New York gave her a great ticker tape parade.

In 1937 she planned an around-the-world flight in a new twin-engined Lockheed Electra which, because of all its navigation instruments, she called a "flying laboratory." In 1937 she took off for her flight around the world with Fred Noonan as her navigator and co-pilot. They went on to Puerto Rico, Venezuela, and Brazil. From Brazil they flew to Senegal, then to the Sudan, Eritrea, Ethiopia, Karachi, landing in India, June 15. The next big hop was to Thailand. John P. V. Heinmuller in his book *Man's Fight to Fly*, wrote, "It was June 20 before they got to Siam, having called at Rangoon where Miss Earhart made a $25 bet with the pilot of a Netherlands airline and won it by beating him to Bangkok." After a visit to New Guinea, they took off July 1 for the little Howland Islands, 2,556 miles away, the most difficult hop of her career.

The world knows the rest of the story. The Navy and Coast Guard picked up a weak message from Miss Earhart: "Fuel running out, position doubtful." Search parties of American warships whose planes scouted 36,000 square miles of sea within six hours failed to find her and her navigator.

(Courtesy of the Norwegian Polar Institute)

The king penguin.
(Courtesy of George T. Guzzio)

The White-Tie Aquatic Stars

This white-tie aquatic star posed for a photographer who was a member of the Norwegian-British-Swedish Antarctic Expedition in 1949–1952. Members of the American Polar Philatelists (who also issue a fascinating journal, *Icecap News*) can suggest the delight and fascination of polar exploration as philatelists.

Varied type collecting gives one a great deal of adventure, regardless if you follow just the Arctic (North Pole) or the Antarctic (South Pole) or both. There are a few collectors who are enamored of all things related to the white-tie aquatic star, the penguin.

The King penguin *(Aptenodytes patagonicus)* and the Emperor *(Aptenodytes forsteri)* are about four feet high and live mainly in Antarctica. The handsome King penguin is a perfect philatelic example of a well-centered stamp from the Falkland Islands, which lie three hundred miles east of the Straits of Magellan at the southern limit of South America. Many other species of penguins are found in the Antarctic Islands, many of whom have been company for lonely explorers.

AQUATIC CHAMPIONS

Penguins are, each and every one of them, great swimmers. They can outswim most little fish, which is their main diet. Their quill-less wings make efficient paddles and usually work alternately with rotating motion. In ages past, the penguin turned away from flight and took to the water to earn its living.

After the penguin has its dinner in the water, it returns to the edge of the ice floe about six feet above its head. It swims in close, measures the distance with a watery eye, and heads out some 30 feet. It revs up to 60 miles per hour under water. Just short of the floe, it planes upwards and becomes a hurtling aerial torpedo.

The penguin is a fearless creature, but then they encounter few enemies. The polar explorer Robert E. Scott observed, "Penguins would hop up in a group and become the appreciative audience listening to the crew of Scott's, singing."

The fetching personality of the Rockhopper penguin *(Eudyptes cristatus)* is caught in the set of stamps from Tristan da Cunha, an island in the South Atlantic Ocean midway between the Cape of Good Hope and South America—an area of just 40 square miles.

The emperor penguin and explorer.
(Courtesy of George T. Guzzio)

Rockhopper penguin and egg.
(Courtesy of George T. Guzzio)

Rockhopper penguins fishing.
(Courtesy of George T. Guzzio)

THE PENGUIN WHO WASN'T THERE

Can you detect the penguin who got ditched and never made it to the stamp?

This is such a small deviation, but to have found the penguin wasn't there was ingenious. The original postal card was evidently discovered by a well-known philatelist, Mary Ann Owens, who collects elephants on stamps. While in Switzerland, she found this card with the imprinted stamp and sent it to her penguin-collecting friend George Guzzio.

Original design for stamp.
(Courtesy of George T. Guzzio)

The imprinted stamp
without the penguin.
(Courtesy of George T. Guzzio)

Antarctica—Admiral Richard Evelyn Byrd

Expeditions, like war, are won by preparation.

Admiral Richard E. Byrd

The most famous American explorer of Antarctica was Admiral Richard E. Byrd. On November 29, 1929, Admiral Byrd flew over the South Pole with his crew, Bernt Balchen, Capt. McKinley, and Howard June, and returned to his base camp called "Little America."

The purpose of the Second Byrd Antarctic Expedition to the South Pole was "to survey unmapped regions and to perfect methods of navigation under the most difficult circumstances imaginable." Rear Admiral Byrd and his crew started out from Boston in October 1933. They reached "Little America" in January 1934.

With only a radio for a companion, Admiral Byrd and company remained at an advanced base 125 miles from the main party for six months. He did not see a living thing outside of his crew during the entire period. During this time, he kept a diary in which he wrote of his astonishment at the attitude of nations toward each other as the "folly of follies." Byrd said that unfortunately international relations were still primitive and twenty thousand years behind the civilized individual in his conduct toward his neighbor.

President Franklin D. Roosevelt, then governor of New York, presented Byrd with the Distinguished Service Medal of the state. As president, Roosevelt designed the Byrd Antarctic Expedition stamp, which Byrd signed.
(From the collection of the late J. P. V. Heinmuller)

A cover cancelled at the
Little America base, 1935.
(Courtesy of George T. Guzzio)

ADMIRAL R. E. BYRD
1933-1935

John P. V. Heinmuller, particularly interested in the instruments so necessary for the Antarctic fliers, wrote: "All direction-finding instruments are worthless at the Pole, where the longitudinal meridians of the earth converge to what must have seemed a pinpoint to Byrd and his men. Only the exactitude of time calculations enabled him to find his way back, five hundred miles each time, to the base of Little America."

Antarctic Philately

Antarctic philately covers a broad international area. The first seven nations to claim bases in the Antarctic were Argentina, Australia, Great Britain, Chile, France, New Zealand, and Norway. Following these were Belgium, Japan, South Africa, USSR, USA, Poland, Czechoslovakia, Netherlands, Romania, East Germany, and Brazil. In 1961 the Antarctic Treaty was signed, pledging peaceful uses and scientific cooperation in Antarctica.

The philatelic involvement in polar exploration can be highly specialized. The covers of specific expeditions are fascinating. Sales of polar covers often contributed to the cost of the different expeditions from various nations.

ZIP block of the Antarctic
Treaty stamp.

Russian stamp.
(Courtesy of George T. Guzzio)

Japanese *mihon* or specimen
overprint.
(Courtesy of George T. Guzzio)

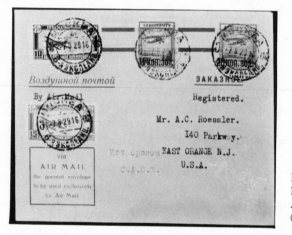

First flight polar cover from
Moscow to New York via the
Arctic Ocean.
(Courtesy of Ray Hofmann)

The first-flight polar cover that went from Moscow to New York via
the Arctic Ocean and the Bering Sea left Moscow August 7, 1929.

It was carried on a twin-motor plane called *The Land of the Soviets,*
with a crew of four. The commander and first pilot was Shestakov,
second pilot was F. Bolotov, navigator was A. Sterligov, and mechanic
was D. Fufaev. This long journey from Moscow to New York stopped
at Seward, Alaska.

Ten American covers were picked up at Seward, postmarked September 29, 1929. They were backstamped in New York City, November 2, 1929. One cover was taken on in Seattle, Washington, postmarked October 18, 1929. This accounts for the great rarity of this first
flight cover from Moscow to New York.

Registered cover from Moscow to New York World's Fair.
(Courtesy of Ray Hofmann)

This registered cover (No. 63), addressed to Grover Whalen, who was chairman of the New York World's Fair, 1939, was carried on an attempted nonstop flight from Moscow to the United States. The cover was dispatched from the Moscow Foreign Post Office on April 28, 1939, and carried aboard the aircraft *Moskva* (Moscow). The aircraft landed the same day at Miscou Island, New Brunswick, Canada, in the Gulf of St. Lawrence. All items of mail were postmarked at the Lighthouse Post Office there.

Howard Hughes

Howard Hughes sought to make a contribution to science and aviation on a grand scale and he accomplished it. Much of the progress in the field of aeronautics in the United States can be credited to him.

Hughes organized his "Round-the-World Flight" to promote the progress of aviation. In 1937, he began actual preparation, placing an order with Lockheed for a special monoplane powered by two 1,100-hp Wright Cyclone engines, each one alone capable of sustaining flight. The plane was named the *New York World's Fair 1939.*

The crew consisted of Howard Hughes, pilot; Col. Thomas F. Thurlow, co-pilot and navigator; Richard R. Stoddart, radio engineer; Harry F. Connor, navigator; and Edward Lund, flight engineer.

As a result of his around-the-world flight, Hughes invented a rubber life raft and a portable radio transmitter.

Later on, Howard Hughes and his Hughes Aircraft Co. turned out missiles including the Falcon, TOW, Phoenix, and Maverick. Most of the satellites of the COMSAT series (earth-orbiting relay stations that make possible transoceanic television transmission and telephone calls) are the result of his total attainment, blurred by the public's fascination with his Hollywood attainments which made stars out of Jean Harlow, Paul Muni, George Raft, Jane Russell, and Lana Turner. Perhaps Olivia de Havilland expressed a viewpoint he never heard, when she told the press, "I remember him with gratitude." United States aviation had progressed a staggering distance—from the Wright Brothers at Kitty Hawk to Howard Hughes and on to the conquest of space.

Howard Hughes. (Courtesy of Ray Hofmann)

Cover carried on Howard Hughes around-the-world flight, and signed by the navigator. (From the collection of the late J. P. V. Heinmuller)

NASA's space shuttle orbiter
Enterprise. (Courtesy of NASA)

The Conquest of Space

The Space Shuttle: A New Era

When the *Enterprise,* named after the "Star Trek" spaceship, became the name of the first space shuttle orbiter, a further step toward man's life in space was underway. In NASA's official space shuttle press kit, they state, "ALT [Approach Landing Test] is a series of flights with a modified Boeing 747 Shuttle Carrier Aircraft (SCA) serving as a ferry aircraft and airborne launch platform for the 67,500 kilogram (75-ton) Orbiter named the *Enterprise.*"

The great *Enterprise,* the workhorse of the space shuttle, is as big as a commercial jetliner. It is to be launched into a low earth orbit in early 1979, with its three main engines being augmented by a pair of solid rocket boosters. The orbital flight of the *Enterprise* will take place sometime in the early 1980s. Right on schedule, the rollout of the first space shuttle orbiter, *Enterprise,* OV–101, took place on September 17, 1976, at Palmdale, California.

A launch point to start a space collection could well be following the entire career of the *Enterprise.* Your first research data can easily be obtained by writing to the National Aeronautics and Space Administration's Public Relations Division. Dates of schedules, step by step, are listed. Then, too, there is the Space Unit of the American Topical Association, one of the most popular national stamp clubs, which was started in 1957 before *Sputnik I* surprised the world. The Space Unit Study Group through their bimonthly journal, *The Astrophile,* gives specific information on how to obtain official cachet covers relating to launches in all their phases. The articles by observers of space launchings are themselves collectors' items. Their space stamp and cover checklists are invaluable. Most popular are their quality space cover auctions which enable members to pick up items not too easy to locate.

The exchange between members on all ongoing space activities worldwide is another reason so many people enjoy this club.

Détente in Space

The Apollo-Soyuz Test Project joined two spacecraft—the United States's *Apollo* and the Soviet Union's *Soyuz*—for 40 hours before they returned to earth. It was the beginning of détente in space. The American astronauts and the Russian cosmonauts exchanged gifts, signed documents, took pictures, and ate dinner together on this first international space flight.

The Apollo-Soyuz flight proved that two dissimilar craft can join together in orbit. This means that astronauts from any nation who become stranded in space could conceivably be rescued by a spacecraft from any other nation.

Enterprise rollout cover.

Apollo-Soyuz first-day cover. (Courtesy of The Posthorn, Inc., New York)

Apollo-Soyuz U.S. Navy Recovery Force, Pacific cover.
(Courtesy of The Posthorn Inc., New York)

The vast aspects of space collecting include COMSAT, the United States member of the fifty-nation consortium that mans the INTELSAT network, which is a series of commercial satellites launched by NASA for the Communications Satellite Corporation (COMSAT) to form the Commercial Satellite System.

Stamp clubs exist close to space centers, and cancel covers, such as the Johnson Space Stamp Club that is close to the Johnson Space Center.

The "Fakes"

The vistas of collecting space are staggering. Where is the beginning? Historically, the Chinese were the first to experiment with rockets, around A.D. 1232. Some space philatelists specialize in unmanned space shots, including space flight tracking and data networks; others track down suborbital flights, which include Alan Shepard's, followed by the orbital flight of Col. John Glenn, Jr.

Because space is such a challenging new collecting area, it is also a sphere of serious cover "rip-offs." *A Study of "Suspect" Space Covers* (by Lester E. Winick, president of the Space Unit of the ATA, and Dr. Reuben H. Ramkissoon) is a spectacular 117-page handbook which exposes frauds in the space cover world. They present photos and detailed descriptions of genuine NASA covers and the fakes. These relate mostly to the various Apollo missions.

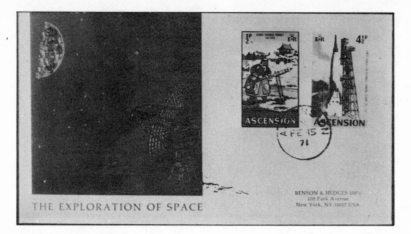

Early Chinese rocket and American manned orbital flight commemorated on stamps from Ascension.
(Courtesy of The Posthorn Inc., New York)

APOLLO 15

The most famous fraud that made newspaper headlines took place when on *Apollo 15* astronaut Al Worden carried one hundred of the "Moon Phases" covers as part of his personal preference kit. These one hundred were noted and authorized by NASA.

So much criticism resulted from the *Apollo 15* covers that NASA confiscated seventy of the one hundred covers, which are now in a safe at NASA headquarters in Washington, D.C.

It is said that some five hundred and possibly two thousand of the same cover exist, identical in all details, but not flown. At a Senate hearing on the matter, a spokesman for the U.S. Senate Committee on Aeronautical and Aerospace Science said, "We have minutely examined a flown and an unflown 'Moon Phases' cover, side by side, and could not find any differences." He continued, "Once these covers left the hands of the astronauts, there is absolutely no way of telling a flown cover from an unflown cover."

At the same time a well-known German dealer made one hundred covers which were signed by astronauts Scott, Worden, and Irwin. They are genuine and scarce.

Actually awareness of the fraudulent aspects in all of philately results from live contact with leaders in the areas one collects, always being certain that the seller allows you to have your purchase expertized, returnable if it is rejected as "not genuine." You must also be certain that the seller can be found if you should wish to return the stamp or cover. Actually by joining a group like the ATA Space Unit, you do keep up with the latest information that should keep you off the fraudulent track in the field of space. The address is: ATA Space Unit, Box 3123, Poughkeepsie, NY 12603.

When space travel becomes commonplace, these items will be as valuable as the Penny Black is now.

Apollo 15 cover flown to the moon and back and signed by astronauts Scott, Worden, and Irwin.
(Courtesy of Thomas Range)

Maritime Philately

One sphere of collecting that has infinite charm and romance, as well as a bit of nostalgia, is ships on stamps. Wolf Spille, a maritime philatelist and ship historian, is totally enthralled by the history of sailing vessels, especially passenger ships. He has won gold medals exhibiting "150 Years of Passenger Ships." In observing the public at stamp shows, one notices that his exhibit seems to create the most interest.

What makes this topical so inviting is that a good deal of material necessary to create an interesting collection is attainable on a modest budget. This includes stamps, errors, proofs, booklet panes, a variety of covers, postcards, and cancels.

In telling the story of "150 Years of Passenger Ships," Mr. Spille starts out with the 3-cent United States stamp which depicts the S.S. *Savannah,* which was built in 1819. Although the ship was stranded in 1822 in Long Island, she performed her first trans-Atlantic voyage with the aid of steam.

The S.S. *Royal William* was built in Quebec and made a trans-Atlantic crossing in 1833, almost continuously under steam. She was sold to the Spanish Navy in 1834 and renamed the *Isabel.* Mr. Spille writes of these famous voyages, and the vessels following them, that "in the next twenty years . . . the general public became convinced that steamers weren't floating teakettles in danger of blowing up and scalding the people on board to death."

In his collection covering the pioneer days is the interesting cover that was carried on the British steam packet, the S.S. *Sirius,* built in 1838 at Leith-Wood. The *Sirius* was originally built for the short Cork-London run. However, she was the first steamer to cross the Atlantic under steam alone, and to the philatelists' pleasure, the first steamer to carry trans-Atlantic mail.

The letter written within, dated April 28, 1838, from Philadelphia, is colorful: "By the time this reaches you, all England will resound with

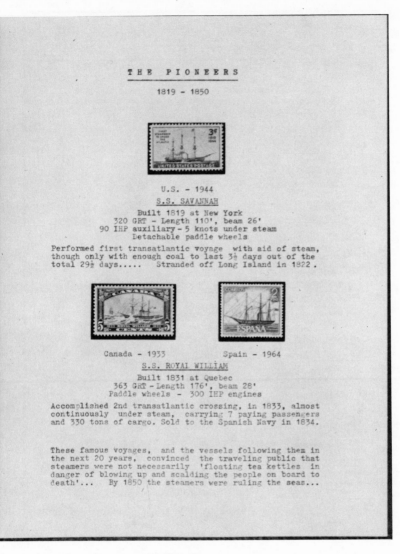

A page from the collection of Wolf Spille.

the praise of the success of the British Packet Company in their attempt to establish a line of packets from Great Britain to New York. Your famous Dr. Lardner proved on paper that the thing was impossible. Your navigators have proved by fair experiment the reverse." And on writing about the *Sirius*, he says, "The *Sirius* from London and Cork reached in perfect safety, New York, in eighteen days, for the better part. But the *Great Western* was close upon her heels. She

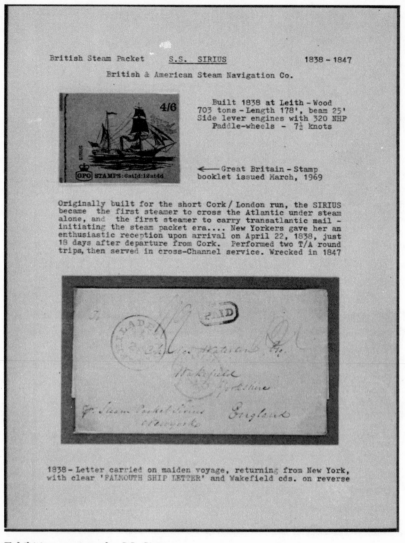

British Steam Packet   S.S. SIRIUS   1838 - 1847

British & American Steam Navigation Co.

4/6

Built 1838 at Leith - Wood
703 tons - Length 178', beam 25'
Side lever engines with 320 NHP
Paddle-wheels - 7½ knots

⟵ Great Britain - Stamp
booklet issued March, 1969

Originally built for the short Cork / London run, the SIRIUS
became the first steamer to cross the Atlantic under steam
alone, and the first steamer to carry transatlantic mail -
initiating the steam packet era.... New Yorkers gave her an
enthusiastic reception upon arrival on April 22, 1838, just
18 days after departure from Cork. Performed two T/A round
trips, then served in cross-Channel service. Wrecked in 1847

1838 - Letter carried on maiden voyage, returning from New York,
with clear 'FALMOUTH SHIP LETTER' and Wakefield cds. on reverse

Exhibition page on the S.S. *Sirius.*
(Courtesy of Wolf Spille)

arrived at New York in just fifteen days from Bristol and had nearly
got in before her precursor. Oh! What cheering, what congratulations.
The guns roared, the people shouted, all New York was mad. And well
might we have expected rejoicings, at the first prospect of a new era
in steam navigation."

In Mr. Spille's grouping, "The Last and Glorious Epoch," the page
on the passenger liner M.S. *Gripsholm,* which was renamed *Berlin,*

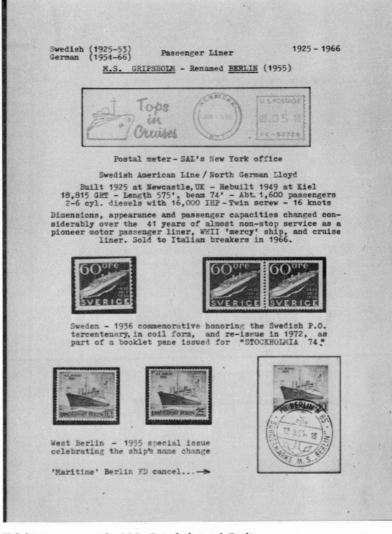

Swedish (1925-53)
German (1954-66)   Passenger Liner   1925 - 1966

M.S. GRIPSHOLM - Renamed BERLIN (1955)

Postal meter- SAL's New York office

Swedish American Line / North German Lloyd

Built 1925 at Newcastle, UK - Rebuilt 1949 at Kiel
18,815 GRT - Length 575', beam 74' - Abt. 1,600 passengers
2-6 cyl. diesels with 16,000 IHP - Twin screw - 16 knots

Dimensions, appearance and passenger capacities changed considerably over the 41 years of almost non-stop service as a
pioneer motor passenger liner, WWII 'mercy' ship, and cruise
liner. Sold to Italian breakers in 1966.

Sweden - 1936 commemorative honoring the Swedish P.O.
tercentenary, in coil form, and re-issue in 1972, as
part of a booklet pane issued for "STOCKHOLMIA '74."

West Berlin - 1955 special issue
celebrating the ship's name change

'Maritime' Berlin FD cancel...➔

Exhibition page on the M.S. *Gripsholm* and *Berlin*.
(Courtesy of Wolf Spille)

shows a "Tops in Cruises" Swedish American Line postal meter out
of the Swedish American Line's New York office. The Swedish coil
stamp issued in 1936 depicting the *Gripsholm* was reissued in 1972
as part of a booklet pane for the International Philatelic Stamp Show,
"Stockholmia," held in Sweden in 1974. Shown also are the stamps
issued by West Berlin in 1955 celebrating the ship's name change.

In the section "Famous Blue Riband Holders of the 20th Century,"

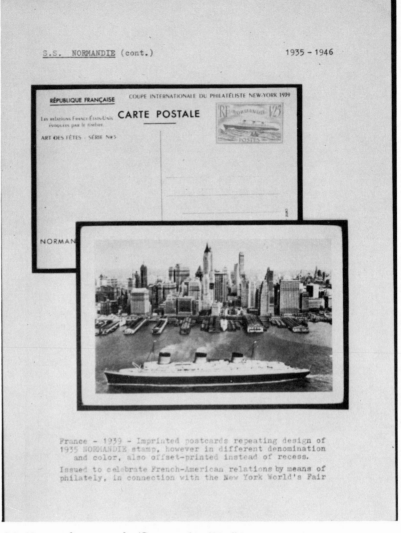

France – 1939 – Imprinted postcards repeating design of
1935 NORMANDIE stamp, however in different denomination
and color, also offset-printed instead of recess.

Issued to celebrate French-American relations by means of
philately, in connection with the New York World's Fair

S.S. *Normandie* postcards. (Courtesy of Wolf Spille)

one can identify a bit more: the S.S. *Normandie*, the S.S. *Queen Mary*,
the S.S. *United States*, and the S.S. *Queen Elizabeth*.

The Carte Postale from France shows an imprint design of the
French *Normandie* stamp which was issued to celebrate French-
American relations by means of philately in connection with the New
York World's Fair.

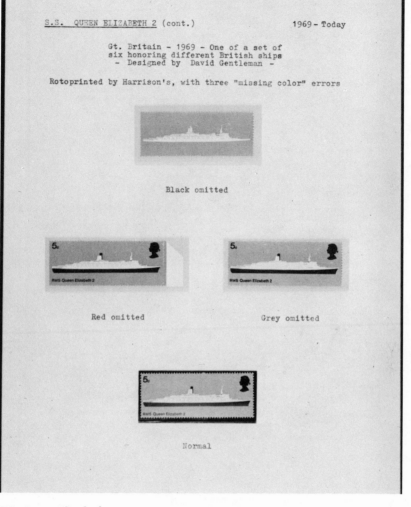

S.S. *Queen Elizabeth* errors. (Courtesy of Wolf Spille)

The final page presents missing colors on the stamp of the S.S. *Queen Elizabeth.*

To the person who might consider exhibiting, both Mr. Spille's introduction and bibliography might serve as a guide in how one gold-medal winner planned and succeeded in getting together an exhibit that is his creation and his fun with stamp collecting.

You might even consider the magnificent area of sailing ships . . . alone. This, too, is an involvement with beauty—the sail and the sea.

BIBLIOGRAPHY

Of the vast amount of books and documentary material, due to space
limitations, herewith only the most frequently consulted sources:-

Philatelic_References

(Unless otherwise indicated, various volumes from 1960s to date)

Catalogues: Periodicals:
  - Scott's   - Illustriertes Briefmarken
  - Michel   Journal (1880s-90s)
  - Stanley Gibbons   - The American Philatelist
  - Sanabria   - S.P.A. Journal
  - Berck   - Topical Time
  - Glasewald (1953)   - Watercraft Philately
  - American Stampless   - Gibbons Stamp Monthly

- Ships on Stamps, by E.W. Argyle (England, 1970-74)

Thematic_References

- The National Archives, Washington (Microfilm copies in N.Y.)
- North Atlantic Steam Navigation, H. Fry (London, 1895)
- Lives of the Liners, F.O. Braynard (New York, 1947)
- Passenger Ships of the World, E.W. Smith (Boston, 1963)
- The Engine Powered Vessel, W.A.Baker-Tre Tryckare (1965)
- The Blue Riband of the Atlantic, T. Hughes (Cambridge, 1973)

- Lloyds Register (London, various vols. 1835 to date)
- Sea Breezes (Liverpool, 1950s to date)
- Fairplay Shipping Journal (London, 1960s to date)
- Journal of Commerce (New York, 1960s to date)

Yugoslav   Panamanian   German M.S. EUROPA
M.S. ISTRA   S.S. OCEANIC   ex KUNGSHOLM (1965)
Blt. 1965 - 5634 GRT   Blt. 1965 - 27644 GRT   Blt. 1953 - 21514 GRT
426 passengers   1,200 passengers   785 passengers

St. Vincent - 1974 special issue honoring cruise ships of today

Bibliography page. (Courtesy of Wolf Spille)

Exhibiting at Stamp Shows

The road to philatelic achievement is the satisfaction and recognition for the pleasure you have in accumulating a fine collection, be it classical or topical. Newcomers are heartily welcomed. First efforts for exhibiting, usually at a local stamp show, can be a joyous surprise, when to your amazement you've won an award!

What exhibiting does is enable you to organize the best of your material. This helps you to develop a more defined want list and set higher goals for yourself. It narrows your view of what you actually need and halts your buying of unrelated material.

Some dealers study your exhibit, and over a period of time find items you more than welcome when they send them to you on approval. Once the philatelic press prints your name and award won, collectors with mutual interests begin to contact you, opening all sorts of new vistas. This is usually the point at which you join a stamp club specifically related to your collecting interests.

Stamp exhibition at the Eden Musee, 1889. Of the three stamp clubs who got together to sponsor this exhibition, the Staten Island Philatelic Society still remains. It is the oldest society of its kind in the United States.
(Courtesy of *Minkus Stamp Journal*)

A Philatelic Adjudication Sheet

The ATOZ Stamp Club was formed largely because of a deep concern and interest in setting guidelines on rules for judging exhibitions, whereby judges at stamp shows could rate every exhibit on a point system. This also enabled an exhibitor to study the judges' viewpoint on his exhibit. This way you learn where you have gained high points and, as well, become aware of your weak points. With this adjudication sheet you are able to get a report of your exhibit toward further philatelic development.

THE ATOZ PHILATELIC ADJUDICATION SHEET

PRESENTATION: 20 points

> Appearance *(check for mounting, arrangement, pattern, color, eye appeal, cleanliness, and neatness):* 12 points

> Balance *(in proportion to write-up and relative material):* 8 points

PHILATELIC KNOWLEDGE: 45 points

> Knowledge *(look for various philatelic elements used in exhibit and check the quality and amount of knowledge shown about the subject and material):* 15 points

> Information *(regarding the stamp or stamps themselves):* 15 points

> Research *(maximum points for original research; for secondary research, 4 to 10 points):* 15 points

CONDITION: 10 points *(Check cancels and centering based on the issue. Physical appearance of material based on scarcity and availability.)*

COVERAGE: 10 points *(Check if material shown is adequate to cover the story, theme, or title of the exhibit.)*

RARITY: 15 points

> Historical value *(actual scarcity of material—how often seen)*

> Collector value *(difficulty of finding the material at all)*

INTERPHIL '76, Philadelphia, Pennsylvania. International exhibitions occur in the United States once every ten years.
(Courtesy of the American Philatelic Society)

Gold Medal Topical Winner

Miss Honor R. Holland, who collected the fifty state flag stamps in a previous chapter, collects lions as a topical. By attending stamp shows, she studied the exhibitions and met many fine collectors. From this, she finally got enough courage and decided that one fine day she would try to exhibit. Even if she won nothing, it would be a challenge.

From the start she knew she wanted to create a collection that could not be completed. At least she would have something original, and she was well aware of the challenge she was encountering.

She began by going to small stamp dealers, plowing through the "penny boxes," and began to pick up either used or mint stamps to get the feel of the infinite variety of stamps her topic embraced worldwide.

She chose to develop a classical approach to a topical with the conviction that aesthetically this would be most satisfying, and philatelically what a topical should be like. She came to realize that actually every page of her exhibit could in itself contain an entire subexhibit.

When one visits a stamp exhibition for the first time, the general reaction is "How did this exhibit ever get put together?" This is exactly how she proceeded.

Honor R. Holland, president, ATOZ Stamp Club; member of Royal Philatelic Society, London; vice president, Junior Ambassadors, Inc.

List of Tools Used to Make Up Lion Exhibit

- Catalogues, both U.S. and foreign, as well as specialized catalogues
- Tongs
- Perforation gauge
- Watermark detector tray and fluid
- Mounts
- Coloraid Paper—a matte finish heavy paper in subdued pastels and gray, or brighter colors appropriate to a theme (as the pale blue used for a U.N. collection)
- Cutter—of the type usually used for photographs
- All reference material compiled
- Elmer's glue
- Acetate sheet protectors
- Paper cut to 11″ × 11½″ from local stationery store. (She has a preference for large-size pages. Many exhibitors use 8½″ × 11″, or 9″ × 12″ pages.

The Lion Exhibit's Development

To cover the subject the exhibit was divided into three parts:

   I. The real animal which included its existence in antiquity
  II. The lion as symbol
 III. The lion in heraldry

Since most of the material in the heraldic section is nineteenth century and has been researched, studied, and extensively written up, this fact had to be taken into consideration by pointing it out in the title page. Therefore the unusual material had to be looked for.

Topical information, layout of exhibit and contents described. This page must indicate the scope of the exhibit.

The text throughout has been kept to the top and bottom of the page. Where possible, information about the topic has been kept to the top of the page and philatelic information to the bottom. Identification of material was made in the text, leaving the material clear of all distractions.

Items were mounted in Hawid mounts, affixed to Coloraid and trimmed to size on a cutter. The material ready for display on a page was then stuck down in prearranged format, using a dab of Elmer's glue. The finished page was put in an acetate sheet protector anchored by a small piece of masking tape, thus enabling it to be handled without displacement.

Typing of text was done paragraph by paragraph, cut to the same width throughout, cut horizontally, and stuck down at the top and bottom of each page.

Pages $11'' \times 11\frac{1}{2}''$ were chosen to display material in an uncrowded way, numbered on peelable labels for easy handling by show volunteers and for her reference.

Layout was determined by having twelve pages or sometimes even twenty-four laid out on a large flat surface, such as the floor, bed, or table. For layouts on the floor or on a bed, use a sheet to put the pages on. This is where the critical faculties count the most. Are the items balanced? Is it top-heavy? Is there too much text? Too many covers? Too many stamps? Can the pages be interchanged without disturbing the continuity? Have the best items been chosen?

The Gir lion has an old reputation for comparative harmlessness and nowadays has become quite a tourist attraction. His dimensions are much the same as for the African race. He is stockier and sturdier than his cousins, with a bigger tail-tuft. A comparative lack of mane, which earned him the nickname "camel-tiger," is considered an adaptation to the lower altitudes of his present home. These points may be readily observed in the 1963 issue of India shown here.

Block on partial cover from Madras to New York, 1964.

India: Gir Lion. Mint stamp; used stamps, multiple on piece, postmarked item. Gift from another collector. Used to establish only genuine non-African lion.

Research is the most important ingredient. In a topical the research on the subject is one ingredient and philatelic research is the other. The two should blend and one should not overwhelm the other.

Libraries are a vast source of information. Articles from the philatelic press are important. Buy, borrow, or beg books on the subject. Compile reference material by photocopying pertinent data. Contact the authorities in the field, for they can be most helpful in eliminating unnecessary studies.

A detailed analysis must be done of each stamp. This means taking careful note of everything shown on a stamp and how it relates to the

The fables of Jean de la Fontaine always illustrate a philosophical point. He was honoured by the Republic of Niger with an issue of three stamps one of which graphically depicts the story of "The Lion and the Rat." It shows a lion in a rage at having been entangled in a net from which his strength alone could have freed him if he had gone about it the right way. A rat is shown patiently gnawing his way through the strands of the net, showing up the fact that "Patience and taking your time can accomplish more than force and rage."

Government control stamped die proof, not in colour of issue, signed by C. Durrens who designed and engraved the airmail stamp issued in November of 1972. The colours of issue were brown, turquoise green and bright purple.

La Fontaine Fable. Proof. Purchased from a stamp dealer. Used to show symbolic use of lion.

subject. A good magnifying glass is essential, however sharp one's eyes are. You'll be surprised what you will find.

The material chosen should venture into every phase of philatelic research: printing methods, perforation methods, paper, inks, postal history. Everything must be checked carefully before an item is chosen: the centering, gum, history as shown by cancellations, unusual uses of a "common" stamp. Friendships with other collectors can be most important and it is courteous to enclose a return addressed envelope with postage when one is writing for information or help.

Catalogues give a lot of basic information. If the material has been

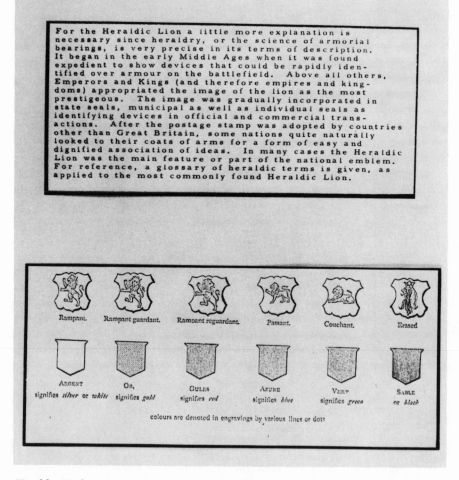

For the Heraldic Lion a little more explanation is necessary since heraldry, or the science of armorial bearings, is very precise in its terms of description. It began in the early Middle Ages when it was found expedient to show devices that could be rapidly identified over armour on the battlefield. Above all others, Emperors and Kings (and therefore empires and kingdoms) appropriated the image of the lion as the most prestigeous. The image was gradually incorporated in state seals, municipal as well as individual seals as identifying devices in official and commercial transactions. After the postage stamp was adopted by countries other than Great Britain, some nations quite naturally looked to their coats of arms for a form of easy and dignified association of ideas. In many cases the Heraldic Lion was the main feature or part of the national emblem. For reference, a glossary of heraldic terms is given, as applied to the most commonly found Heraldic Lion.

Rampant. Rampant guardant. Rampant reguardant. Passant. Couchant. Erased

Argent Or, Gules Azure Vert Sable

signifies *silver* or *white* signifies *gold* signifies *red* signifies *blue* signifies *green* or *black*

colours are denoted in engravings by various lines or dots

Heraldic Explanatory Page. Necessary to explain topic.

extensively written up and studied, resort to specialized catalogues. Apart from *Scott's,* it's good to get hold of *Minkus, Stanley Gibbons* (British), *Michel* (German), *Yvert et Tellier* (French), *Galvez* (Spain), *Bolaffi* (Italian), *Prinet* (Belgian), *Mueller* (Swiss), *Facit* (Scandinavian), *Higgins and Gage* (in English for postal stationery), *Holmes* (Canadian), etc.

Read and study exhaustively. Write down the pertinent facts, then see how it looks on an exhibit page. Rewrite to fit and until you are

According to the first Book of Ezekiel, four creatures were revealed to him all of which had sprouted wings. The Winged Lion has been traditionally associated with the Apostle Mark; subsequent founder of the Alexandrine Church, martyred and canonised. The Lion of Saint Mark was adopted by the City of Venice as a heraldic device.

Local stampless letter of 1847 showing the Lion of Saint Mark in the official seal of the "Commissario di Guerra"

Stampless Cover. Postal history. Obtained at auction.

satisfied that, although some things had to be left out, the essence and pertinent facts have been retained. This is where most of the work comes in when making up an exhibit.

Never pass up an opportunity to look at someone else's exhibit or collection. You may just find that extra stamp, a way of doing things that spurs you on, or solve a problem.

This information and technique can be applied to most exhibits, and it is a method that has been used for a prize-winning exhibit.

It was quite natural that the Lion should be chosen as a device on Tibetan stamps. Quite apart from the legend accompanying Buddhism, it is conceivable that there were lions in the Himalayas millennia ago. Adapting to the snow it would have a white coat. In heraldic terms the Tibetan Lion can be classified as Passant Guardan.

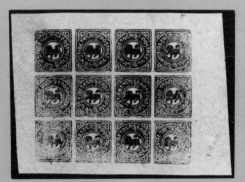

Twelve individual wooden blocks were carved and held together in a form, inked and then used for handprinting, making each stamp vary from the others. This denomination, first issued in 1912, shows a constant error in positions 6 and 7 namely "POTSAGE" instead of POSTAGE. This particular sheet shows a further error which occurs only in the last printing namely 'EOSTAGE' in position 12.

Tibet. Entire sheet with two errors. Birthday gift.
Used to establish widespread use of heraldic lion.

Timothy A. Holmes, marathon
runner and stamp collector.

Timmy's Trunk

The nonphilatelist is a peculiar bird. At least that's what I thought of
Timothy Holmes at our first meeting, which wasn't philatelic, but
rather through a mutual friend in Africa.

One fine day he mentioned that his great-grandfather, Henry Elliott, was a postmaster in the early 1870s in Canada, and his grandfather, Jabez Elliott, had been an ardent stamp collector from the age
of fifteen (1890) up to the time he died, carrying on the collection the
postmaster had begun. One day, rather shyly, Timmy mentioned, "As
a matter of fact, I have a trunk full of stamps, mint and used, lots of
covers and postal stationery, that ranges mostly in the 1870s." Those
of us listening were startled.

Timmy was the first person we had met with a trunk full of nineteenth-century classics of Canada who had never even opened the
trunk. For weeks he would bring in little batches of material to show
us. Our enthusiasm got him involved. He was pleased to discover that
some of his covers were so valuable. He kept the trunk mainly, until
he began to collect, as a sentimental possession. His mother, a Canadian, had traveled around the world, but always kept the trunk because of the tremendous admiration she had for her father who had
lovingly built up his father's early nineteenth-century Canada collection. The trunk contains bundles of queen's heads wrapped in thread,
packed by the hundreds.

Postal Stationery

Following this fan of five cancellations on Canada's first postcard,
issued in 1871, addressed to Henry Elliott, are different type cancels.

This stampless cover addressed to Henry Elliott from Coburg, Upper Canada, was cancelled October 27, 1849, and went to Darlington, Upper Canada, arriving October 27, a distance of 23 miles. The rate was 4½ pence for a collect letter. Both cancels are town cancels of the 1839 serif style.
(Courtesy of Timothy A. Holmes)

Canada's first postcard of 1871. Various type cancels and shades.
(Courtesy of Timothy A. Holmes)

The top cancel is a number (36) in a double ring or two-ring cancel denoting town of posting #38 which was Bowmanville. Following is a duplex device, town/date, in circle. (Town Toronto; date August 22; Ontario, in circle combined with a "grid killer.")

The third and fourth postcards show homemade canceling devices that were made by local postmasters. The circle in the third postcard could have been made by a cork, wood, or leather device which was

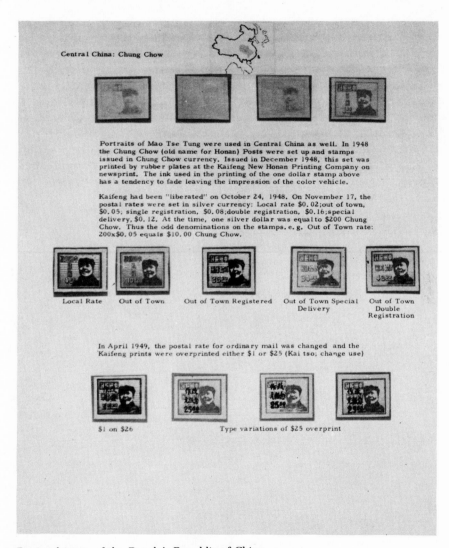

Central China: Chung Chow

Portraits of Mao Tse Tung were used in Central China as well. In 1948 the Chung Chow (old name for Honan) Posts were set up and stamps issued in Chung Chow currency. Issued in December 1948, this set was printed by rubber plates at the Kaifeng New Honan Printing Company on newsprint. The ink used in the printing of the one dollar stamp above has a tendency to fade leaving the impression of the color vehicle.

Kaifeng had been "liberated" on October 24, 1948. On November 17, the postal rates were set in silver currency: Local rate $0.02;out of town, $0.05; single registration, $0.08;double registration, $0.16;special delivery, $0.12. At the time, one silver dollar was equal to $200 Chung Chow. Thus the odd denominations on the stamps. e.g. Out of Town rate: 200x$0.05 equals $10.00 Chung Chow.

Local Rate   Out of Town   Out of Town Registered   Out of Town Special Delivery   Out of Town Double Registration

In April 1949, the postal rate for ordinary mail was changed and the Kaifeng prints were overprinted either $1 or $25 (Kai tso; change use)

$1 on $26   Type variations of $25 overprint

Regional issues of the People's Republic of China.
(From the collection of Timothy A. Holmes)

used at Cobourg, Ontario. The fourth postcard had a cork cancel used at Toronto, Ontario, and the bottom postcard is the standard cancel used by the post office, date July 5, at Bowmanville.

These are all hand cancels because machine cancels were not introduced until the 1890s. All these cards shown were used in the 1870s.

The New

Someday Timmy plans to dig into the trunk. In the meanwhile, in his leisure time, he's become a collector of Red China, one of the most popular collecting enthusiasms, particularly for the younger generation. These early stamps portraying the late Mao Tse-tung are quite difficult to find. The analysis of these elusive stamps shows that even if Timmy hasn't gone through his trunk, he has, in the amusement of enjoying his stamp-collecting friends, become a gold-medal winner with his display of early Red China. He's waiting for time to dig deeply into his family trunk, not only filled with the Canadian classics, but with a pride of owning a collection that is now a four-generation saga, from great-grandfather to grandfather to mother to son.

The United Nations

There are few, if any, stamp-issuing sources that will strike as responsive a chord, pro or con, as the United Nations is likely to do (the only entity, by the way, that is not a country but allowed to issue stamps). Born out of the ashes of World War II, the failures of the League of Nations, and perhaps with more love and goodwill of people around the world than almost any other of man's dreams, the United Nations became a stamp-issuing body in 1951 after signing an agreement with the United States. The United States Postal Service mans the U.N. Post Office in New York. In the European Office of the United Nations in Geneva, Switzerland (in the old home of the League of Nations which came to an end in 1946), the Swiss PTT runs the U.N.–Geneva Post Office.

What makes the U.N. an attractive area for the collector? Well, for one thing, it is possible to complete a collection of mint singles of the United Nations.

In the days of the League of Nations, the Swiss PTT issued special stamps—"service stamps" as they are called—for use in the Palais des Nations in Geneva. These were stamps of Switzerland overprinted "Societé des Nations Unies" and the stamps were used on the official correspondence of the League. The Swiss also issued stamps for the International Labor Organization and the Universal Postal Union in Bern, which are now agencies of the U.N., as are the International Telecommunications Union (ITU), the World Health Organization (WHO), and the World Meteorological Organization (WMO), for whom the Swiss PTT still issues special stamps. These stamps can only be used in the respective headquarters buildings of the organizations and for the most part are used on official mail. In The Hague in the Netherlands, the International Court of Justice has its own special stamps issued by the Dutch government that are available to the court for official mail (hardly ever found mint). In Paris the French PTT issues special service stamps for use by the United Nations Educational, Scientific, and Cultural Organization (UNESCO).

The stamps of the United Nations are often called "messengers of peace," for they serve to call attention to the activities, programs, problems, and solutions of the United Nations and, therefore, the world. The money derived from the sale of the stamps in New York is distributed in a complicated way. The U.N. pays the United States for each piece of mail actually sent out from the building, but it retains the money made from the sale of stamps and first-day covers to collectors, and this money can be very useful to an organization with lofty goals and empty pockets.

Stamps and subjects are chosen by the Design Committee of the U.N., made up of staff members including the head of the Postal Administration. They must select a design that will tell the story without being controversial. Furthermore, the symbols must be universally recognized, such as chains of bondage or doves of peace.

The United Nations at EXPO '67

In 1967, Canada celebrated its centennial by hosting a marvelous world exhibition in Montreal known as EXPO '67. The United Nations was invited to participate and build its own pavilion. However, the

Meeting of the Interdepartmental Design Committee for the United Nations Postal Administration.
(Courtesy of the United Nations/M. Tzovaras)

problem was one of money. In order to raise a portion of the necessary
funds, it was suggested that the U.N. issue stamps for use only in the
Pavilion of the United Nations in Canadian denominations. The subjects most obvious for the designs of the stamps were adaptations of
the decorative panels on the doors of the public entrance to the General Assembly building in New York. These doors were a gift from
Canada to the United Nations when the building was under construc-
tion. Unfortunately, the Canadians objected to the designs of the
stamps because the ladies portrayed were bare-breasted. One of the
suggestions was to add the U.N. emblem to cover their nudity; however, reason prevailed when someone noted that tens of thousands of
visitors to the U.N. had seen the ladies in all their splendor on each
and every door leading into the New York building. The stamps were
issued along with another lovely stamp depicting the Pavilion on the
United Nations. The set is an interesting one for study because of its
short usage and its variety of cancels.

Design with U.N. emblem
which was rejected.
(Courtesy of the owner)

Accepted design.
(Courtesy of the owner)

Of the many lovely issues of the United Nations, none compares with the attractiveness of the first set of definitives that went on sale in 1951. Indeed, many collectors concentrate their efforts in studying these issues, for they remained in use for many years.

First-day cover signed by Trygve Lie.

One of the most telling stamps in the grouping was a simple blue engraved issue of an adult's hand grasping the hand of a child. It symbolized as no other the exact meaning of UNICEF. It has many philatelic possibilities, and is one of the very few that has the engraver's initials on the stamp (see "S.H." on the bottom of the child's sleeve). One of the most desirable items in this collection is a first-day cover signed by the late Secretary General, Trygve Lie. His signature is itself a rarity, and adds value to the cover. It is for this reason that United Nations collectors get involved with autographs as well. They complement the collection and, because of the nature of the organization, add special meaning.

To give you an idea of what a United Nations collection can be, here are some pages from the collection of Richard E. Beresford concerning just one design: the design of the 2-cent and $1 issue of the United Nations, New York, the 10-Swiss franc issue of the United Nations, Geneva, of 1970, and a copy of the design used to commemorate the twenty-fifth anniversary of the United Nations by Brazil.

The beautiful color of the stamp issued for the high denomination of the Geneva United Nations office (SF10.00) was the result of a United Nations Design Committee meeting. One member present pointed out the blue of the British 10 shilling Machin Head definitive and suggested, "Why not this shade of blue?" And thus it was chosen.

Other items of interest to the United Nations collector are meters, first flight covers, special events, souvenir cards, and show imprints.

Issued by the United Nations
1951

Issued by the United Nations
1970

Issued by Brazil
1970

Following a world-wide contest for the first series of stamps to be issued by the United Nations, the design of J. F. Doeve of the Netherlands was selected for the 2¢ and $ 1. When designs were again being selected for the first series of stamps in Swiss denominations, this design was again picked to serve as the highest denomination of any UN stamp.

The same year that the UN 10 Swiss Francs was issued, Brazil selected this design (and color) for its commemorative issue for the 25th Anniversary of the United Nations.

The selected pages that follow tell the story and show the usage of this design that spans over 19 years.

Title page of U.N. exhibit.
(From the collection of R. E. Beresford)

10 Shilling Issue
5 March 1969

10 Francs Swiss
issued 17 April
1970

The United Nations was required to issue a 10 Franc stamp under the terms of the agreement between the UN Postal Administration and the Swiss PTT. The Design Committee selected the 2¢ $1 design of the 1951 issue. The Graphics Unit of the UN were asked to modify the design from five languages to two (French and English) and to make the necessary art work. The color was suggested by a British member of the Design Committee who had just received a copy of the new 10 Shilling British definitive. The Committee agreed to the choice of the 10 Shilling blue and this stamp along with the art work was sent to the printer of the new 10 Franc stamp - Setelipaino of Finland. The stamps were steel engraved with marginal notations of value for the Swiss postal clerks and printed on glazed paper in an initial quantity of 2,250,000.

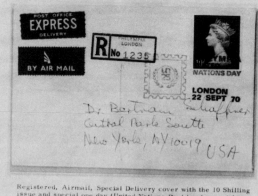

Registered, Airmail, Special Delivery cover with the 10 Shilling issue and special one day (United Nations Day) hand cancel from The International Stamp Exhibition - Philympia, 22 September 1970. Receiving New York postmark dated 24 September 1970.

How a stamp color was chosen.
(From the collection of R. E. Beresford)

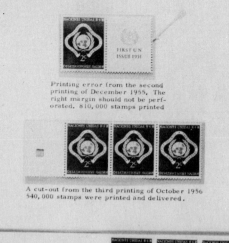

Printing error from the second
printing of December 1955. The
right margin should not be perforated. 810,000 stamps printed

A cut-out from the third printing of October 1956
540,000 stamps were printed and delivered.

Inaugural flight of American Airlines from New York to Pago Pago, Samoa
on 2 August 1970. Backstamped in Pago Pago 2 August. Stamps from first
printing of 1951.

An exhibit page showing error, first flight cover and a "cutout"—punches used
by the printer for accounting purposes which varied from printing to printing
and are a study in themselves.
(From the collection of R. E. Beresford)

Chief of the U.N. Postal Administration, Mr. Ole Hamann, with actress Kim Hunter.
(Courtesy of the United Nations)

In New York, Mr. Ole Hamann, Chief of the U.N. Postal Administration, is shown here with actress Kim Hunter. Mr. Hamann is unique in that he was one of the designers of the original issue stamps in 1951.

The Famous # 38

The key to every stamp collection is always the elusive stamp that is uncommon and hard to obtain. That is the story of the tenth anniversary souvenir sheet of the United Nations issued in 1955. This little piece of paper cost only 15 cents on the first day of issue and now

The famous U.N. souvenir sheet on a first-day cover signed by the designer.
(Courtesy of Kenneth S. August)

commands $300. There were two printings and the second issue of 50,000 makes it even more valuable.

The design was created by Claude Bottiau of France, who was on the United Nations graphic arts staff.

Human Rights Day first-day cover signed by Eleanor Roosevelt. (Courtesy of Kenneth S. August)

Human Rights and Eleanor Roosevelt

It would be impossible to mention the United Nations without mentioning Eleanor Roosevelt. When she was appointed by President Truman to the United Nations, she accepted the post with some apprehension. She was on the committee to draw up the Universal Declaration of Human Rights for the United Nations. She fought many battles against opponents and in the end, she read the Declaration to the General Assembly and received an unprecedented ovation. The United Nations celebrates Human Rights Day each December 10. In the rose garden of the United Nations Headquarters in New York, there is a bust of Mrs. Roosevelt. Over the years tourists have "polished" her nose to a bright shine as they have reached out to touch this unusual memorial.

Collectors' Items

In creating any collection, it is of interest to enhance the pages with items that are a little different, unusual, or hard to find. In addition to interesting autographs, the unusual is often created for shows or by societies. These items which seem so "available" at the time become scarce and eventually sought by collectors.

Examples of this were created by the Club of U.N. Collectors over the years. A special event cover marking the visit of the *Apollo 8* astronauts to the United Nations (occasions when the United Nations building is closed to the public, thus making that cancel more difficult

"We saw the earth the size of a quarter, and we recognized then and we reported then that there really is one world. We are all brothers. If it was a triumph at all, it was a triumph of all mankind . . . truly the United Nations is the hope of the world."

A "special event" cover marking the visit of the *Apollo 8* astronauts to the United Nations, January 10, 1969, and signed by then astronaut Frank Borman.
(Courtesy of the Club of U.N. Collectors)

Original drawing by Henrik Starcke.
(Courtesy of the Club of U.N. Collectors)

Starcke describes the concept behind this striking statue:

Just as the natural growth of a tree trunk gives promise of still greater life, the sculpture must inspire those present with the thought that the great human dream will achieve reality. The statue must clearly be a symbol of the fundamental ideals dominating the existence of the Trusteeship Council and the United Nations itself.

The same ideals dominate on smaller scale the activities of the Club of United Nations Collectors. Besides contributing to a wider appreciation of the purpose and character of the United Nations, the Club believes Mankind and Hope belong together in reality as well as in art.

Today, still less than a year old, CUNC celebrates its one thousandth member. He joins collectors from five continents of all ages and outlooks and vocations who aspire, as one U. N. stamp puts it, "To live together in peace with one another."

Bull's-eye U.N. hand cancel in souvenir folder.
(Courtesy of the Club of U.N. Collectors)

Special flight cover.
(Courtesy of the Club of
U.N. Collectors)

to find). A page from a souvenir folder, the front of which had an original drawing by Henrik Starcke (done for the club) and a beautiful "bull's-eye" hand cancel on the Starcke art stamp inside. Added to this minicollection is a special flight cover bearing the two Starcke art stamps with first-day cancel and a receiving cancel at the Copenhagen airport.

There are a number of societies dedicated to United Nations collectors. The oldest is the U.N. Philatelic Society which is made up of mostly United Nations staff members. The Club of U.N. Collectors, Box 400, Madison Square Station, New York, N.Y. 10010, we have mentioned. The United Nations Philatelists, 4114 R. Ave., Anacortes, Wash. 98221, faithfully activates "in-depth" United Nations philately. An older organization is the U.N. Study Unit, 82-63 88th Place, Glendale, N.Y. 11227.

In England, there is the U.N. Study Group-GB and another club, Friends of U.N. Philately. Others include the U.N. Collectors of Australia and UNO-Philatelie E.V., Sedanstrasse 11, D–5000, Cologne, West Germany.

An example of a U.N.
show imprint used at most
shows the U.N. attends.

And the Juniors

A young collector, Billy Mai-
sannes (age seven) fascinated
with the world of stamps.
(Courtesy of LeRoy Wollney)

We are the music makers
And we are the dreamers of dreams
Wandering by lone sea-breakers,
And sitting by desolate streams,
World-losers and world-forsakers,
On whom the pale moon gleams:
Yet we are the movers and shakers
Of the world forever it seems.
                    Arthur William Edgar
                    O'Shaughnessy

"The United Nations," wrote thirteen-year-old Jimmy Pawelczyk, "can be described only as a handful of man's dreams. Their mere colored pieces of paper carry the very idea that men dreamed long ago—world peace, not the threat of nuclear war that could destroy our planet." Thousands of other youngsters collect United Nations stamps because the story behind each stamp, such as peaceful uses of outer space, human rights, world conservation, world health, and education for progress are meaningful to them and to the future.

INJUNPEX '74

It was fitting, and a distinguished milestone in junior philately, when on July 5, 1974, the First All-Junior Stamp and Literature Exhibition (INJUNPEX) held the opening ceremonies at the United Nations. This event celebrated the fifth anniversary of the Club of U.N. Collectors which cosponsored the All-Junior exhibition with the American Philatelic Society and the United Nations.

The opening of INJUNPEX '74 at the United Nations. Capt. Charles F. Juechter, USCG, Chairman, at left; Kenneth S. August, Junior Chairman, center; Mr. George Martin, American Philatelic Society; and Mr. Ole Hamann, right, Chief of the U.N. Postal Administration.
(Courtesy of the United Nations)

The author with the founder of the Club of U.N. Collectors, R. E. Beresford, administrator, Education and Publicatons Programs, The Philatelic Foundation.

Young people have always been wonderfully curious about the world they live in and, even more so, interested in the many places that exist that are different from what they know. The world of stamps "opens the windows of their minds." In stampdom there are two schools of thought concerning junior collecting. The first is to give the kids anything, meaning torn stamps, CTOs (canceled-to-order, mostly from eastern European countries), etc., on the basis that they don't know anything anyway.

Scattered throughout the nation are teachers in schools and leaders in stamp clubs and philatelic organizations who lend their talents in concentrated efforts dedicated to encourage junior philately. These outstanding individuals support the second school of thought in recognizing the importance of education through stamp collecting.

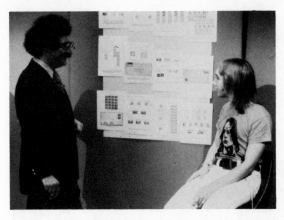

John A. Carlson, one of the junior exhibitors of INJUNPEX '74 with Gene Shalit on the NBC "Today" show.
(Courtesy of NBC)

Special souvenir card issued for INJUNPEX '74.
(Courtesy of the Club of U.N. Collectors)

The Junior Ambassadors

One such national organization is Junior Ambassadors, Inc. Their purpose is to educate juniors in a qualitative training approach to stamp collecting. Very simply put, adult advisors help juniors and the juniors help their fellow members. They work as a team and by invitation to direct teaching programs in a class within a school in cooperation with teachers, principals, and PTAs.

Young people find companionship, means of expression of their individuality, and, by virtue of the hobby, the necessity to do research and read up on history and other facts that they otherwise might not do on their own. They compete locally, nationally, and internationally with their exhibits or their writing and come in contact with as many diverse opinions and views as there are people. Some can take advantage of traveling. Others become interested in languages. The spirit of competition trains the juniors to learn to win and lose with dignity.

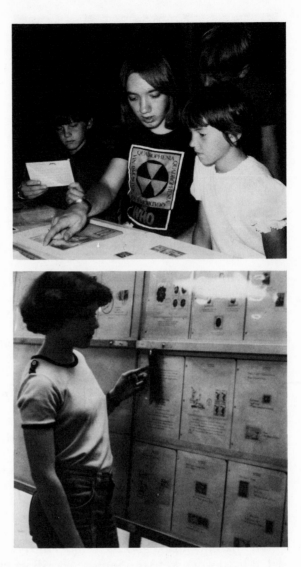

A junior workshop session.
(Courtesy of LeRoy Wollney)

Miss Jean Burger becomes
an award winner.
(Courtesy of LeRoy Wollney)

A First Family of Philately—United States

"Daddy" Sibum, president of the Pocono Philatelic Society, often says, "When I was a boy, I collected by myself. I never had any guidance, the kind my children are getting now. How I would have enjoyed it!" His daughter Vicki has been chairman of the junior shows and was appointed the youth representative of the Stamp Advisory Committee of the U.S. Bicentennial Administration, Washington, D.C. Today, at nineteen, she is a member of the Adult Advisory Board of

The Sibum family. From left to right, Herman, Sr., Libby, Bruce, Vicki, Wayne, and Herman, Jr.

Junior Ambassadors and was a charter associate member of the Collectors Club of New York.

Following in Vicki's footsteps are her three younger brothers. Only the mother doesn't collect stamps. She collects the albums and the exhibits, helps out with the typing and proofreading, and manages a feast for family and friends as they talk about stamps.

A First Family of Philately—Guadalajara, Mexico

INJUNPEX '75 was the idea of a junior, Fernando Santoscoy. He had attended INJUNPEX '74 in New York. With the sponsorship of the Federacion Mexicana de Filatelia, A.C., and the Jalisco Filatelico, A.C., he organized INJUNPEX '75 in the beautiful Federal Palace in Guadalajara. There were juniors and junior collections from all over the world. For a week, each day was a fiesta. There was a beautiful United Nations souvenir card and seven special covers and cancels for each day of the show.

The parents mixed and the juniors mixed, but through it all with a lot of hard work were the Santoscoys. All six children had a job. It was only natural that the Sibums and the Santoscoys would meet and all had in common the exhaustion and exhilaration that goes into putting together a big stamp show.

SUPPORTIVE PARENTS

One enormous factor in the bringing of the stamp world into the world of a youngster is the understanding and support of the parents. The interplay of parents becomes basic as any young collector pro-

The Santoscoy family. From left to right, Alicia, Guillermo, Luis, Mother, Martha, and Fernando. (Dr. Santoscoy, the father, and a son were gone to the market when this picture was taken.)

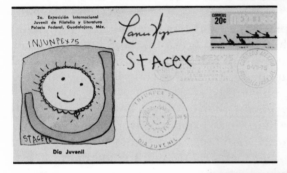

One of the INJUNPEX '75 covers. Designed by Stacey Wyman and signed by her and by her father, Lance Wyman, who designed the Mexican stamp on the cover and has designed stamps of the United States.

Two award winners, Marcela Ochoa and Alejandro Sierra, INJUNPEX '75.

gresses. One typical letter from a junior regarding attendance at a junior show says, "I'm all set to go, but only two things stand in my way: my mother and my father. My mom says I am too young to be traveling alone, and my father goes along with my mom."

The headlines in your paper about youth behavior don't present the thousands upon thousands of children and parents who are constructively growing up with love and the many traditional values of home life that are often thought to be extinct. In stamp collecting, the family can have an integrated play time that is unique.

A Father Looks at His Junior Philatelists

In the junior stamp world, every adult is the "father of . . ." or "the mother of . . ."—the juniors are the stars. How does a father react to the philatelists closest to his heart, his children? The Rev. Walter J. Brown says, "As the father of junior philatelists, the hobby provides me with both mysteries and real gratifications.

"First, the mysteries. How can a child leave socks all over his room, bring papers home from school looking like they had a narrow escape from a shredder, but get angry and frustrated if a stamp is mounted slightly off center or has the least little nick missing from a corner? How can a child who can't find her coat most of the time find the dates which cover the use of a particular canceling machine in an individual post office? How can a child forget to brush his teeth but remember and rattle off the displacements of half a dozen of the ships pictured on his stamps? I really don't understand these contradictions, but they are all true of my young philatelists.

"Though the mysteries remain, there are clear benefits for the children and for me. They are living in an expanding world which not only includes perforations, Scott numbers, cancellations, colors, dies, proofs, coils, and all the other technical nitty-gritty, but cultural, historic, economic, social, and political dimensions as well. Any country's

The Rev. Walter J. Brown with his daughter, Carey.
(Courtesy of Anne Brown)

history, heroes, and pride are displayed artistically in its philatelic production. Often economic failure due to inflation, revolution, or external political pressure is engraved and distributed on each piece of mail for all the world to see.

"Frequently now each child reports that some class in school is dealing with material which is already familiar because of the stories told by stamps.

"There is the expanding world of friends and acquaintances who share the hobby, which brings joy to the heart of a father. Like other concerned fathers, I worry about my children's social relationships and the potential negative influence of some friends. Within the associations with other collectors, both juniors and adults, there exists a wholesome warmth. These are people who are seriously concerned about worthwhile values and the emerging maturity of the young people. No parent could ask for more for their children's social development.

"As long as you don't tell anyone, particularly my children, to me stamps are stickers that one puts on an envelope to pay the freight on the mail truck. At the same time they have become a gateway to new worlds filled with challenge and excitement for my kids. So I'll gladly go to bourses, pay frame fees, drive to meetings, and support them in this adventure in any way I can. It's worth it. Where else can you both mail a letter and get an education for 13 cents?"

The Son, Paul Brown

The younger of Mr. Brown's philatelists was recently assigned by his fifth-grade teacher to present a lecture with visual aids to his class and prepare a paper to hand in on his hobby. This is what he wrote:

"Before 1840 stamps were not used to send letters. Instead of putting a postage stamp on a letter, you would take it to the post office and send it. The person receiving the letter was required to pay for it if he wanted it. It was thought to be rude if the sender paid the postage because it implied that the receiver was too poor to pay for it. In this system the post office was losing money because the receivers were not paying for some letters.

"The first stamp issued in the whole world was the English Penny Black in 1840. It was called the Penny Black because it was black and gray and was worth one penny. Pictured on this stamp is Queen Victoria. She was the only person in England who got to send letters free.

"The first official stamp issued in the United States was issued July 1, 1847. Ben Franklin's picture was chosen for this stamp

Paul Brown (right) with Mr. Ole Hamann, Chief, U.N. Postal Administration, New York.
(Courtesy of LeRoy Wollney)

PHILATELY

Mrs. Marion Evans
520 Minooka Ave.
Moosic Pa.
18507

by Paul Brown

because he was the first postmaster general of the United States. In the 130 years since then, the U.S. has issued about 2000 different stamps.

"Nowadays all countries to my knowledge issue postage stamps. Some of the countries issue so-called stamps intended only for collectors. These are stamps to watch out for because the countries who print them are just making a profit every time somebody buys one. If you see a stamp that is 3–D, made out of silver or gold foil, made like a record, or printed on a sheet of steel, then you're sure that it is a stamp that's not really a stamp. Some are a bit harder to detect because they look like real stamps. They are cancelled on the front but have never been really used on a letter because the glue on the back has not been disturbed. The worst thing about these phony stamps is that they are very attractive and so it's usually kids who get ripped off buying them. Some of the Bicentennial stamps issued around the world were phonies, and lots of kids bought them because they didn't know any better.

"Most kids collect stamps from all around the world. This helps educate children as to where countries are and what the big issues and events are that get pictured on stamps. Sometimes when a child gets a stamp from an unusual country, he gets very excited and it's a lot of fun. But after awhile when you've gotten stamps from most of the countries, it gets boring.

"A child can also learn from having a topical collection. This is a collection of one certain subject on the stamps of different countries. Some kids enjoy space on stamps, and others would like dogs or horses. But as I said before, you'd better watch out for phony stamps in these popular topics.

"Some kids would enjoy a country collection, which is a collection of the stamps, covers, and postal stationery from one country. You might choose a special country because your ancestors used to live there, or you might pick a country because it's unusual and it interests you.

"There is another kind of collection called a classical collection. In this way of collecting, you study one stamp or a series of stamps. You try to get it in all its colors, dies, different perforations, mint, used, on different envelopes, as a coil stamp, as a booklet pane, or any other form in which it comes.

"Besides these ways of collecting, there are people who like to collect other material related to the mails, like cancellations, postal stationery, postmarks, and envelopes or covers cancelled aboard ships or research vessels. Some people who like to do research write articles for stamp magazines and publish books.

"No matter what you collect, from worldwide to classicals, you will always be learning something new and you'll always be making new friends."

A Mother's View

"With regard to juniors and stamp collecting," says Anne Brown, "I am of the very firm opinion that parent involvement is most important. Of course, this is equally true of a whole variety of other areas of children's lives, from schoolwork to music to problems with the bully down the street. There is a unique joy in learning along with your child which makes some of the rigors and difficulties of parenthood a little less overwhelming. I've always liked learning along with the children in most things. If your ego can't take that posture of equality in ignorance becoming knowledge, however, you can always manage to research a little yourself, on the sly, and just ahead of the children, and then you can dazzle the little devils with your knowledge and erudition. This is sort of fun, too! They don't *have* to know that you are really only a chapter ahead of them!

"Stamp collecting in its various permutations is an ideal family activity—there are so many different ways to enjoy the hobby that every member of the family is sure to find something to interest them, even if it only involves being the cheering section (they're important, too!). Yes, you will become accustomed to stamp hinges picked up from the floor by your unwary bare feet, soaking pans of stamps in odd places, and stamps and covers and journals jumping out of drawers where you know *you* didn't put them. Whether or not the entire household gets deeply involved, it is vitally important that at least one parent be interested in the activity with the children. I have known kids who managed to become fine young collectors without interest and support from their parents, but it surely is a tough way to go. Attending stamp meetings, shows, and bourses, helping out financially with stamp acquisitions, frame fees for shows, philatelic memberships and publications, and a host of other activities supportive of the hobby and in some cases vital to its pursuit are real obstacles to a child without a parent to help.

"Our family has been pleased by the interesting friends our children have made through their stamp activities, these friends are by now all over the world because the children have been involved in junior philatelic activities for several years. The disciplines my children are learning in researching and writing are a joy to my soul, since I am unhappy about the passing superficial treatment these areas are getting in schools these days. I am additionally unimpressed with the ways in which I see many youngsters 'killing' time. Most seem to have lots of it on their hands and they are all too often destructively inventive in finding ways of filling this vacuum in their lives. Again, if you are involved in an exciting process of discovery with your children, there never seems to be a problem of filling time, and constructively at that. Stamps have provided our family with untold hours of recreation, taught our children some disciplines they wouldn't have learned otherwise, given them the opportunity to learn to win with humility and lose with grace, enabled them to travel to places they'd never have gone, and made friends they would have had no other occasion to meet. How could you possibly beat a package like that?"

Officers of the P.S. #1 Stamp Club with its president, Miss Stephanie Dinkins, in the center.
(Courtesy of LeRoy Wollney)

To Turn on Children to Learning

Throughout the country, there are teachers and some grade school principals directing stamp clubs. One such school is Public School #1 in Staten Island, New York. Robert Burger, the principal and a collector himself, set up a program for his fifth through seventh grades whose ages range from nine to twelve years. He appointed one of his teachers, Mrs. Arna Cochran, to take charge.

"As educators," he explained, "we are always looking for ways to turn on children for learning." He recognizes that stamp collecting motivates children in school studies and is especially valuable when linked up with classroom work. The stamp lessons elicit more enthusiasm for school itself.

The hobby enhances many skills. Children learn to use reference sources such as *Scott's Catalogue* and the encyclopedia. The quest for information sends children beyond a stamp catalogue to many other sources of information. Stamps strongly support the school curriculum.

> This stamp was made in 1932. He was the first president of the unitedstates His name is George Washington. He led the army to fight the British. Then he went to Mount vernon to see Martha.
>
> Mike Wronski

A short essay on a stamp, by Mike Wronski.

The Old Man from the Mountain

One of the most beloved leaders of junior philately is Ray Patton, "the old man from the mountain." For more than ten years he has nurtured and developed the juniors of the Pocono Mountain Philatelic Society in Stroudsburg, Pennsylvania. His group may well be the oldest in the United States, but the "old man from the mountain" is still the youngest friend the juniors ever had. Ray Patton is but one example of many unsung individuals worldwide who dedicate their experience wholeheartedly to the education of young people through stamp collecting.

Bruce Sibum and Ahmed El (right) with their awards at the Pocono Mountains Philatelic Society's all-junior stamp show.
(Courtesy of LeRoy Wollney)

A New Invitation to Learning

Many great people have influenced stamp collecting. Three that have been mentioned in this book, Theodore E. Steinway, Alfred Lichtenstein, and Louise Boyd Dale, would no doubt be pleased to see young people following in their footsteps.

A vast new arena of youth communication now exists where the high standards of knowledge and enjoyment are found to make a hobby of generations appear with joy, usefulness, and new leadership.

Junior philatelists and their adult supporters in major cities throughout the world have shown through stamp exhibitions, classes, school studies, and stamp clubs the potential that governments can strongly support: making the educative force of stamp collecting and its companion, writing, a totally new invitation to learning.

John H. Steinway with Paolo DeMaria, who share an interest in music and stamps.
(Courtesy of Anthony DeMaria)

Jim Craig, a junior who has graduated to associate member of the Collectors Club of New York.
(Courtesy of LeRoy Wollney)

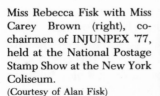

Miss Rebecca Fisk with Miss Carey Brown (right), co-chairmen of INJUNPEX '77, held at the National Postage Stamp Show at the New York Coliseum.
(Courtesy of Alan Fisk)

Printing, Ink, Paper, and Glue

The press that printed
the first stamps.

How Is a Stamp Made?

If you have ever ordered an engraved invitation or calling card,
then you are underway to understanding how a stamp becomes a
stamp.

When the first stamp was issued, it was to have certain special
qualities, qualities which have never really changed to this day: 1) Be
an obvious statement that the postage was paid and how much; 2) be
easy to account for and handle; 3) be as secure as possible from forgery
and reuse.

The firm of Perkins, Bacon, and Petch received the contract for the
first stamp and it was not as simple to produce as it sounds. Rowland
Hill's watercolor sketch was the basis for the design. However, it took
the skill of the engraver's hand to turn out the finished product. The
Perkins process of printing from engraved plates was based on the
original design being hand-engraved into soft steel, called a die. This
piece of steel or die can be worked and reworked until all the flaws
are out and all the details in. It is then treated so that it becomes
"hard." This hardened die is then used to make a transfer roll or plate.
Simply, it is a way of repeating the design over and over on the final
printing plate. The transfer roll is much like your negative for a photograph. Everything is in reverse to what will be printed. When the
transfer die is also hardened, it is used to make the plate from which
the stamps are printed. The image or picture on the plate is in reverse.

In the case of the first stamp, the design included what is still called
"machine work," a type of work in which Perkins specialized. This
fancy scrollwork was produced on a lathe, much like the kind of
machine that turns out fancy table legs. In the case of engraving, it
makes fine geometric ovals, circles, and lines which no hand, however
skilled, could hope to duplicate. This work is common on most paper

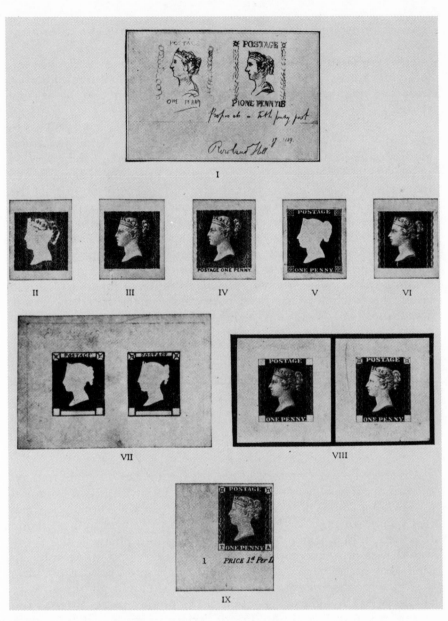

Steps in the production of the world's first stamp, the Penny
Black. Fig. I is the drawing by Sir Rowland Hill of what he
thought a stamp should look like. Figs. II through VIII are
the various engraver's steps in achieving the final postage
stamp, Fig. IX.
(Courtesy of the British Post Office)

money and is used both for the beauty aspects and also to prevent forgery.

This combination was so successful that the "Penny Black" was not forged for thirty years and when it was, the forger took a few liberties with the design and added some things that were not on the original stamp.

Once a sheet of stamps is to be printed, the steel plate is affixed to the bed of the press. In the older issues (and today's fancy invitations and stationery), the stamps were produced on simple hand-operated presses. When the plate was secure on the press, ink was applied to the surface. It was dabbed so that it would sink into the lines of the steel. Once the plate was covered with ink, the ink was removed with a squeegee so that the ink trapped in the lines remained but the surface of the plate was clean. A sheet of paper was then laid over the plate and through pressure applied to the back of the paper, the ink would be forced upwards to the paper from the plate. This process is commonly known as engraving, recess printing, or intaglio. Over the years, the machinery has been perfected and the speed increased. Sometimes "wet," really damp, sheets of paper were used and they are briefly mentioned in catalogues as "wet" and "dry" printings. The printing was done from the same plates but with a "wet" printing; the paper shrinks as it dries so the image of the stamp becomes smaller than with a dry printing. One of the best examples (and one which is a lot of fun) is the early airmails of China, which vary considerably, as they were for the most part "wet" printings.

Photogravure

Anyone who has seen a lot of pop art posters has no doubt noticed the rather large blowups of cartoon characters with bright lines and dots of color. These dots on the original cartoon were usually so small that you never noticed them—that is, your eye never noticed them. It is the common way every newspaper prints a photo. And it is the way that stamps are produced by photogravure and lithography. In photogravure, a fine line screen is used to separate a picture into little dots. A screen is exactly what it looks like—finely made screen wire or fabric. As the light or reflection of the picture passes through the screen, it is transferred into dots of various sizes: large dots for dark areas and small dots for light areas. In photogravure, the plate is like a photographic negative, and it is developed chemically so that the dots are etched into the plate as the lines were cut in the engraving plate. Again, it is these dots that hold the ink and transfer it to the paper. Both in photogravure and lithography it is possible to produce a full-color picture by breaking it down into four or more colors. Four is the usual number and the four colors consist of cyan, magenta, yellow, and black. For fancy artwork, sometimes as many as seventeen different colors may be used.

An old lithographic stone bearing the transfers of the India 1854 essays.
(Courtesy of the Royal Philatelic Society, London)

Lithography

Lithography can be summed up in two short statements. Lithography is based on the principle that oil and water don't mix. In lithography, the printing surface is above the plate, not cut into it.

All of the factors that apply to photogravure apply to lithography except that in lithography the dots in the printing are larger. The original lithography was done with stones, literally polished stones, that were treated chemically to make them like photographic plates. A line or picture laid down on this stone in a greasy way would be developed—that is, an acid solution would be applied to the plate which would be repelled by the grease but not the other areas. Thus the greasy area would be higher than the nongreasy area. Water would be laid on the stone and then an ink roller, much like a rolling pin, would be rolled across the stone. The ink would stay on the raised area and the water below. Laying a piece of paper on the surface of the stone and applying pressure would transfer the image to the paper. Toulouse-Lautrec, the famous French artist, was one of the first to use this form of printing for some of his most famous posters. (Some of these have been reproduced on stamps by engraving, no less!)

Again, this is the primitive way lithography was done, and today there are high-speed presses that roll out millions of printed pieces an hour. The metal plate has replaced the stone, and in between is a rubber blanket or roller that actually transfers the image from the plate to the paper. Lithography is cheaper than most processes and is good for long runs, like printing three billion United States Christmas stamps.

A block of Romanian stamps with the wrong stamp in the form.
(Courtesy of R. E. Beresford)

Typography

Typography is also known as letterpress. Some books you read are printed this way and you can often notice that the back of the page is marked with the feel of where the type hit the paper. If you can envision making the type a stamp design, you can see that this would be an easy way of printing. Great Britain used this process a great deal, especially for the colonial issues where the design was the same but the names changed. Romania used it as well and one of their more interesting errors occurred when they put a 25 value stamp in the form with a 5 value stamp.

The Printing Press

The United Nations, since 1951, has printed 954 million stamps. In the United States, the Bureau of Engraving and Printing produces and delivers approximately 27 billion postage stamps to over 5,300 sepa-

A "special stamp" issue. This one is printed se-tenant (two designs together). On sale for a long period of time and printed in large quantities. The same design is imprinted on two different envelopes as well. Printed in six colors on the gravure press.
(Courtesy of the U.S. Postal Service)

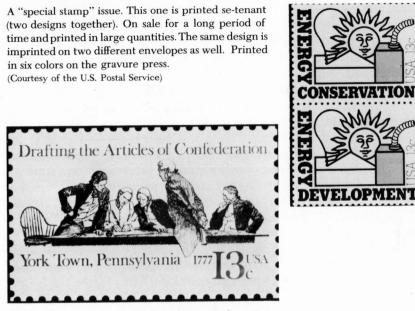

A "commemorative" stamp which is issued in a smaller quantity for a shorter period of time. This stamp was engraved in two colors and printed on tan paper.
(Courtesy of the U.S. Postal Service)

rate post offices. It also produces millions of stamps for use in the Canal Zone.

Stamp production in the United States is probably greater than anywhere else in the world. Since 1894, the Bureau of Engraving and Printing has constantly been required to produce more and more stamps as the public use of mails increased, as did the use of commemorative stamps.

The Bureau of Engraving and Printing produces six classes of stamps: regular, international airmail, special, postage due, memorial and commemorative. Regular refers to the stamps always on hand at the post office (which we call definitive issues), special refers to special delivery and seasonal stamps such as Christmas. Memorial stamps are issued to honor American statesmen (usually presidents) who die. Commemorative stamps honor events of historical importance, anniversaries, expositions, and great people. These are issued in limited quantities.

Because of the staggering quantities of stamps produced in the United States and the requirement that each and every stamp be perfect in all respects (that's what makes the errors so rare), the printing equipment is both unusual and yet represents all of the phases of the printer's art. While the United States still produces engraved stamps on a mass basis, many nations in the world do not. They have shifted over to the colorful gravure and offset processes, which delight the eye and, incidentally, sell stamps.

A few years ago a press release on the Christmas stamp came along announcing that some three billion stamps would be printed and distributed. Most of these were used on Christmas cards and were discarded and destroyed.

In September 1976, the United States Postal Service announced that the 1976 Christmas stamps would be printed on two different presses: 70 percent of the Currier and Ives issue would be printed on a new webfed eight-color combination gravure-intaglio press installed at the Bureau of Engraving and Printing, the remaining 30 percent were produced on the Andreotti press. They differed in two distinct ways: On the Andreotti press, five plate numbers would appear in the margin of the sheet of stamps and the inks used were solvent based. On the new press, the plate numbers "float," that is, they appear in different positions depending on the rotation of the printing cylinders, the margins around the stamps are different and narrower, and also the color of the stamps is slightly different due to the fact that the ink is water-based on the new press.

The press, when fully employed, is to be capable of printing regular, commemorative, or booklet stamps on a web of pregummed, coated paper, phosphor-tagging them, precanceling them and printing on the back if desired, perforating, cutting, and delivering stacks of 100 sheets.

Phosphor Coating or "Tagging"

With the advent of high-speed machines that sort mail, it was found that by applying a substance like phosphor to the face of a stamp, the mail sorters could process the mail and "face it," that is, have all the mail address and stamp up so that the stamps could be cancelled.

Many countries have experimented with phospher tagging. In Britain, there are phospher bars on the definitive stamps that can denote the class of mail (1 bar for first class, 2 bars for second, etc.). The cylinder number of the phosphor appears on some of the sheet margins and indeed the whole area of phosphor tagging is a new and fascinating field. To understand it and, moreover, see it, you must invest in an ultraviolet light and then read some of the fine publications that have appeared on the subject. With more and more countries using phosphor on their stamps, there is a lot of future in studying these issues.

Gum

Once the stamp came into being it was obvious that something would have to be used to affix it to an envelope. The solution was what we call gum, which for the most part is a simple dextrose solution. Even today, not all stamps are gummed. Brazil and the People's Republic of China are two examples of countries where not all stamps issued were necessarily gummed. The factors were in general the climate. Damp, humid air makes gummed stamps a mess to handle. Without the gum, the stamps tend to stay flat and are easier to handle.

Where stamps were not gummed, it was common to have a glue pot and brush available in the post office to affix the stamps. That is why some stamps seem to be nailed down on old covers. Usually this gum leaves a brownish tinge around the edge of the stamps.

Advances in glue and gum have been made and now there are special gums to be used in tropical climates that resist dampness to some extent. In fact, to look at the back of a stamp with this type of gum is to usually say that there is no gum there at all. It usually has a dull, if any, luster.

To make stamps more appealing, there have been attempts at flavoring the gum so that in licking them, the taste would be strawberries, mint, or many other things. The public in the main never did go along with these experiments very well and so, stamps remain tasting rather tasteless—which seems to please the public by and large.

Since World War II, a lot of fuss has been made about the gum side of a stamp with premiums being paid for stamps with "original gum and never hinged." Since stamp hinges were the only thing available in the old days prior to hingeless mounts for stamps, most of the older and more valuable stamps were hinged in albums and these tiny marks could be detected on the surface of the gum of the stamp. Many fine stamps were condemned because of this gum-no-hinge philosophy. As a result, a whole new business developed of regumming stamps to make them appear as though they had never been hinged. Some of the experts in this field are really excellent in producing a dark crackled glue of the 1880s that can fool most any collector. When it is a good stamp for good money, be sure and have it checked by reputable experts for its originality.

Paper

Ever since the first "Penny Black," the paper for stamps has had its own special characteristics. Fancy watermarks were used to prevent attempted forgery, silk and fiber threads were mixed in with the soft paper to make its imitation difficult. Depicted here is a "Dandy Roll," which is the name given to the roller that impresses a design—in this

A "dandy roll" for multiple crown watermark. (Courtesy of the Royal Philatelic Society, London)

case a crown—in the soft paper pulp just before it goes into the drying process. The design disturbs the soft fibers just enough to create the pattern—in this case the crown—when the paper dries. Held to the light, it will show through. When printed it may be seen when wet or when moistened with an agent such as lighter fluid.

The varieties of paper used for stamps are almost as endless as anything else we have discussed. The Swiss have used paper with silk threads for years, and the famous Swiss firm of Courvoisier, printers of many of the world's most beautiful stamps, use this paper for most of their issues. In Tibet, paper was made from bark and plants, giving it a soft, porous quality.

Ink

While we mention Tibet, we might add that they once printed stamps using enameled paint instead of printing ink. It was easier and on hand at the time. Ink in stamp printing also varies and great care should be taken when soaking a stamp, especially an older issue. Check to see if the stamp catalogue has anything to say about the inks. Often there will be a warning that if soaked, the ink may wash off the stamp. This is true of certain Austrian and Dutch issues for Indonesia. The basic idea was the old one—to prevent reuse of the stamps, but it does not make it easy for the collector.

With the outbreak of World War I, there was a change in printing inks, for many of them came from Germany. Fugitive inks have been used and aniline inks, inks which penetrate the very paper on which the stamp is printed. Fugitive inks are those that will run or wash off.

Inks can have phosphorescent qualities which will also show up under the ultraviolet light. These glowing qualities can help you discover various printings of a stamp that by eye you might not be able to detect.

Again, with inks, paper, glue, and methods of printing, many books and studies have been written on almost all facets of stamp production and even certain issues.

The Bureau Specialist issued monthly by the Bureau Issues Association is one fine place to start learning about American stamps and their production. For information, write to: Bureau Issues Association, 19 Maple Street, Arlington, Maine 02174.

The Universal Postal Union

The most harmonious, functional, and international operation in existence is the Universal Postal Union. It is so successful yet hardly anyone knows about it.

In 1862 Abraham Lincoln's postmaster, Montgomery Blair, sent a circular letter to all countries with which the United States had diplomatic relations. In it he wrote, "Many embarrassments to foreign correspondents exist which can be remedied only by internationally concerted action."

A postal clerk in his own country could pick out denominations of stamps by their color with ease. That's why, in fact, different colors were chosen. When looking at a foreign stamp, however, he was confused. There was no uniformity of color or uniformity of rates. In 1868 the U.S. Post Office published a "Table of Postage Rates to Foreign Countries" that included 540 different basic rates. Dr. Heinrich von Stephan, postmaster of the North German Confederation, recognized what he termed "intolerable confusion, worse yet, a state of veritable chaos." In 1874 he brought together delegates of twenty-one nations at Berne, Switzerland, and out of this came the foundations of the Universal Postal Union. By 1885 membership included 86 countries and by 1900 there were 113 nations. Today the UPU includes the entire world. It's a rare specialized agency in the United Nations in which there is no turmoil. It is a remarkable, simplistic touch that nations of the world *can* get together for a common good. Perhaps it is the love for the magic of a stamp that allows it to be the conduit of success in international cooperation—an interesting thought to contemplate as you receive a letter from any part of the world.

Recommended Reading

Useful Handbooks

Foundations of Philately by Winthrop S. Boggs, D. Van Nostrand Co. Inc. 1942.

Linn's World Stamp Almanac—how to order stamps, identifying stamps, museums and libraries, stamp production, stamp laws, the world's stamp clubs, philatelic literature, and postal history. Compiled and edited by the staff of *Linn's Stamp News,* published annually by Amos Press, P.O. Box 29, Sidney, Ohio 45365.

Stamp Collectors Guide Handbook by Samuel Grossman, Bonanza Books, Division of Crown Publishing, 1957.

Stamp Collectors Encyclopedia by R. J. Sutton, Revised Edition, Bonanza Books, Division of Crown Publishing, 1971.

Standard Handbook of Stamp Collecting by Richard McP. Cabeen, Thomas Y. Crowell, 1957.

United States Stamps and Stories edited and published for the United States Postal Service by Scott Publishing, 1972.

Overall Introductions to Stamp Collecting

Collecting Postal History: Postmarks, Cards and Covers by Prince Dimitry Kandrouroff, Larousse & Co. New York, 1973.

Illustrated Encyclopedia of Stamp Collecting by Otto Hornung, published by Hamlyn, London, 1970.

Philately and Postal History—An Introduction by Col. Leonard H. Smith, Jr., published by N. H. Smith, Clearwater, Florida 1970.

Stamp Collecting, Stanley Phillips, published by Stanley Gibbons, London 1972.

Stamp Collectors Guide to Europe by Jon L. Allen and Paul H. Silverstone, ARCO Publishing Co., N.Y. 1974.

Bibliography

Age of Faith by Ann Fremantle and the editors of Time-Life Books (from the Great Ages of Man Series, published by Time-Life Books, 1965).

All About Horses by John Elsey, European Review column in *Stamp Collector*, August 7, 1976.

All About Stamps by Mauritz Hallgren (Alfred A. Knopf, 1940).

Ancient America by Jonathan Norton Leonardo and the editors of Time-Life Books (from the Great Ages of Man Series, published by Time-Life Books, 1967).

An Informal History of the Collectors Club by William W. Wylie, reprinted from the *ANPHILEX Catalogue*, 1971.

Aristocrats of Philately by Dr. Norman Hubbard, INTERPHIL '76 catalogue, 1976.

Around the World by Elizabeth and Klaus Gemming (Barre Publishers, 1968).

Art Nouveau (National Postal Museum bulletin, London).

Background to Philately by Leslie R. Roy and B. Rodgers Tillstone (Blanford Press, London, 1953).

Benjamin Franklin by Beatrice Hessel, *Minkus Stamp Journal*, Vol. IX, No. 2, 1976.

Bookletry by John Caffrey, *APS Journal*, April 1976.

British Elizabethan Stamps by David Potter (B. T. Batsford, Ltd., London, 1971).

British Postage Stamps by John Easton (Faber & Faber, Ltd., London, 1953).

British Postage Stamps of the Nineteenth Century by Robson Lowe (National Postal Museum, London, 1968).

Castiglione and Chinese Art by Warren M. S. Yang, *Minkus Stamp Journal*, Vol. VIII, No. 1, 1973.

A Child's World of Stamps by Mildred Dupree (Parents Magazine Press, N.Y., 1973).

China Directorate General of Posts, Philatelic Bulletin, No. 23, 1971.

Collecting Postal History: Postmarks, Cards and Covers by Prince Dimitry Kandaouroff (Postal Covers, Box 26, Brewster, N.Y. 1973).

Collecting Stamps for Fun and Profit by Frederick Collins (P. D. Appleton Century Co., 1936).

Color Treasury of Stamp Collecting by Uberto Tosco (Crescent, Div. of Crown Publishers, 1972).

Essays and Proofs of British North America by Kenneth Minuse and Robert

H. Pratt (Essay and Proof Society of North America).

The Fabulous Ferrari, by Gustav Detjen, Jr., *Stamp World* reprint.

The Fine Art Stamps of France, edited by Pierre de Brimont (*Historical Album,* published by P. Ruinart, Rue des Terraux, Lausanne, Switzerland, 1964).

Foundations of Philately by Winthrop S. Boggs (D. Van Nostrand Co., Inc., 1962).

Harris Stamp Collectors Guide and Companion, published annually by H. E. Harris & Co., Inc., Boston, Mass.

The Hindenburg by Michael Macdonald Mooney (Dodd, Mead, 1972).

Hindenburg Crash Mail: The Search Goes On by Arthur Falk.

The History of the Letter: From the Late Middle Ages by Ludwig von Bertalanffy. *Postal History Journal* (reprint), January 1973, Vol. XVII, No. 33.

How to Prepare Stamp Exhibits by C. E. Foster (The New Mexico Philatelic Association).

Illustrated Encyclopedia of Stamp Collecting by Otto Hornung (Hamlyn, London, 1970).

Journal of the Rossica Society of Russian Philately, No. 82, 1972.

The King's Stamps by A. G. Rigo de Righi and Alain de Cadenet (National Postal Museum, London).

La Poste (Dans Les Temps Anciens et Modernes) by Paul Gerherd Heurgren (Stockholm, Sweden, 1924).

Last Two Million Years (Reader's Digest Association, 1973).

The Letter Box by Jean Young Farrugia (Centaur Press, Fontwell, Sussex, England, 1969).

The Life of Mozart by Hans Conrad Fischer and Lutz Besch (Macmillan, 1969).

Man's Fight to Fly by John P. V. Heinmuller (Funk & Wagnalls, 1944).

The Medieval Machine: The Industrial Revolution of the Middle Ages by Jean Gimpel (Holt, Rinehart & Winston, 1976).

NASA Space Shuttle Kit, Release #77–16, NASA, Washington, D.C.

Newfoundland Airmails, 1919–1939 by R. E. R. Dalwick and C. H. C. Harmer (H. R. Harmer, Ltd., London, 1933).

New Zealand: The Great Barrier Islands (1898–1899) Pigeon Post Stamp by P. J. Reg Walker, H. L. Chisholm, H. M. Goodkind (Collector's Club Handbook, 1969).

Old Post Bags by Alvin Harlow (D. Appleton & Co., 1928).

The Origin of Posts: Italy, Early 15th Century by Ludwig von Bertalanffy. Supplement to *The Philatelist and Postal Historian* (December 1962).

The Overland Mails by LeRoy R. Hafen (Arthur H. Clark Co., Glendale, Calif., 1926).

Pageant of Civilization as Told by Postage Stamps by F. B. Warren (The Century Co., New York, 1926).

The Paper Chase by Alvin F. Harlow (Henry Holt, 1940).

Paper Gold by Karl Wagenheim (Peter H. Wyden, 1976).

People and Pianos by Theodore E. Steinway (Steinway & Sons, 1961).

Perforated Insignia by Floyd A. Walker, *Collectors Club Philatelist,* November 1975.

Philatelic Terms Illustrated by Russell Bennett and James Watson (Stanley Gibbons, Ltd., London, 1972).

Philately and Postal History by Col. Leonard H. Smith, Jr. (N. H. Smith, Clearwater, Florida, 1970).

Pictorial Treasury of U.S. Stamps (Collector's Institute, Ltd., Omaha, Nebraska, 1974).

Pigeon Posts—New Zealand—The Great Barrier Islands—1898–1899 by J. Reg Walker (Collector's Club Handbook, 1968).

Political Campaign Covers by Barbara Mueller, *Minkus Stamp Journal*, Vol. VII, No. 4, 1972.

The Pony Express and How It Saved the Union (State Historical Society of Colorado, 1960).

Pony Express: The Great Gamble by Roy S. Bloss (Howell–North Press, Berkeley, California, 1959).

Postage Stamps and Postal History of Newfoundland by Winthrop S. Boggs (Quarterman Publications, Inc., Lawrence, Mass., 1974).

Postal History Primer by Calvet Hahn (Calvet Hahn, New York, New York, 1975).

Postillion to Prince by Sonia Krivenko, *Topical Time*, March–April 1967.

The Queen's Jewelry by Sheila Young (Taplinger Publishing Co., New York, 1969).

Rocket Mail Catalogue by Ellington and Zwisler (published by John W. Nicklin, distributed by Perry Zwisler, Holyoke, Mass., 1967).

The Romance of Stamp Collecting by Ernest A. Kehr (Thomas Y. Crowell Company, Inc., 1947).

Royal Mail by F. George Kay (Rockliff Publishing Corp., Ltd., London, 1951).

Royal Philatelic Society, London, 1869–1969 (printed by Robert Maclehose & Co., Ltd., for the Society; the University Press, Glasgow, 1969).

So You Want to Invest in Stamps by C. Ellis Millbury (The Hobson Book Press, 1945).

Space Topics, A Study of Suspect Space Covers by Dr. Reuben A. Ramkisson and Lester C. Winick, *Astrophile Supplement*, January 1975.

Speedy: A History of U.S. Special Delivery by Henry M. Gobie (published by Wilhelmina M. Gobie, distributed by David G. Phelps, North Miami Beach, Florida, 1976).

Stamp Collecting by Stanley Phillips (Stanley Gibbons, Ltd., London, 1972).

Stamp Collectors Encyclopedia by R. J. Sutton, Revised Edition (Bonanza Books, Div. of Crown Publishing, Inc., 1971).

Stamp Collectors Guide to Europe by Jon B. Allen and Paul H. Silverstein (Arco Publishing Co., New York, N.Y. 1974).

Stamp Collectors Handbook by Samuel Grossman (Longacre Publishing Co., New York, 1973).

Stamps and Music by James Watson (Faber & Faber, London, 1962).

Standard Handbook of Stamp Collecting by Richard McP. Cabeen (Thomas Y. Crowell Company, New York, 1957).

Techniques of Philately by L. and M. Williams (Heinemann, London, 1969).

These Stones Will Shout by Mark Link, S. J. (Argus Communications, Niles, Ill., 1975).

U.S.: The 24¢ Airmail Inverted Center, 1918 by Henry M. Goodkind, Collector's Club Handbook, 1956.

Washington Report by Belmont Faries. *Minkus Stamp Journal,* Vol. XI, No. 3, 1976.

Weill's Deal in the World's Rarest of Stamps, Smithsonian Magazine, January 1973.

The World of Art by Elizabeth and Klaus Gemming (Barre Publishers, Barre, Mass., 1968).

The Year of the Rose by R. C. Balfour (*Illustrated London News* for the Royal National Rose Society, 1976).

Acknowledgments

Her Majesty Queen Elizabeth II for graciously permitting illustrations from The Royal Philatelic Collection; His Serene Highness Prince Rainier III who graciously wrote the introduction and granted permission to illustrate certain items from his private collection; John C. Marriott, Keeper of the Royal Philatelic Collection of Her Majesty Queen Elizabeth II; H. G. Rigo de Righi, Curator, National Postal Museum, London, for his valuable assistance as well as illustrations; H. Chiavassa, Director of Posts, Monaco, for his kind help and generous assistance; Y. C. Shih, Director of Posts, Directorate General of Posts, Republic of China.

Bernard D. Harmer, President, Harmers International. His assistance was invaluable. His excellent staff, especially Keith A. Harmer, Christopher R. Harmer, Alison M. Harmer, Meme Schwarts and Emily Odell, provided illustrations, checked philatelic data, as well as making major contacts throughout the philatelic world. Harrison D. S. Haverbeck, a veritable encyclopedia of knowledge, who flawlessly answered hundreds of questions with patience and friendship; E. Herbert Mayer, for lending material from his postal history collection on military history.

Robert P. Odenweller for his learned and informative section on "Creating a Classic Collection," his description of the work of The Philatelic Foundation, and his expertise in the proofreading of this book; Robert H. Pratt, for his illustrations and descriptions of the Newfoundland proofs; John Steinway, for his material on his distinguished father's collection, as well as his store of interesting stories relating to Theodore E. Steinway; Fred Faulstich for lending material from the collection of the noted postal historian Edith Faulstich; James T. De Voss, Executive Secretary, American Philatelic Society, for information and illustrations; Gustav Detjen, Jr., Executive of the Franklin D. Roosevelt Society, for material on Franklin D. Roosevelt.

Special thanks to the Collectors Club of New York members. In particular, Louis Grunin, Ray Hofmann, Abbot Lutz, Ira Seebacher, Philip Silver, and Ira Zweifach. Special thanks must be given to Mrs. Josephine Eldridge, the Collectors Club librarian, for her patience and help; the Anne Boyd Lichtenstein Foundation for illustrations; The Philatelic Foundation, New York. Special thanks to William H. Miller, Jr., and curators Peter Robertson and Brian Green, whose response for technical information was most helpful.

ATOZ Stamp Club, New York: Thanks to the following members for their generous assistance: R. E. Beresford, for his selected pages of United Nations,

6.3 ¢ precancels, Founder of the Club of U.N. Collectors, N.Y.; Lawrence Black, for his information on stamp shows and philatelic literature, President of the Vatican Society, N.Y.; Lauretta Garabrant, representative, North Jersey Federation of Stamp Clubs, for her selected pages of Switzerland. Melvin Garabrant, Vice President, American Topical Association, President, Europa Study Unit for his information and illustration relating to Europa; George T. Guzzio, National Director of Judges Accreditation of the American Topical Association, American Philatelic Society, for lending illustrations on music on stamps and his generous guidance on a variety of philatelic areas; Honor R. Holland, President, Executive Secretary, Collectors Club of New York, for her material on the "U.S. State Flags" and pages from her exhibit "The Lion." Timothy A. Holmes, Staff Member, The Philatelic Foundation, New York, for his selected pages on the Beaver issue of Canada as well as stamps from the People's Republic of China; Thomas E. Range, Treasurer, Space Unit, ATA, for his advice on "space"; Irwin Rosen, President, New York chapter, Fine Arts Philatelists, for his selection of "Art on Stamps" from his collection and research on the history of art through the ages; Dr. Murray Sherman, Program Chairman, for his help on "space"; Wolf Spille, Founder and President, Maritime Collectors Club, for selected pages from his collection; Doris Tusty, Member of the Board of Directors, Greater New York Area Girl Scouts, for her research material and illustrations on Thurn and Taxis.

With special thanks to the following governments and government agencies: Austrian PTT; Bhutan Permanent Mission to the United Nations; British Post Office; Bureau of Engraving and Printing, Washington, D.C.; Directorate General of Posts, Republic of China; National Aeronautics and Space Administration, U.S.A.; Norwegian Polar Institute; Swiss PTT; United Nations Headquarters, New York; United Nations European Office, Geneva; United Nations Postal Administration, New York; United Nations Postal Administration, Geneva; United States Postal Service, Washington, D.C.

With special thanks to the following societies and organizations: American Philatelic Society; American Topical Association; ATOZ Stamp Club; Collectors Club of New York; Europa Study Unit; Essay and Proof Society of North America; Anne Boyd Lichtenstein Foundation; Junior Ambassadors, Inc.; Royal Philatelic Society, London; Society of Philatelic Americans; Franklin D. Roosevelt Philatelic Society; The Philatelic Foundation.

And museums: National Gallery of Art, Washington, D.C.; Peabody Museum of Archeology and Ethnology, Harvard University; State Museum of Berlin, German Democratic Republic; The Franklin D. Roosevelt Library, Hyde Park, New York; The Oriental Institute, University of Chicago; Swiss Postal Museum, Berne, Switzerland; National Postal Museum, London.

Others deserving special thanks: Adrien Boutrelle, photographs; H. E. Harris, Inc. Boston, Mass.: Wesley P. Mann, Jr., John A. Carlson; Lighthouse Publications, Inc., New York: W. Tinnemeier; Minkus Publications, Inc. New York: Don Kampa; StanGib, Ltd., New York: G. N. Oakden; *Stamps Magazine*, New York: Jim Morton, August Perce; *Stamp Show News:* Lee Gill; Scott Publications, New York: Harvey Warm, Paula Pines; LeRoy Wollney, photographs.

Special thanks to the following for their articles in this book: Paul Brown, The Rev. Walter Brown, Anne Brown.

For the "aristocrats" of philately, thanks to the following: Bernard D. Harmer; Dr. Norman Hubbard; Hiroyuki Kanai; Anne Boyd Lichtenstein Foundation, New York; Thurston Twig-Smith, *Honolulu Advertiser;* Raymond and Roger Weill, New Orleans; Irwin R. Weinberg.

No book is ever complete without help. Special thanks indeed to: Nicholas Ellison, a unique editor for his guidance and encouragement; Lydia Link for the designing of the entire book; Richard E. Beresford and Honor R. Holland for seeing the book from concept to completion, helping with the selection of material, ideas, and layout. Last, but by no means least, my warmest appreciation goes to Anne Brown, who handled the typing of the manuscript with efficiency and endless patience and handled the correspondence worldwide relating to the development of this book.

The Chinese writer Tai T'ung wrote a book on the history of Chinese writing of which he said, "Were I to await perfection, my book would never be finished. I have made shift to collect the fruits of my labors as I find them. Such a rough draft is the present book." I well realize how much has been omitted, but I sincerely hope *Funk & Wagnalls Guide to the World of Stamp Collecting* will bring endless enjoyment to thousands of newcomers to the most exciting hobby in the world.

Viola Ilma

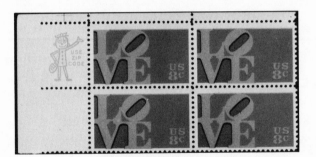

An expressive commemorative stamp.

Index

Page numbers in *italics* indicate illustrations.

National Postal Museum, London,
England, 131
Netherlands
Erasmus of Rotterdam stamp, *117*
German Shepherd (dog) stamp, *34*
Newfoundland, 36, 37, 176
composite die proof, *38*
finished die proof and stamp as issued,
39
from Newfoundland, *34*
registered cover, *35*
St. Pierre and Miquelon stamp, *34*
2p scarlet vermilion of 1857, *176*
Newfoundland Airmails (Harmer), 193
New Yorker, The, 172
New York Times, 112
New Zealand, *follows page 148*
Iceberg rose stamp, 9
Nonsporting (dog) Group stamps, 41, 42
Norway, 130

Observation, value of in collecting, 3, 8
Ochoa, Marcela, *303*
Odenweller, Robert P., 180–188
Owens, Mary Ann, 254, 255

Paderewski, Ignace Jan, 46, 50
Pakistan, Stars and Crescent stamp, *7*
Pan American Exposition, 173
Paper, 319, 320
first use of, 94
Paper Gold, 137
Papyrus, 91, 92
Parcel post, 88
Parchment, 92
Partridge, W. Scott, 63, 64
Paterson, Campbell, 186
Patton, Ray, 310
Pegram, General John, 219
Pegram, Hetty, 218–220
"Pellicles," 239
Pemberton, Edward L., 139, 140, 142
Penguins, 253, 254
Penny Black, 131, *follows page 148,* 150,
305, 314
Penny post, 121, *122*
Penny Red, *1*
Perfin, 73
Perfins Club, The, 77
Perfin Stamp Society, 73
Perforation gauge, 32, 33
Perforations, 37, 72
"Perfs," *see* Stamps, perforation of
Pergamon library, 92
Perkins, Bacon & Co., 132
Perkins, Bacon and Petch, 312
Persian postal system, 90, 92
Peru, 86, 87, 141

Philatelic Foundation, 48
education, 189
expertization, 190
Philatelic research, 141
Philatelic Sales Office, Washington, 161
Philatelic Society, London, The, 140,
141, 144
Philatelist, The, 140, 164
Philately
Confederate States, 218–223
junior, 298–311
maritime, 266–275
origin of name, 44
rarest philatelic items, 170–179
ripoffs in, 169
Philbrick, Frederick A., 139, 141, 144
Phillips, Charles J., 144
Phosphor bands, *136*
Phosphor coating, 318
Photogravure, 314, 315
Piatigorsky, Gregor, 47
Pigeon post, 229, 230
Siege of Paris, 238, 239
Pike's Peak Express, 224
Pocono Mountain Philatelic Society, 301,
310
Poland
Airedale (dog) stamp, *39*
Fox Terrier (dog) stamp, *39*
Frédéric Chopin stamp, *76*
Paderewski stamp with his autograph,
47
Pons, Lily, 46
Pony Express
first rider, 225, 226
first route of, 226
founder of, 224
and the Gold Rush, 224, 225
riders, 227, 228
Postage stamps
moments of triumph on, 105, 106
prepaid adhesive, 133
world's first, 131–133
Postage Stamps of New Zealand, 182
Postal History Primer, 212
Postal Stationery, 59, 60, 283–286
Postal Stationery Catalogue, see *Higgins
and Gage*
Postal systems
Charlemagne's, 96
Chinese, 94, 95
Egyptian, 91, 92
English, 120, 121
French, 118
Greek, 88
Japanese, 94
Mexican, 88
Persian, 89, 92, 93